Persuasive Legal Writing

ASPEN COURSEBOOK SERIES

Persuasive Legal Writing

Third Edition

Louis J. Sirico, Jr.
Professor of Law and Director of Legal Writing
Villanova University Law School

Nancy L. Schultz
Professor of Law
Chapman University School of Law

. Wolters Kluwer

Law & Business

AUSTIN   BOSTON   CHICAGO   NEW YORK   THE NETHERLANDS

Aspen Publishers
Attn: Permissions Department
76 Ninth Avenue, 7th Floor
New York, NY 10011-5201

To contact Customer Service, e-mail customer.care@aspenpublishers.com, call 1-800-234-1660, fax 1-800-901-9075, or mail correspondence to:

Aspen Publishers
Attn: Order Department
PO Box 990
Frederick, MD 21705

Printed in the United States of America.

1 2 3 4 5 6 7 8 9 0

ISBN 978-0-7355-0746-3

Library of Congress Cataloging-in-Publication Data
Sirico, Louis J., Jr., 1945-
    Persuasive legal writing / Louis J. Sirico, Jr., Nancy L. Schultz. — Third edition.
        p. cm
    Revision of: Persuasive writing for lawyers and the legal profession. 2nd ed. c2001.
    ISBN 978-0-7355-0746-3
        1. Legal composition. 2.   Law—United States—Language. 3.   Law—United States—Methodology. I.   Schultz, Nancy L., 1957- II.   Sirico, Louis J. Persuasive writing for lawyers and the legal profession. III.   Title.
    KF250.S54 2011
    808' .06634—dc22

                                                                                2010051404

About Wolters Kluwer Law & Business

Wolters Kluwer Law & Business is a leading provider of research information and workflow solutions in key specialty areas. The strengths of the individual brands of Aspen Publishers, CCH, Kluwer Law International and Loislaw are aligned within Wolters Kluwer Law & Business to provide comprehensive, in-depth solutions and expert-authored content for the legal, professional and education markets.

CCH was founded in 1913 and has served more than four generations of business professionals and their clients. The CCH products in the Wolters Kluwer Law & Business group are highly regarded electronic and print resources for legal, securities, antitrust and trade regulation, government contracting, banking, pension, payroll, employment and labor, and healthcare reimbursement and compliance professionals.

Aspen Publishers is a leading information provider for attorneys, business professionals and law students. Written by preeminent authorities, Aspen products offer analytical and practical information in a range of specialty practice areas from securities law and intellectual property to mergers and acquisitions and pension/benefits. Aspen's trusted legal education resources provide professors and students with high-quality, up-to-date and effective resources for successful instruction and study in all areas of the law.

Kluwer Law International supplies the global business community with comprehensive English-language international legal information. Legal practitioners, corporate counsel and business executives around the world rely on the Kluwer Law International journals, loose-leafs, books and electronic products for authoritative information in many areas of international legal practice.

Loislaw is a premier provider of digitized legal content to small law firm practitioners of various specializations. Loislaw provides attorneys with the ability to quickly and efficiently find the necessary legal information they need, when and where they need it, by facilitating access to primary law as well as state-specific law, records, forms and treatises.

Wolters Kluwer Law & Business, a unit of Wolters Kluwer, is headquartered in New York and Riverwoods, Illinois. Wolters Kluwer is a leading multinational publisher and information services company.

SUMMARY OF CONTENTS

TABLE OF CONTENTS

Chapter 6
Adopt a Persuasive Writing Style

Chapter 7
Write Compelling Introductions

Chapter 8
State Your Facts Persuasively

Chapter 9
Use Authority Persuasively

Chapter 10
Make Equity and Policy Arguments

Chapter 11
Writing for Nonlegal Audiences

Chapter 12
Writing for Legal Audiences

Chapter 13
Five Pitfalls in Persuasive Writing

Chapter 14
Advocacy and Ethics

Appendices

Appendix A
Magic Words: Writing with Flair

Appendix B
Review Exercise

When new lawyers begin to practice their profession, they usually have acquired a sufficient knowledge of legal doctrine and at least a satisfactory proficiency at legal analysis. However, they often do not yet understand how to think and write like advocates.

Despite experiences like moot court, students spend most of their academic years objectively analyzing and evaluating court opinions and other legal documents. As a result, they may prefer objective writing, because it entails less risk than advocacy: They do not have to take a position and defend it against assertive critics.

However, as many practitioners have told us, novice lawyers have difficulty switching from neutral writing to persuasive writing. For example, when writing an intra-office memo for a senior attorney, they may not be aware that they should be playing the advocate. They may be content with synthesizing and applying the relevant cases, statutes, and regulations. However, the senior attorney also wants to know if it is possible for his or her client to win. Therefore, novice lawyers also should be proposing ways to overcome the legal obstacles they have identified.

Even when writing a brief, they may fail to write as assertively as they should. They also may not recognize that all sections of the brief, including the table of contents and statement of facts, are places for attractively portraying the client and its argument.

When beginning lawyers try to write like advocates, they sometimes misunderstand what persuasive writing is. They may think that learning persuasive writing requires learning a set of gimmicks — for example, referring to your client by name and calling the other party by an abstract title like "the plaintiff" or "the appellee."[1]

Although gimmicks may sometimes help — if the reader has not already seen them one time too many — they are not the key. Novice lawyers also may think that persuasive writing requires them to adopt an overblown

---

1. Rule 28(d) of the Federal Rules of Appellate Procedure requires you to be clear in identifying parties:

> In briefs and at oral argument, counsel should minimize use of the terms "appellant" and "appellee." To make briefs clear, counsel should use the parties' actual names or the designations used in the lower court or agency proceeding, or such descriptive terms as "the employee," "the injured person," "the taxpayer," "the ship," "the stevedore."

dramatic style. If so, they might have been more successful had they lived in an earlier era. They also may think that persuasive writing requires ignoring strong arguments by opposing counsel and even ignoring adverse precedent. However, ignoring the opposition means giving up the opportunity to counter important arguments, and sometimes even violates ethical rules.

In this book, we provide you with the keys to persuasive writing. They are not particularly dramatic. They consist of writing simply and clearly, and consistently putting your best foot forward, while still arguing ethically and remembering to write for your audience.

By mastering these skills, you can stand out from your peers. Anyone who has read the briefs of practicing lawyers knows that too many are badly organized and barely comprehensible. Some skirt prohibitions by distorting critical facts and ignoring damaging precedent. You can easily produce a better work product.

If you organize your work product carefully and adopt a clear English style, you will have taken the most important steps to make your writing persuasive. If you also train yourself to structure your sentences, paragraphs, and documents in a way that encourages your reader to focus on your important arguments and react positively to them, you will become a consummate advocate.

For example, suppose you represent the defendant, the Slope Corporation, an employer that is being sued for its employee's negligence. Jones, the employee, sold outdoor power equipment and used his own car to carry out his job duties, and the Slope Corporation gave him a monthly car allowance. An accident occurred while Jones was driving after regular work hours in the car that he used while working.

Slope is being sued under a respondeat superior theory. Under the theory, the injured person can sue an employer for an employee's negligence where the employee acted within the scope of employment at the time of the negligent incident. Smith, the injured person, argues that Slope is liable under respondeat superior and seeks money damages. Smith argues that Jones hit Smith while operating a car that Slope did not own, but that Jones used while working and for which Jones received a monthly allowance.

Slope argues that Jones was not acting within the scope of his employment. It argues that Smith cannot demonstrate that it is liable for its employee's actions.

In constructing your argument, you might start by writing this paragraph:

> Slope Corporation argues that Smith should not be granted monetary relief because Jones was not acting within the scope of his employment when he caused the accident. The fact that Jones caused the accident using his own vehicle poses a challenging barrier to recovery. The fact that Jones was no longer engaging in his job responsibilities when the incident occurred should ensure that the plaintiff should not be awarded damages based on the employee's conduct. So the case law holds.

Although this paragraph is grammatically correct and contains the pertinent information, it is far from being a compelling piece of advocacy. You could make the paragraph far more persuasive if you revised it this way:

> Because Jones caused the accident while he was off-duty, Smith cannot recover from Slope Corporation under a respondeat superior theory. As the case law holds, a court can award damages under respondeat superior only when the employee acts within the scope of employment. Here, Jones was driving his car after work hours for his own purposes. Thus, even if Smith finds that Jones's car is comparable to a corporate-owned vehicle, Slope is not liable.

As you can see, you can improve your persuasiveness measurably by presenting your argument in an assertive way, reordering the presentation, and revising your sentences to make them more compelling. In this example, the three most effective techniques for improving persuasiveness are presenting information in an order that is easy to follow, using topic sentences (thesis sentences), and ending the sentences in an assertive way.

In this book, we teach you how to write persuasively. A glance at the table of contents will give you a general idea of the lessons we present.

We begin with a look at the big picture: a historical perspective on the key components of persuasion, a discussion of the psychology of persuasion, and an introduction to the importance of good storytelling. We then offer suggestions that work at a macro level: making your argument as simple as possible, adopting an assertive style, and organizing your writing. We also offer tips that will help with specific aspects of your document: writing effective introductions, presenting facts skillfully, and structuring your sentences and paragraphs to be persuasive.

We also discuss aspects of persuasion that are unique to legal argumentation: using authority effectively and making equity and policy arguments. We emphasize the importance of tailoring your arguments to your audience. We offer a summary of the most common pitfalls of persuasion and the most important ethical rules governing advocacy. Finally, we conclude by introducing you to rhetorical flair by presenting a collection of paragraphs that employ classical rhetorical devices and by giving you a final exercise that will give you an opportunity to apply your newly learned lessons.

As you read the book, you will discover that the lessons are fairly simple and sometimes self-evident. These characteristics are evidence that they work. If the strategies were so subtle that you did not recognize them, you would know that they would not appeal to your common sense or to that of your audience.

The difficulty with learning persuasiveness lies in learning to apply the lessons and also in knowing when to reject them. To help you, we include a large number of examples with an emphasis on revising passages to make them more persuasive. At the end of several chapters, we also offer exercises that permit you to work on developing your advocacy skills.

A word of caution is in order. Learning to write well is not a matter of learning rules and mechanically applying them. It is not about learning a formula; it is about learning an art. The lessons in this book will help you improve your writing only if you think about why they usually make writing more persuasive and then decide whether they will help improve your particular sentence, paragraph, or document. In writing, creativity and reflection play a significant role.

Because good writing is an art, there is always room for improvement and room for disagreement. There are different ways to express the same idea effectively. For example, when you examine the many illustrations in this book, sometimes you will come across ways to make the good illustrations even more persuasive. By reflecting on the revisions that you would make, you will improve your understanding of the art of writing.

Before you begin studying these lessons on advocacy, you should give some thought to how you plan to internalize them. Although we have made an effort to limit the number of lessons, there are still quite a few, probably too many for you to make part of your writing style all at once.

Here are our suggestions. Begin by reading the chapters carefully. Working through the examples will give you experience in employing the relevant lesson. For more experience, complete the exercises. When you are drafting a brief or other major document, turn to the table of contents and use it as a checklist.

To improve your writing on a daily basis, pick the two or three lessons that you think will make the greatest improvement in your writing. Consciously apply them to your writing. When you start to apply them almost automatically, pick two or three more lessons and begin to apply them. Little by little, you can incorporate all the lessons into your writing style.

On a final introductory note, we want to say thank you to our student research assistants who were of great help in working on this edition. A big thanks to Marshall Burstein of Villanova and Dhruv Sharma and Brian Wolensky of Chapman.

Persuasive Legal Writing

CHAPTER 1

A Brief Historical Perspective

LOGOS
PATHOS
ETHOS

These words will be familiar to students of rhetoric, particularly those of you who have encountered Aristotle at some point in your educations. Rhetoric often carries pejorative connotations, with some considering it to be nothing more than the use of words essentially devoid of substantive meaning but designed to inflame passions and prejudices — "empty rhetoric." Historically, however, it is simply the use of language to accomplish particular goals, especially to persuade. As noted by James Boyd White, "[t]he ancient rhetorician Gorgias (in Plato's dialog of that name) defined rhetoric as the art of persuading the people about matters of justice and injustice in the public places of the state, and one could hardly imagine a more compendious statement of the art of the lawyer than that."[1]

Lawyers use rhetorical tools constantly, both orally and in writing. This chapter offers some historical context for understanding why legal persuasion is constructed in particular ways, and points out that the techniques you will learn in this book originated long ago, and have withstood the test of time, now measured in millennia.

I. RHETORICAL COMPONENTS AND RESPONSIBILITY

Aristotle is universally cited as the author of the fundamental tenets of persuasion theory. He introduced the three core attributes of persuasion mentioned at the beginning of the chapter. What are logos, pathos, and

---

1. James Boyd White, *Law as Rhetoric, Rhetoric as Law: The Arts of Cultural and Communal Life*, 52 U. Chi. L Rev. 684, 684-85 (1985).

ethos, and how do they inform our thinking about persuasion? In the words of Aristotle himself:

> Of the modes of persuasion furnished by the spoken word there are three kinds. The first kind depends on the personal character of the speaker; the second on putting the audience into a certain frame of mind; the third on the proof, or apparent proof, provided by the words of the speech itself. Persuasion is achieved by the speaker's personal character when the speech is so spoken as to make us think him credible. We believe good men more fully and more readily than others: this is true generally whatever the question is, and absolutely true where exact certainty is impossible and opinions are divided. This kind of persuasion, like the others, should be achieved by what the speaker says, not by what people think of his character before he begins to speak. It is not true, as some writers assume in their treatises on rhetoric, that the personal goodness revealed by the speaker contributes nothing to his power of persuasion; on the contrary, his character may almost be called the most effective means of persuasion he possesses. Secondly, persuasion may come through the hearers, when the speech stirs their emotions. Our judgements when we are pleased and friendly are not the same as when we are pained and hostile. It is towards producing these effects, as we maintain, that present-day writers on rhetoric direct the whole of their efforts. This subject shall be treated in detail when we come to speak of the emotions. Thirdly, persuasion is effected through the speech itself when we have proved a truth or an apparent truth by means of the persuasive arguments suitable to the case in question.[2]

In other words, a persuasive argument consists of more than the presentation of facts and rational, logical conclusions based on those facts and applicable principles, although such logical appeals are obviously a critical component of persuasion. Audiences are affected as well by emotional appeals — Aristotle suggests that we may be more likely to be persuaded in some emotional states than others — and by their perception of the credibility of the advocate, which will tend to be influenced by the advocate's character, reputation, knowledge, and presentation. We will deal in more depth with the emotional and ethical aspects of persuasion in Chapter 2, but here are a few examples of how speakers have used these types of appeals in various contexts.

---

2. Aristotle, *Rhetoric, http://classics.mit.edu/Aristotle/rhetoric.l.i.html*. Aristotle's *Rhetoric* is obviously in the public domain, and can be accessed in many ways, both in hard copy books and on the web. We offer one source here, but a simple search may lead you to other equally useful resources. If the long web address does not get you to *Rhetoric*, try shorter versions of it and use the links on the website to get there.

Here are some historical, and in the opinion of these authors, effective emotional appeals:

Elizabeth Cady Stanton (1848) Keynote, First Woman's Rights Convention

We should not feel so sorely grieved if no man who had not attained the full stature of a Webster, Clay, Van Buren, or Gerrit Smith could claim the right of the elective franchise. But to have drunkards, idiots, horse-racing, rum-selling rowdies, ignorant foreigners, and silly boys fully recognized, while we ourselves are thrust out from all the rights that belong to citizens, it is too grossly insulting to the dignity of woman to be longer quietly submitted to.

Frederick Douglass (July 4, 1852)

The rich inheritance of justice, liberty, prosperity, and independence bequeathed by your fathers is shared by you, not by me. The sunlight that brought light and healing to you has brought stripes and death to me. This Fourth of July is yours, not mine. You may rejoice, I must mourn. To drag a man in fetters into the grand illuminated temple of liberty, and call upon him to join you in joyous anthems, were inhuman mockery and sacrilegious irony. Do you mean, citizens, to mock me by asking me to speak today?

Fellow citizens, above your national, tumultuous joy, I hear the mournful wail of millions! Whose chains, heavy and grievous yesterday, are, today, rendered more intolerable by the jubilee shouts that reach them. If I do forget, if I do not faithfully remember those bleeding children of sorrow this day, may my right hand forget her cunning, and may my tongue cleave to the roof of my mouth! To forget them, to pass lightly over their wrongs, and to chime in with the popular theme would be treason most scandalous and shocking, and would make me a reproach before God and the world.

Clarence Darrow (May 19, 1926, murder trial of Henry Sweet)

Gentlemen, I feel deeply on this subject; I cannot help it. Let us take a little glance at the history of the Negro race. It only needs a minute. It seems to me that the story would melt hearts of stone. I was born in America. I could have left it if I had wanted to go away. Some other men, reading about this land of freedom that we brag about on the Fourth of July, came voluntarily to America. These men, the defendants, are here because they could not help it. Their ancestors were captured in the jungles and on the plains of Africa, captured as you capture wild beasts, torn from their homes and their kindred; loaded into slave ships, packed like sardines in a box, half of them dying on the ocean passage; some jumping into the sea in their frenzy, when they had a chance to choose death in place of slavery.

They were captured and brought here. They could not help it. They were bought and sold as slaves, to work without pay, because they were black.

Emotional appeals to notions of justice and injustice such as these are likely to be effective if the communicator effectively evokes feelings of outrage or sympathy, or both. We believe the three advocates above have done so effectively, and from different perspectives, although all three try to get the audience to identify with the victims of the injustice. The more the audience can identify with a particular perspective, the easier it is to persuade them to act upon that perspective.

Emotion can also be evoked by creating positive identification, through shared experience or ideals, as in the following example:

Nelson Mandela (May 1994, Inaugural Speech)

Let there be justice for all.
Let there be peace for all.
Let there be work, bread, water, and salt for all.
Let each know that for each the body, the mind and the soul have been freed to fulfill themselves.
Never, never and never again shall it be that this beautiful land will again experience the oppression of one by another and suffer the indignity of being the skunk of the world.
Let freedom reign.
The sun shall never set on so glorious a human achievement.[3]

Here are some examples of communicators using various methods to enhance their ethical appeal.

The first two speakers address their reasons for communicating, telling the audience that their messages come from deep personal conviction, which has been demonstrated consistently in their previous actions and communications. Sincerity is an aspect of ethical appeal that is highly likely to enhance persuasiveness.

Daniel Webster (January 26, 1830)

Mr. President, I have thus stated the reasons of my dissent to the doctrines which have been advanced and maintained. I am conscious of having detained you and the Senate much too long. I was drawn into the debate with no previous deliberation such as is suited to the discussion of so grave and important a subject. But it is a subject of which my heart is full, and I have not been willing to suppress the utterance of its spontaneous sentiments. I cannot, even now, persuade myself to relinquish it without expressing once more my deep conviction that since it respects nothing less than

---

3. Reprinted in Hywel Williams, *Great Speeches of Our Time* (Quercus 2008).

the Union of the states, it is of most vital and essential importance to the public happiness. I profess, sir, in my career, hitherto, to have kept steadily in view the prosperity and honor of the whole country, and the preservation of our federal Union.

Mohandas Gandhi (before sentencing in trial for sedition, March 23, 1922)

I wanted to avoid violence, I want to avoid violence. Nonviolence is the first article of my faith. It is also the last article of my creed. But I had to make my choice. I had to either submit to a system which I considered had done an irreparable harm to my country, or incur the risk of the mad fury of my people bursting forth, when they understood the truth from my lips. I know that my people have sometimes gone mad. I am deeply sorry for it, and I am therefore here to submit not to a light penalty but to the highest penalty. I do not ask for mercy. I do not plead any extenuating act. I am here, therefore, to invite and cheerfully submit to the highest penalty that can be inflicted upon me for what in law is a deliberate crime and what appears to me to be the highest duty of a citizen.

Here are three notable figures in American history, who bring to their communications a built-in ethos that comes of long and distinguished service, directly addressing their own feelings and perceptions on the subject of their communications. You will note that each expressly adds a healthy dose of humility to the message. Putting yourself in the message can often add to your credibility, by reminding the audience that you see yourself as only human and allowing them to identify with you more readily. It is, admittedly, more difficult and probably less appropriate to do this in a written communication, at least in a formal writing such as a brief to a court. It might, however, have applicability in letters to clients or other types of legal writing.

George Washington: Farewell Address

In looking forward to the moment which is intended to terminate the career of my public life, my feelings do not permit me to suspend the deep acknowledgement of that debt of gratitude which I owe to my beloved country, for the many honors it has conferred upon me; still more for the steadfast confidence with which it has supported me . . . here, perhaps, I ought to stop. But a solicitude for your welfare, which cannot end but with my life, and the apprehension of danger, natural to that solicitude, urge me on an occasion like the present to offer to your solemn contemplation, and to recommend to your frequent review, some sentiments which are the result of much reflection, of no inconsiderable observation, and which appear to me all important to the permanency of your felicity as a people. These will be offered to you with the more freedom, as you can only see in them the disinterested warnings of a parting friend, who can possibly have no personal motive to bias his counsel. Nor can I forget, as an encouragement to it, your indulgent reception of my sentiments on a former and not dissimilar occasion.

Benjamin Franklin to the Constitutional Convention (September 17, 1787)

Mr. President, I confess that I do not entirely approve of this Constitution at present, but, sir, I am not sure I shall never approve it: for, having lived long, I have experienced many instances of being obliged, by better information or fuller consideration, to change opinions even on important subjects, which I once thought right, but found to be otherwise. It is therefore that the older I grow, the more apt I am to doubt my own judgment, and to pay more respect to the judgment of others.

Thomas Jefferson: Inauguration

Friends and fellow citizens, called upon to undertake the duties of the first executive office of our country, I avail myself of the presence of that portion of my fellow citizens which is here assembled, to express my grateful thanks for the favor with which they have been pleased to look toward me, to declare a sincere consciousness, that the task is above my talents, and that I approach it with those anxious and awful presentiments which the greatness of the charge, and the weakness of my powers, so justly inspire.

Here is a more modern speaker using different tools that affect his ethical appeal. In the first excerpt, Colin Powell directly addresses the expectations of the audience, and acknowledges that he is likely dealing with a wide range of expectations. He does so with a bit of humor, also a useful rhetorical tool (although, again, not as useful in most legal writing as it may be in spoken communication). The subject of audience expectations and how to adapt to them is covered at length in later chapters.

Colin Powell, Commencement Speech at Howard University (May 14, 1994)[4]

The real challenge in being a commencement speaker is figuring out how long to speak. The graduating students want a short speech, five to six minutes and let's get it over. They are not going to remember who their commencement speaker was anyway. P-O-W-E-L-L. Parents are another matter. Arrayed in all their finery they have waited a long time for this day, some not sure it would ever come, and they want it to last. So go on and talk for two or three hours. We brought our lunch and want our money's worth. The faculty member who suggested the speaker hopes the speech will be long enough to be respectable, but not so long that he has to take leave for a few weeks beginning Monday. So the poor speaker is left figuring out what

---

4. Reprinted in William Safire, *Lend Me Your Ears: Great Speeches in History* (Norton 1997).

to do. My simple rule is to respond to audience reaction. If you are appreciative and applaud a lot early on, you get a nice, short speech. If you make me work for it, we're liable to be here a long time.

Here, from the same speech, is an ethical appeal that goes to the heart of who the speaker is. He provides perspective on where he comes from, which might help some to assess the credibility of his message:

I am a direct descendant of those Buffalo Soldiers, of the Tuskegee Airmen, and of the navy's Golden Thirteen, and Montfort Point Marines, and all the black men and women who served this nation in uniform for over three hundred years. All of whom served in their time and in their way and with whatever opportunity existed then to break down the walls of discrimination and racism to make the path easier for those of us who came after them. I climbed on their backs and stood on their shoulders to reach the top of my chosen profession to become chairman of the American Joint Chiefs of Staff. I will never forget my debt to them and to the many white "Colonel Griersons" and "General Howards" who helped me over the thirty-five years of my life as a soldier. They would say to me now, "Well done. And now let others climb upon your shoulders."

Here are a few other examples of modern speakers establishing their ethos[5]:

Jesse Jackson, Democratic National Convention (July 1984)

Leadership must heed the call of conscience, redemption, expansion, healing and unity. Throughout this campaign, I've tried to offer leadership to the Democratic Party and the nation. If, in my high moments, I have done some good, offered some service, shed some light, healed some wounds, rekindled some hope, or stirred someone from apathy and indifference — then this campaign has not been in vain.

Nelson Mandela Inaugural Speech (May 1994)

We are both humbled and elevated by the honour and privilege that you, the people of South Africa, have bestowed on us, as the first president of a united, democratic, non-racial and non-sexist South Africa, to lead our country out of the valley of darkness.

Barack Obama (March 2008)

I am the son of a black man from Kenya and a white woman from Kansas. I was raised with the help of a white grandfather ... and a white grandmother. ... I've gone to some of the best schools in America and lived in one of the world's poorest nations. I am married to a black American

---

5. Reprinted in Hywel Williams, *Great Speeches of Our Time* (Quercus 2008).

who carries within her the blood of slaves and slave-owners. . . . I will never forget that in no other country on earth is my story even possible. . . . It is a story that has seared into my genetic makeup the idea that this nation is more than the sum of its parts — that out of many, we are truly one. . . .

There is no question that the effective use of language and rhetorical tools can have a profound impact on an audience. To the extent that an advocate seeks to persuade an audience to undertake an action, for example, to convict an individual of a crime, the advocate bears a significant responsibility to use his or her tools appropriately. On the power of rhetoric, and the need to use rhetorical tools wisely, Aristotle again offers insights that resonate through the centuries:

> Rhetoric is useful (1) because things that are true and things that are just have a natural tendency to prevail over their opposites, so that if the decisions of judges are not what they ought to be, the defeat must be due to the speakers themselves, and they must be blamed accordingly. Moreover, (2) before some audiences not even the possession of the exactest knowledge will make it easy for what we say to produce conviction. For argument based on knowledge implies instruction, and there are people whom one cannot instruct. Here, then, we must use, as our modes of persuasion and argument, notions possessed by everybody, as we observed in the Topics when dealing with the way to handle a popular audience. Further, (3) we must be able to employ persuasion, just as strict reasoning can be employed, on opposite sides of a question, not in order that we may in practice employ it in both ways (for we must not make people believe what is wrong), but in order that we may see clearly what the facts are, and that, if another man argues unfairly, we on our part may be able to confute him. No other of the arts draws opposite conclusions: dialectic and rhetoric alone do this. Both these arts draw opposite conclusions impartially. Nevertheless, the underlying facts do not lend themselves equally well to the contrary views. No; things that are true and things that are better are, by their nature, practically always easier to prove and easier to believe in. Again, (4) it is absurd to hold that a man ought to be ashamed of being unable to defend himself with his limbs, but not of being unable to defend himself with speech and reason, when the use of rational speech is more distinctive of a human being than the use of his limbs. And if it be objected that one who uses such power of speech unjustly might do great harm, that is a charge which may be made in common against all good things except virtue, and above all against the things that are most useful, as strength, health, wealth, generalship. A man can confer the greatest of benefits by a right use of these, and inflict the greatest of injuries by using them wrongly.[6]

---

6. Aristotle, *Rhetoric*, *http://classics.mit.edu/Aristotle/rhetoric.l.i.html*.

Thus, Aristotle demonstrates a great faith in the power of persuasion to achieve just ends, while recognizing that there is a risk that unscrupulous writers and speakers can use these tools for less noble goals. He points out the importance of examining issues from both sides, while suggesting that truth will emerge from such an examination because it is "easier to prove and easier to believe in."

A modern writer offers a somewhat more cynical view of the lawyer's use of rhetorical tools:

> To be effective, the lawyer must confine his overclaiming in order to preserve his credibility. Thus, when he writes his statement of facts he will "lawyer" those facts, but he will do so gently enough that his reader will accept his statement as "the facts." The standard by which lawyers consistently measure their rhetoric is a standard of effectiveness. To pursue any of these conventions so far as to render them counter-productive is to fail in our rhetorical purpose. Second, so long as it may serve our purposes, we lawyers have nothing against the truth. Indeed, under such circumstances, we are quite prepared to put it to good use. Third, and this actually illustrates my point about the truth, lawyers — or at least good lawyers — tend to read texts differently than they speak about them. Thus, if, in the good lawyer's speaking, texts tend to have one true and objectively ascertainable meaning, that same lawyer is likely to read and think about those texts as if they were highly inde-terminate pots of rhetorical possibilities that could be put to work in the service of his various projects. Finally, good lawyers understand, at some level, that persuasion requires more than the simple application of the principles of deductive logic and narrowly rational argumenta-tion. This broader understanding of rhetoric is most evident in those lawyers who are particularly effective in dealing with juries, in selling legal services, in transactional negotiations, and in politics.[7]

Again we see the recognition of credibility as an important foundation of persuasion, as well as recognition of the fact that lawyers can manipulate legal authorities to serve particular ends. In addition, we see the recogni-tion that logic alone is not determinative of persuasive power. Thus, the influence of Aristotle's ancient views continues, even when the message is less idealistic.

II. FURTHER THOUGHTS AND DEVELOPMENTS

After Aristotle, significant contributions to the development of rhetorical theory were made by Roman orators such as Cicero and Quintilian. Build-ing on the work of Aristotle, they continued to develop the importance of

---

7. Gerald Wetlaufer, *Rhetoric and Its Denial in Legal Discourse*, 76 Va. L. Rev. 1545, 1559-60 (1990).

the three aspects of logos, pathos, and ethos to persuasion, as well as developing an organizational strategy that largely remains intact today.[8]

Quintilian's Institutio Oratoria includes twelve books on how orators should be educated that still influence the thinking about and teaching of persuasive techniques. Aristotle, Cicero, and Quintilian offered advice for lawyers that retains a great deal of validity today. For example, they emphasized:

(1) the importance of using emotion as a means of stressing sympathetic facts;

(2) the importance of understanding your judge's background and perceptions;

(3) the importance of not making every argument you can think of, lest you bore the judge and detract from your stronger arguments; and

(4) the importance of communicating confidence and belief in your case.[9]

On the subject of ethical appeals, Quintilian suggested that "he who would have all men trust his judgment as to what is expedient and honorable, should possess and be regarded as possessing genuine wisdom and excellence of character."[10]

The goal of this brief historical introduction to rhetoric was to help you understand some of the context for much of what we try to teach in this book, and the continuity of principles that inform the teaching of and thinking about techniques of persuasion. In the rest of the book, we develop these principles and offer concrete suggestions for implementing them.

---

8. For an excellent application of Greco-Roman rhetorical principles to the writing of Supreme Court briefs, see Michael Frost, *With Amici Like These: Cicero, Quintilian and the Importance of Stylistic Demeanor*, 3 JALWD 5 (2006).

9. Michael Frost, *Ethos, Pathos and Legal Audience*, 99 Dick. L. Rev. 85 (1994). This article offers an extensive analysis and historical perspective on these elements of persuasion.

10. Quintilian, *Institutio Oratorio, III*, viii, 13.

CHAPTER 2

The Psychology of Persuasion

One author of this book received an e-mail offering the following:

How To Talk Anyone Into Anything, Anytime!

Could you imagine being *so persuasive* that people just naturally go along with whatever you say? The reason I ask is, there's this great new report on the Net. It's called TOTAL PERSUASION, and it has a lot of powerful stuff in it. Like a question that will instantly turn anyone into PUTTY IN YOUR HANDS . . . a subliminal technique that establishes your credibility in a matter of *seconds* . . . a way to get other people to trust you (this is so easy you'll wonder if it should be ILLEGAL) . . . and a lot more!

Have you ever wanted to get people to INSTANTLY accept your ideas by thinking THEY came up with them? This report has a great way to do it. And it works. You can use this technique to get hired for a better job, or get yourself more money when you're selling something. Or even get a bank to INSIST you take the loan you asked them for in the first place!

This stuff's almost too good to be true. But it is for real, because it comes from a master persuader who has studied ancient war strategies, sales, marketing, and deep psychological communication techniques. He has the most advanced persuasion training in the world, and he's a highly regarded teacher himself. It's truly amazing stuff. You'll also learn a secret about winning arguments that will really surprise you! When you use this technique, you secretly take the wind out of the other person's sails, and before they know it they're agreeing with you!

Unfortunately, this is probably many people's idea of persuasion; they believe that the goal is to manipulate other people to do what you want them to do. In reality, persuasion is nothing more than the successful communication of an idea from one person to another, with the result that the reader or listener ends up agreeing with the speaker or writer. We can be persuaded of many things, major and minor; our attitudes can undergo significant shifts, or relatively minor changes of direction. Sometimes simply to be informed is to be persuaded; other times it takes more than information to shift an attitude. So how does this process work? How do we persuade someone else to adopt our way of thinking?

There may be as many theories on that subject as there are people to ponder it. Nevertheless, there are some relatively clear principles of persuasion:

1. It is easier to persuade someone if the other person understands the message; that is, persuasive messages are clear messages. We devote substantial space in other chapters in this book to suggestions regarding how to send clear messages.
2. Effective use of emotion can be very persuasive.
3. Persuasive arguments are credible arguments; credibility can be a function of the speaker as well as the message.

Emotion and credibility are the primary focuses of this chapter — in other words, we come back to Aristotle's pathos and ethos.

I. PATHOS

The effective use of emotion involves creating a response in the audience that makes the audience want to do things your way. It means the audience not only believes at an intellectual level that you are right, but feels it at a gut level and wants to do something about it.

> Legal decision making is enriched and refined by the operation of emotions because they direct attention to particular dimensions of a case, or shape decision makers' ability to understand the perspective of, or the stakes of a decision for, a particular party.[1]

One way you can create this response is to make the audience feel as though they have experienced the same thing your client did — in other words, your client's story is not an abstract set of facts, but a personal story the audience can relate to. Justice Oliver Wendell Holmes, Jr., observed that "the life of the law has not been logic: it has been experience."[2] Emotions are a fundamental aspect of the human experience. As one distinguished English barrister has observed, "[M]ost human action is prompted by feeling. . . . One distorts reality by suggesting that emotion is an unreliable guide to a true decision on fact, and that there is therefore something suspect in evoking or displaying emotion."[3]

---

1. Abrams & Keren, *Who's Afraid of the Law and Emotions?*, 94 Minn. L. Rev. 1997 (2010).
2. Holmes, *The Common Law* 1 (The Legal Classics Library ed. 1985, reprinting 1st ed. 1881).
3. R. DuCann, *The Art of the Advocate* 156 (1980), as quoted in John C. Shepherd & Jordan B. Cherrick, *Advocacy and Emotion*, 138 F.R.D. 619 (1991).

There are several ways to evoke useful and appropriate emotional responses in your audience. One experienced litigator offers these suggestions:

1. Take them there: Visualization — being able to "see" something in your mind's eye — is a powerful persuader.
2. Show the details of reality: Details are important. They are the difference between vague generalizations and compelling pictures that demand the right verdict.
3. Use the present tense. The present tense creates more of a feeling of immediacy that allows the audience to identify with the story and its participants.[4]

If you use these tools — and you will learn more in later chapters in this book about how to do so — you will transport your reader into your client's worldview, with the result that the reader will be more motivated to act in accordance with your recommendations.

You should also think about a way to characterize your case in a simple way that evokes appropriate emotion on the part of the reader. One way to do this is to find a central theme that sums up your case in a way your reader can easily understand. "For example, the issue of personal responsibility could be the emotional theme of a medical malpractice case, or in a criminal case, the CET [Central Emotional Theme] might be the issue of justice."[5] Experienced and effective litigators never underestimate the importance of using such a theme to provide context for the specific arguments they will make in a case. An emotionally compelling appeal is one in which the advocate combines the facts and law into a simple but persuasive theme.

As the ancient Greeks and Romans recognized, like all people, judges are moved by the right combination of reason and emotion. Judges themselves have acknowledged the importance of the proper use of emotion in an advocate's argument. For example, Lord Birkett has written: "[M]any opinions have been expressed from time to time about the character of the highest advocacy and the highest oratory. It would seem to be the view of those best qualified to judge that simplicity of speech, linked with the expression of the deepest feelings of mankind, has always had the power to stir mens' blood in all ages of the world's history."[6]

———

The trick might be to determine which emotions are likely to evoke the response you are looking for. Thus, you need to determine what your judge

---

4. James W. McElhaney, *It's Happening Now: Breathing Life into the Case*, ABA Journal, Oct. 1993, 101-02.
5. David M. Yamins, *Using the Central Emotional Theme in the Courtroom*, N.Y.L.J. April 28, 1993.
6. Birkett, *Six Great Advocates* 109-10 (1961) as quoted in Shepherd & Cherrick, *supra.*

is likely to be passionate about. For example, while juries might be moved by arguments appealing to simple emotions such as sympathy or anger, judges, especially appellate judges, might be more moved by appeals to their desire to do the right thing in a larger, social policy kind of way. If broad and important policies will be served by a ruling in your favor, you might be able to create an emotional response in the judge by persuading him or her that he or she is acting for the betterment, not just of your client, but of a larger segment of the population — in other words, justice will be served by a finding in your favor.

Successful advocates express emotion naturally in a way that complements their unique personalities as well as the facts of their cases. Different emotional "styles" can be equally persuasive before the same judge or jury. Advocates enhance their persuasive abilities when they successfully develop their own emotional styles. In other words, do not try to emulate someone else's style just because it impressed you. If it is not consistent with your personality, it will not ring true and you will lose credibility. If you are a soft-spoken, thoughtful person, express your emotional arguments that way. If you are more strongly emotional or flamboyant, use that to your advantage. You should keep this in mind when you are making written arguments; your emotional writing style should be consistent with the image you will convey at oral argument, although you obviously have somewhat more flexibility in an oral presentation.

Persuasive advocates believe in and care deeply about their client's cause. Successful advocates know how to express their strong, positive feelings for their clients in a manner that touches the emotions of a judge or jury. John Mooy described the emotional interaction between the advocate, as storyteller, and the audience: "When you truly believe in something — a cause, perhaps, or your version of the facts — you speak with a conviction which enables you to lead your audience through your story step by step. This technique is more than sincerity, for you can be sincere yet not be believed. . . . Believability is that intangible that comes from within."[7] This believability may come at least partly from your ethos, or ethical appeal.

II. ETHOS

Effective use of ethical appeals involves subtly persuading your audience of your own credibility. In other words, your arguments should be believed because you are a believable person. As a person of honor and integrity, you would never ask the audience to do anything that wasn't entirely appropriate. As seen in the examples in Chapter 1, the expression of personal humility is a time-honored way of drawing the audience into your circle of persuasion. Most of us are more easily persuaded by people

---

7. Mooy, *Advocacy and the Art of Storytelling*, 10-11 as quoted in Shepherd & Cherrick, *supra*.

who seem like us, rather than by people who try to set themselves apart or place themselves above us.

Because the speaker originates the message, the worth of any communication act depends largely on the speaker's intelligence, character, and attitudes, or at least on how these attributes are perceived by listeners. Writers since the classical period have stressed that able communicators develop as a whole, that one cannot be one type of person as a communicator and another type in other pursuits. Rhetoricians have given this principle a name—the "able man theory."

Why is this concept important to the speaker? Listeners accept your ideas in part because of their impressions of you as a person. They form impressions of your credibility, accepting your ideas because they expect that you know and properly appraise the facts and opinions you express. They may believe that you have an earnest desire to communicate and that you would not purposely mislead them. Further, they may form the impression that your training and experience have prepared you to speak with authority. If your listeners react positively, your chances of communicating successfully multiply several-fold.[8]

Thus, if you convey an impression that you are thoughtful, honest, and well informed, your message is more likely to be well received. It is highly unlikely that this book can do much to affect your basic human qualities, but we can teach you how to put those qualities together with effective persuasive techniques so that your advocacy will have its desired goal. "Although a good communicator must be capable, a capable person may not be an effective communicator."[9] Rhetoric is both a science and an art that can be learned and can enable an otherwise capable person to become a competent communicator.

An important aspect of ethical appeal is the "packaging": People form initial impressions based on what they see. "What you say is important, of course, but so are a few other factors, like how you sound and how you look; what kind of clothes you're wearing on the outside and what kind of mood you're wearing on the inside; whether you are under-prepared or over-nerved; whether you are funny and eloquent, relaxed and in command; and how you react to the unexpected."[10] This advice translates into the written context in the form of attention to detail. Does your written product look professional? Is it free of spelling, typographical, or grammatical errors? Is your research adequate? Do you use words well? Do you communicate confidence in your arguments?

Meeting expectations of the audience is another important aspect of enhancing your ethos. Violating expectations can create a sufficiently negative response that all the knowledge and expertise in the world will not overcome it.

---

8. Glenn R. Capp et al., *Basic Oral Communication* (5th ed. Prentice-Hall 1990), at 7-8.
9. *Id.* at 11.
10. James W. Robinson, *Better Speeches in Ten Simple Steps* (Prima 1989).

I remember one speaker who chose to bend the rules. He was a participant on a panel of international trade experts at a conference that was attended by the governor of California and other top state officials. Rather than stick to his own agreed-upon topic, he began his presentation by saying, "Before getting into my subject, I would like to offer some observations about the presentation of the previous speaker. I understand that this will come out of the time I have been allotted."

Frowns quickly formed on many faces throughout the audience. To make matters worse, he didn't adhere to his time limit He tried to give two speeches in a time slot meant for one. As the clock ticked away, he talked faster and more furiously to cover his topic. The frowns turned into outright resentment.

Ironically, this speaker had the most expertise of any guest that afternoon, but this was all lost as he sacrificed his good will with the audience. He failed because he failed to do his job.[11]

When you are communicating in writing, it is important to know your job. Stick to what you need to say to accomplish your goal. This requires you to have a clear sense of what your goal is — are you trying to persuade a judge to rule on a motion in your favor, or to overturn an adverse decision on appeal? Make the content-appropriate arguments that are likely to sway the judge in your favor, and only those arguments.

If you bring sincerity, frankness, and sometimes even courage to your persuasive efforts, you will fare better. You must be willing to deal with opposing arguments head on. It is important to acknowledge differences of opinion and available alternatives. No one will believe you if you say that yours is the only way — there are always different ways of looking at things!

As one noted legal scholar has observed, character — of both the writer and the reader — is an integral part of persuasion:

> When we advance arguments, we say "be like me" (or, at least, be like the character I am presenting myself to be in this argument). When we respond, "yes, that's what I think" after listening to another's arguments, we expose and foster an aspect of our own character, advancing a conception of who we consider ourselves to be. Arguments soothe, nurture, move people toward a conception of themselves. They also offend, disturb or repel us. . . .
>
> A person's character has traditionally been seen as the summation of who a person is, the integration of an individual's personality. To read for character, then, involves an evaluation of considerable importance: Being persuaded by an argument is a way of becoming who one is. The nature of our character is always open: We are constantly in the

---

11. *Id.* at 11-12.

process of defining ourselves. While sometimes we stick to an argument, to some definition of ourselves, at times others' arguments convince us and we change our minds. . . .

[A] kind of character much admired in modern society is a person who is able to keep an open mind, able to challenge her/his most fundamental assumptions and, if convinced, to change her/his way of life. . . .

My claim is that you will be persuaded by what I have had to say to the extent that these kinds of evangelical appeals find a place in your own character, to the extent that they appeal to an aspect of yourself and to a way in which you experience the world that you recognize and want to nurture. Ask yourself why you had these reactions. Was it because my arguments were "based" on something that you "know" to be "true" or "false"? Or was it because we had, or failed to have, some intersubjective connection—because you either identified or failed to identify with the view of world to which I have been appealing?[12]

Professor Frug's argument brings us full circle, back to the idea that persuasion ultimately is a function of identification—with a person and a viewpoint. Your goal as an advocate is to persuade your legal audience that you should be believed because you are a trustworthy individual, and that they (judge, jury, opposing counsel) should respond as you request because they could easily find themselves in the position of your client and they would want the same result if they did. In other words, the audience is more likely to respond positively if they can, and want to, identify both with you and your cause. This is obviously an oversimplification of the persuasive process, but it does provide a cognitive framework for learning the lessons in this book and for thinking about why advocacy works (or doesn't). You will also learn how to integrate the facts and the law into this framework.

---

12. Jerry Frug, *Argument as Character*, 40 Stan. L. Rev. 869, 873-77 (1988).

CHAPTER 3

Storytelling and Persuasion

The law is fundamentally a human enterprise. In other words, it is about people — clients and the people in their lives, lawyers, judges, juries, witnesses, police officers, and so on. And all people have stories. The job of being an advocate includes figuring out which stories you need to know, and which stories you need to tell. Then you need to find a way to tell those stories persuasively, or to include your understanding of those stories in your strategy for handling a case.

Every good trial lawyer will tell you that putting a case in front of a judge or jury is all about telling the story in the right way.

> If we are to be successful in presenting our case we must not only discover its story, we must become good storytellers as well. Every trial, every presentation, every plea for change, every argument for justice is a story.[1]

There has been plenty of research to show that juries understand a case better if there is a story that makes sense.[2] In fact, the same research shows that if the story doesn't make sense, jurors will fill in the gaps to create a story they can understand. For example, if the prosecutor in a murder case doesn't present a clear motive, jurors will fill it in on their own, according to their experience and beliefs about how people behave. They may decide the murder was about drugs, even though there has been no evidence whatsoever that drugs were involved.[3]

Although it may seem intuitively obvious that telling a story is important in a trial before a jury, it is just as important in a trial or a motion before a

---

1. Gerry Spence, *Win Your Case* (St. Martin's Press 2005); see also Lebovits, *Persuasive Writing for Lawyers — Part I*, 82-Feb. N.Y. St. B.J. 64 (2010) and Perdue, *Grand Openings*, 46-May Trial 46 (2010).

2. See, e.g., Rideout, *Storytelling, Narrative Rationality, and Legal Persuasion*, 14 Legal Writing: J. Legal Writing Inst. 53 (2008).

3. That was the experience of one of the authors of this text when she served on a jury many years ago. There was no clear motive in the prosecution case, so the jury decided it must have been about drugs, despite the complete lack of evidence.

judge, or in an appellate brief.[4] This goes back to the fact that we are all human, even judges, and we understand stories. There are scholarly analyses of this phenomenon if you would like to read them, but our focus in this book is on teaching you how to use that knowledge effectively to represent your clients in an advocacy setting.

What are the elements of a story? Character and plot, certainly. Conflict is an element of many stories, and a likely one if you are representing a client as an advocate. Our court system is all about resolving disputes, or conflict. Good stories have beginnings, middles, and ends. Good stories allow us to get inside the heads of the characters and understand and care about them. Likable characters we can identify with make a story more compelling and keep our interest. Good stories make us want to know what happens next, and how the story ends.

The beauty and challenge of being an advocate is that you are telling the story to the person or people who get to decide how the story ends. Will your client go to jail? Will your client have to pay a substantial sum of money? Who will get custody of the children? Your task is to tell the story in a way that makes the audience want to give your client what he or she wants and deserves under the law. The special challenge of being an advocate in our adversary system is that the lawyers on both sides have to tell their stories using the same set of facts and available law. So the quality of the advocacy, or storytelling, takes on extra importance.

Let's look at a concrete example. Suppose you have a moot court problem involving a public defender who believes that her office is not adequately representing clients of color — African-American and Hispanic clients, specifically.[5] She has done research that she believes supports her claim and has actively tried to persuade her superiors to do something about the problem. They have told her that the issue is more complicated, that they are doing the best they can with limited resources, and that if she goes public with her accusations she might endanger their already limited funding. She chooses to make a presentation on the subject at a local CLE (Continuing Legal Education) seminar after having been warned by her superiors that she could face disciplinary action if she doesn't stop agitating about the subject. After the CLE presentation, the public defender is fired. She claims violations of her First and Fourteenth Amendment rights. Here are the facts as presented in the record:

> Appellant Apalsa Public Defender Service (APDS) is an agency of Apalsa County, a public employer funded by the State of Apalsa and charged with

---

4. See, e.g., Holland, *Sharing Stories: Narrative Lawyering in Bench Trials*, 16 Clinical L. Rev. 195 (Fall 2009) and Sheppard, *Once Upon a Time, Happily Ever After, and in a Galaxy Far, Far Away: Using Narrative to Fill the Cognitive Gap Left by Overreliance on Pure Logic in Appellate Briefs and Motion Memoranda*, 46 Willamette L. Rev. 255 (Winter 2009). Ken Chestek offers empirical support for the idea that judges are persuaded by stories in *Judging by the Numbers: An Empirical Study of the Power of Story*, 7 JALWD 1 (2010).

5. This case was the basis of the Thomas Tang Moot Court Competition in 2009. Reprinted with permission.

the provision of legal services to indigent criminal defendants. Appellant APDS hired Appellee [Achara] Anand, an attorney of Thai descent, in August 2000, shortly after she graduated from law school and became a member of the State Bar of Apalsa. There is no dispute about the fact that APDS, like other public defender services in this state, is underfunded and its staff overworked. According to a statewide survey, as of 2005, 77% of all persons charged with felonies in the state were indigent and APDS attorney caseloads averaged 280 cases per year. Since 1990, Apalsa State Bar committees have consistently recommended that the state legislature double the funding of public defender services. While there have been slight increases in each budget cycle, the number of indigent defendants has also risen, resulting in a drop in the funding available for each case handled by APDS and similar agencies throughout the state. Perhaps as a result, in excess of 95% of all indigent defendants in the state accept guilty pleas.

The record establishes that Anand is a well-qualified, competent, and highly motivated attorney, and that she consistently received outstanding performance evaluations through 2003. During this period she became increasingly concerned with APDS' ability to provide adequate legal representation to indigent defendants and what she perceived to be racial discrimination in the provision of its services. She repeatedly raised these issues in individual meetings with her co-workers and supervisors, as well as in staff meetings. All APDS employees agreed that these were issues of concern but generally attributed the problems to lack of funding. There was no consensus among the staff on any actions Anand proposed to remedy the situation, other than to continue requesting additional monies from the state legislature.

After two years of apparently fruitless discussions, Anand began compiling information on the clients served by APDS. With the assistance of acquaintances with relevant expertise, she analyzed the data by race or ethnicity of the client, hours spent per client, and outcome of each case. Based upon this research, she concluded not only that the assistance rendered by APDS attorneys generally failed to meet what she believed to be standards of competence required by the Sixth Amendment, but that the agency's meager resources were being disparately allocated in a manner which discriminated against Mexican, Mexican American and African American clients. The results of Anand's research have not been disputed in this case.

Facing resistance from her co-workers to discuss the implications of her findings, Anand prepared written materials documenting her evidence and conclusions, and presented these materials in Apalsa County Bar Association (ACBA) CLE sessions from January 2004 through July 2005. Her allegations that the county's indigent defense program might be so poorly funded and staff resources so disparately allocated as to present serious Sixth and Fourteenth Amendment problems generated considerable controversy among members of the bar and the state legislature. During this period Anand's supervisor at APDS held several conversations with Anand during which he acknowledged that the agency was in dire need of additional funding. However, he also emphasized his belief that Anand's controversial presentations were counterproductive, politicizing the question of funding in ways he believed made it less likely that the state legislature would increase their budget. His preferred strategy involved a public relations campaign highlighting the hard work of the public defenders and showcasing "deserving" cases of wrongfully accused citizens represented by APDS, but without mentioning issues of discrimination based upon race or ethnicity.

Anand refused to comply with her supervisor's repeated requests to stop making her presentations on the inadequacies of the services rendered by APDS. In response, her 2004 and 2005 performance evaluations reflected that while she continued to provide excellent legal services to her clients, she was "uncooperative" and demonstrated an "unwillingness" to function as "a member of the APDS team." In 2005, Anand was the only APDS staff attorney whose contract was not renewed.

If you represent the fired public defender, you would tell the story of a dedicated employee who was only concerned about her clients and the clients of her colleagues. You would talk about her desire for justice for the African-American and Hispanic clients, and you would describe her frustration at not being heard by her superiors. You would tell a chronological story of how she first discovered the problem, how she did the research to demonstrate that it was a real problem, how she went to her superiors expecting something to be done only to be told she was endangering both the office overall and her own job, and how she ended up feeling that she had no choice but to go public. She even chose a relatively small-scale venue for her public presentation—she didn't go to the press, which would surely sensationalize the story, but only to a group of lawyers who would likely understand the issues involved. You would make it clear that the public defender was the central character in the story. You might begin the story like this:

> Achara Anand is a well-qualified, competent, and highly motivated attorney. For the first three years of her service as a Public Defender, she consistently received outstanding performance evaluations. That suddenly changed when she discovered and spoke about the fact that her employer, the Apalsa Public Defender Service, was allocating resources in a way that disadvantaged Mexican, Mexican American, and African American clients.

With this beginning, you have established Anand as a sympathetic character we want to root for. You would continue to tell the story in chronological order, developing the plot and the conflict with the employer in such a way that the judges reading the brief will want to find a way to decide in her favor. You would weave the story facts into the legal analysis so that the legal basis for her claim is clear. You will learn more about how to do this in subsequent chapters.

If you represent the Public Defender Service, you would tell the story of a dedicated group of lawyers, trying to represent too many clients with too few resources. The lawyers who run the office must look at the big picture — serving the largest possible number of clients, and keeping resources flowing as much as possible. They are faced with a subordinate who raises an issue of concern, but who cannot seem to understand the damage she is doing — to morale around the office, to client confidence in the services rendered, and to the Office's ability to secure funding in an always difficult political environment. The supervisors counsel the lawyer, they warn her that her actions will have consequences, and yet she goes outside the office to stir up trouble. What choice did they have? The story might begin like this:

> The Apalsa Public Defender Service is a dedicated group of overworked attorneys providing legal services to underserved members of the Apalsa community. The APDS is historically underfunded by the legislature and must make difficult decisions about the allocation of resources while constantly battling for additional funding.

Now you have a different central character, and a different storyline. The sympathy now is with all of the struggling attorneys in the APDS. The conflict is created by Anand without regard for her colleagues and superiors, who are doing the best they can. Again, you would weave the story and the applicable law together in such a way that the judges will want to support the APDS.

Both stories, as noted, must be told in the context of the applicable law. So you do your research, find the most applicable cases, and fit them into your story. You analogize and distinguish relevant facts, and apply the rules that originate in the Constitution. You may find that the story becomes stronger or weaker depending on the available precedent. But the story is always there, and must be the heart of your presentation. If you tell the story well, in a way that feels fair and honest, and that your audience can understand, you put the judges in a position where they want to rule your way, and all that is left is to give them a legal basis to do so.

But what happens if you don't like the story you have to tell? Let's take another moot court example. A 16-year-old has been convicted of the aggravated rape of a classmate, and sentenced to life without the possibility of parole.[6] The rape occurred on an isolated property, in an RV belonging to the defendant's stepfather. It was only discovered because police had been watching the property for drug activity, and on the day of the rape they were using a military-grade optical device to watch activity on the property

---

6. This case was the basis of the American Collegiate Moot Court Association Moot Court Competition in 2009-2010. The problem authors are Kimi King, Lewis Ringel, and Paul Weizer. Reprinted with permission.

from a public highway. The RV was approximately 900 feet from the highway in a wooded area. The case raises Fourth (unreasonable search and seizure) and Eighth Amendment (cruel and unusual punishment) issues. Here are the facts as presented in the record:

William DeNolf, Jr., is a fifteen year old resident of Olympus with two criminal convictions for "serious" crimes. The first was for shooting passersby at a state fair with an air gun. For that, because of his age, he forfeited the right to possess a firearm in Olympus until he was 21 years of age, and he was sentenced to spend six weekends performing community service. The second was a state jail felony charge of cruelty to animals. In light of his age, the fact that this was a first offense, his expression of remorse, and an acknowledgement that he had a substance abuse problem (he admitted he was drunk and high on marijuana at the time of both of the incidents), he was sentenced to four weeks in a juvenile correctional "boot camp," and he was ordered to undergo substance abuse counseling.

In 2009, William DeNolf, Jr. was convicted of the kidnapping and aggravated rape of a high school classmate. The crime was uncovered by a law enforcement task force investigating a conspiracy to grow and distribute marijuana. During the course of the drug trafficking investigation in the City of Knerr, State of Olympus, several agents participating in the joint task force began to suspect DeNolf, Jr.'s step-father, Chester Comerford and an associate, Bobby Bronner, with being major growers. State law enforcement officials provided additional information from confidential informants which strengthened suspicions. The task force, led by Assistant District Attorney for the State of Olympus, Geronimo Gusmano, obtained utility records from the Comerford/DeNolf, Jr. residence and discovered that the family owned two properties: a residential home and a wooded area of approximately twenty-five acres on the outskirts of the Knerr city limits. The utility company provided a spreadsheet for estimating average electrical use for both properties. Task force officers concluded that the electrical usage at the wooded property was abnormally high, while the main residence was slightly below average in electrical usage. From this, the task force began to concentrate on the wooded property as the possible site for the drug operation.

For nearly three months, the task force observed the wooded property from a public highway. In particular, the task force focused on a thirty-five foot long recreational vehicle parked near the center of the property. The team found that Comerford and Bronner often visited the property using a truck, taking in items in boxes and removing items in black bags — typically remaining for brief periods of time. On several occasions, however, they did spend the night. The recreational vehicle was never moved during this surveillance period. It had four flat tires, but otherwise it appeared in good working order. Had the tires been replaced, or fixed, the vehicle could have been readily driven off the property, except that it did not have a current registration, nor insurance.

At 6:30 on the morning of January 17, 2009, from an unmarked police car parked on the nearest public highway adjacent to the property, Detective Kristin Paige of the Knerr police department examined the recreational vehicle, located some nine hundred feet away, utilizing a CYCLOPS-237 optical device which she had used on patrol in Iraq where she had served in the military as a reservist. This device is a mechanical monocular vision-enhancing device which has not only military applications, but is also popular among bird and wildlife enthusiasts because distant objects can be detected, magnified, and various images recorded digitally through a camcorder which can be attached. The device measures motion in the lens and sends an audio beep so that the observer can focus more closely on motion within the viewfinder. It does not pick up actual sounds coming from objects. It is useable for both day and night-vision, and with enhanced camera lenses available for additional, but expensive costs, the viewing range and quality are considered to be the highest level available on the public market. The CYCLOPS-237 is available in certain specialty catalogues, through U.S. military suppliers, and with a relatively small, but growing, level of public distribution because of its high cost and military applications.

Using the device, Detective Paige identified, through a window with no curtains, the tops of a number of small plants growing under a lamp in the rear of the recreational vehicle parked on the property. No member of the task force could discern these objects using the naked eye from the road; these objects could only be seen with the aid of CYCLOPS-237, and the type of plants themselves could not be readily identified by law enforcement.

Based on the above information, law enforcement sought to obtain a warrant to search the property, including the recreational vehicle. The Olympus state task force decided to go ahead and obtain a warrant because two weeks earlier it had learned that Comerford and Bronner had applied for a state registration permit for the recreational vehicle. Prior to executing the warrant on January 17, 2009, the CYCLOPS-237 was deployed for another visual inspection to determine if the recreational vehicle was occupied. Detective Paige was able to identify movement within the vehicle. Specifically, she was able to identify not only DeNolf, Jr., but she could also see the shadow of another person within the vehicle. She could not see specific motions, nor could she identify the persons. Detective Paige testified that she believed the two persons appeared to be fighting during different times of the observation, but that there was no indication of an immediate struggle. At one point William DeNolf, Jr. did come outside with what appeared to be a bloody nose and mouth. All of Detective Paige's observations were recorded digitally and introduced at trial.

Detective Paige, along with fourteen members of the drug task force, entered the wooded area and searched the interior of the recreational vehicle. Inside, authorities discovered DeNolf, Jr. along with a young girl approximately 15 years of age, subsequently known as Jane Doe, whose injuries were severe and required immediate medical attention, emergency surgery, and hospitalization. Doe reported that she had been abducted by DeNolf, Jr. 24 hours earlier at gunpoint while they were walking home from school and taken to the isolated property where she was repeatedly raped and sodomized by DeNolf, Jr.

A complete search of the vehicle produced more than one hundred tomato and bell pepper plants. No drugs or drug paraphernalia were found on the property.

Fifteen year old William DeNolf, Jr. was convicted in a one-day trial by an Olympus State trial court for first degree aggravated rape and first degree aggravated kidnapping of a minor. Judge Julie Burt sentenced Mr. DeNolf, Jr. to life in prison without the possibility of parole. There was no evidence that Mr. DeNolf, Jr. was mentally challenged. While he had a discipline problem at school and a record of disruptive behavior, along with physical violence, he did well in his class grades.

Olympus does not have a "three strikes law," but Proposition 417, adopted by the voters of Olympus in November 2008, denies convicted defendants the possibility of parole. It establishes that punishment for "aggravated rape" (defined as "rape accompanied by other heinous acts") would be life in prison without parole. Proposition 417 did not speak to the issue of age or mental capacity.

If you represent the defendant, it is difficult to find a good story to tell. He had been in trouble with the law before, and there is no excusing or justifying his conduct on the day of the rape. So you must look at the case the way most criminal defense lawyers look at their cases when their clients are less than sympathetic — the story you must tell is the story of protecting everyone's rights. So you tell the story of the police out on the highway, using highly specialized equipment to see things they could not see unassisted, without a warrant. You point out that they never did find drug-related activity on the property. You want the audience to think about the importance of our constitutional protections, and to feel that they would not want to be the victims of such surveillance. You might begin the story like this:

> The Olympus police used the CYCLOPS-237, a military-grade optical observation device, to look inside a recreational vehicle parked 900 feet from a public highway, in the middle of a 25-acre, wooded, privately owned property. The police were looking for drugs, but after three months of observation discovered only tomato and bell pepper plants on the property. The recreational vehicle had four flat tires and had never moved from the property during the entire period of observation.

You want the reader to picture the secluded nature of the property, and see the analogy between the recreational vehicle and a home. You establish the intrusiveness of being observed by the police from 900 feet away. You also establish that the police never found what they were looking for. Now the central character is all of us — the American people — and the conflict is with the abuse of authority. The story is one that evokes the fear of living in a police state without privacy. We have essentially taken Mr. DeNolf out of the story, as it is more than difficult to sympathize with him.

On the Eighth Amendment issue, you could talk about the tragedy of putting children away for life, with no hope of rehabilitation or the opportunity to prove they have changed. You might talk about how teenage boys are not fully formed human beings and how science proves they lack impulse control. You wouldn't ask the audience to sympathize with the boy as he is, but as he might become. If he matures and sees the error of his ways, and could become a contributing member of society, shouldn't he be given the chance to do so? You wouldn't argue that he shouldn't be punished, but that he should have hope for a better future if he eventually proves that he deserves another chance.

EXERCISE

Draft an introductory paragraph for the defense's Summary of Facts in the brief on the Eighth Amendment issue.

The government's story is easier in many ways. You tell the story of why the police believed there was drug activity on the property, and how they spent a lot of time observing so they would get the evidence they needed. You talk about the serendipitous sighting of the boy and the discovery of the rape — it has to be a good thing that they caught the rapist and saved the girl from further harm. On the Eighth Amendment issue, you talk about the need to keep some particularly dangerous people out of the general population, even if they are young when they commit horrible crimes. You might begin the story this way:

> On January 17, 2009, Detective Kristin Paige and other members of a law enforcement task force discovered a 15-year-old girl who had suffered serious injuries, which required immediate medical attention, in the course of being raped. The officers arrested William DeNolf for the aggravated rape. The officers were present at the scene of the rape because of an ongoing drug investigation.

Now you have humanized the law enforcement officers by using the name of the lead detective. You have made the officers the "good guys" because they found an injured victim and perhaps prevented even further injury. They caught the "bad guy." No one wants to believe that such a discovery is a bad thing, right? So you have set the stage for finding a legal justification for the actions of the officers, and established them as the protagonists in your story.

Let's go back to the elements of good storytelling — character and plot. In our first example, we have specific characters on both sides — the public defender and her superiors. We can ask the audience to identify with them because they are both trying to do the right thing. We can set up a plot with specific dangers — to the African-American and Hispanic clients, or to all the clients of the Public Defender's Office. There is inherent interest and conflict in the plot. The audience should care what happens. We can tell the story in a logical, chronological sequence from both sides — there is an easy-to-identify beginning, middle, and end.

In the second example, the characters are harder to identify with. Some people would be happy to identify with the police, whereas others would not. No one is likely to want to identify with the rapist, but if we make him a more generic character he could be anybody's child and possibly deserving of another chance. In the end, the story has to be a broader one — it has to be the story of all of us, and the rights we hold dear enough to include them in our Constitution. The plot is less about what happened on that specific day than it is about the kind of society we want to live in.

So you have to make choices in your storytelling. Whose story do you need to tell? How do you make it compelling? How do you encourage the audience, which in your case has so much power, to give the story the ending you want it to have? The tools of good storytelling are developed more in the remainder of the book. You will also learn more about the use of legal authority in support of your stories.

Learning to merge the elements of good storytelling, the human aspects of every legal case, with high-quality legal analysis will make you an exceptional advocate. You will find that your work becomes both more fun and more rewarding as you learn the keys to excellence.

CHAPTER 4

Make Your Argument Clear and Credible

I. MAKE YOUR ARGUMENT AS SIMPLE AS POSSIBLE

British political leader Lord Home once explained how he digested complex material: "When I have to read economic documents, I have to have a box of matches and start moving them into position to simplify and illustrate the points to myself."[1] Your goal is to present your arguments so simply that the reader does not need to carry around a box of matches and does not get the urge to use the matches for their usual purpose. The most important key to persuasive writing is to make your arguments as simple as possible.

If you make your critical arguments sound unnecessarily complicated, you can expect to hurt your case. The more difficult it is to understand your arguments, the more likely it is that the reader will give up or, even worse, reach a conclusion opposite from the one that you are advocating. You are more likely to persuade the reader with arguments that seem logical and simple and sound like common sense. Stick to your main arguments and write them so that they are easy to understand.

Here is a simple method for rooting out excessive complexity. Try to state your argument to a legal associate in just a few sentences. If he or she cannot follow your train of thought, revise your words and try again.

A. Present Information in an Order That Is Easy to Follow

The quest for simplicity begins with the sentence. Consider this example, in which you are describing the actions of the trial court in a way that suggests that the court was wrong:

> In summary, the trial court barred the defendants from explaining to the jury that their conduct was lawful according to their beliefs and barred them from substantiating the facts predicating those beliefs so as to show their beliefs to be reasonable by calling expert witnesses.

---

1. *Oxford Dictionary of Modern Quotations* 533 (Tony Augarde ed., 1991).

To understand the sentence's message, you probably had to read it more than once. Although the sentence is grammatically correct, it requires too much effort to comprehend. When you force a reader to piece together the meaning of an unnecessarily complicated sentence, you are not writing as persuasively as you could be.

In this sentence, the argument sounds particularly complex, because the writer presents the information in a confusing order. In particular, the second half of the sentence requires surprising energy to understand and integrate into the meaning of the entire sentence.

We can make the sentence more digestible and more persuasive by reordering the way in which we present its content. If we wish to keep all the information in a single sentence, we can rewrite it this way:

> In summary, although the defendants believed that their conduct was lawful and had expert witnesses who could show that the beliefs were reasonable by substantiating the facts supporting those beliefs, the trial court barred them from explaining their beliefs to the jury and from calling the expert witnesses.

The underlying argument now seems simpler, because the sentence presents its message in an order that the reader can follow more easily. Although this version is easier to understand, it still requires excessive effort, because it contains too much information for a single sentence. We can simplify the argument more by using three sentences:

> In summary, the trial court refused to permit the jury to hear testimony showing that the defendants believed their conduct to be lawful and that this belief was reasonable. It barred the defendants from explaining to the jury why they believed they acted lawfully. In addition, it barred expert witnesses from substantiating the facts supporting the defendants' beliefs and thus from showing that their beliefs were reasonable.

We can improve comprehensibility even more by adding some verbal signals:

> In summary, the trial court refused to permit the jury to hear testimony showing, first, that the defendants believed their conduct to be lawful and, second, that this belief was reasonable. First, it barred the defendants from explaining to the jury why they believed they acted lawfully. Second, it barred expert witnesses from substantiating the facts supporting the defendants' beliefs and from thus showing that their beliefs were reasonable.

By including the words "first" and "second" as verbal signals, we give the reader a clear idea of the structure of our argument. This version contains the same information as the original. However, because we have simplified the structure of the presentation, the reader will find it more understandable and more persuasive.

B. Focus on Your Main Arguments

When you write a law school exam, you expect to get credit for identifying and discussing the critical issues. You also expect extra points for discussing issues that are barely arguable or exceptionally complicated, even though they would be extremely artificial if raised in a "real-world" legal argument.

The real world has a different system of grading. When you include numerous, complicated, artificial arguments in a legal brief or other persuasive document, do not expect the rewards that you garnered in law school. These arguments will distract the reader from the arguments with real persuasive power. They also may detract from your credibility. Stick to the arguments that have the best chance of winning. Heed the words of Judge Aldisert of the United States Court of Appeals for the Third Circuit:

> With a decade and a half of federal appellate court experience behind me, I can say that even when we reverse a trial court it is rare that a brief successfully demonstrates that the trial court committed more than one or two errors. I have said in open court that when I read an appellant's brief that contains ten or twelve points, a presumption arises that there is no merit to *any* of them.[2]

Deciding on what to focus is not always easy. Deciding to abandon or greatly deemphasize certain arguments is also difficult. However, these decisions may be the critical creative act that brings you success. The painter Hans Hoffman has written: "Every creative act requires elimination and simplification. Simplification results from a realization of what is essential."

We can illustrate this principle with an example from the briefs filed with the Supreme Court in *Stump v. Sparkman*, 435 U.S. 349 (1978). In that case, a mother filed a petition with Judge Harold Stump of the Indiana Circuit Court for authority to have her "somewhat retarded" daughter sterilized. Judge Stump signed the petition and the daughter was sterilized. A few years later, she learned what had happened and brought a civil rights action against several individuals, including Judge Stump.

Judge Stump's lawyers argued that because he was acting in his judicial capacity, he was protected from lawsuits. The daughter's lawyers argued that when he signed the petition, he was not acting in his judicial capacity and therefore could be held liable for violating the daughter's civil rights.

The issue before the Supreme Court is whether Judge Stump enjoys judicial immunity from the legal action. The Court ultimately found for Judge Stump.

---

2. United States v. Hart, 693 F.2d 286, 287 n.1 (3d Cir. 1982) (emphasis in original).

Here are the headings and subheadings from the brief supporting Judge Stump:

I. The DeKalb County Circuit Court of which Harold D. Stump is presiding judge was at all times pertinent to this litigation a court of original, exclusive, general jurisdiction over all causes, matters and proceedings except those expressly removed from it.

II. The doctrine of judicial immunity protects a judge from civil liability for any act within his jurisdiction done in the exercise of his judicial function.

III. A court of general jurisdiction possesses the power of determining its own jurisdiction.

IV. Judicial immunity is not lost through procedural errors, irregularities or deficiencies of a circuit court judge's acts. An "approval" is not an "order."

V. At all pertinent times, Judge Stump acted in his judicial capacity. Judicial immunity exists for any act done by a judge in the exercise of his "judicial function."

VI. In applying the doctrine of judicial immunity, the terms "jurisdiction" and "judicial function" are given broad definition.

VII. Only clear absence of all jurisdiction over the subject matter and that fact known to the judge will bring about a denial of immunity.

VIII. The opinion of the court of appeals is erroneous because it ignores, conflicts with and represents an unwarranted departure from the statutory authorities of the state of Indiana and the precedent of this court.

When you see an argument like this one with eight major headings, you dread having to read it. You know that the analysis will be complicated and probably badly organized. When you discover that the individual headings suggest a poorly structured argument and poorly structured subarguments, you know that reading the brief is going to be a struggle. Although you suspect that the kernel of a significant argument is buried in there somewhere, you do not know where to begin looking for it. You are not in a mood to be persuaded.

Could you reduce this diffuse argument to one with two or three major headings and a limited number of subheadings? Of course. Consider this revised version:

As the presiding judge in a court of general jurisdiction, Judge Stump is immune from civil liability for any act within his jurisdiction done in the exercise of his judicial function.

I. Judge Stump acted within the jurisdiction of the DeKalb County Circuit Court.

A. As a court of general jurisdiction, the DeKalb County Circuit Court determines its own jurisdiction, and, here, Judge Stump decided that he had jurisdiction.

B. Even if a judicial action contains procedural errors, irregularities or deficiencies, a court does not lose jurisdiction and a judge like Judge Stump retains judicial immunity.

C. Judge Stump would lack immunity only if jurisdiction over the subject matter were clearly absent and the judge knew it, plainly not the case here.

II. Judge Stump acted in his judicial capacity and thus within the exercise of his judicial function.

A. Judge Stump acted within his judicial capacity.

B. For purposes of judicial immunity, the term "judicial function," like "jurisdiction," is defined broadly.

As you can see, this revision permits you to focus on the main points, which are in the introductory heading and two major headings. If you need a more detailed analysis, you can look to the subheadings.

Most of the argument in the original appears in the revision. The omitted arguments were either not compelling or distracted the reader from the main arguments. For example, although Headings VII and VIII in the original may be correct and may even have a place in the body of the argument, they do not warrant headings in the outline.

For purposes of comparison, consider the headings for the opposing brief arguing that Judge Stump is liable:

I. A judge is immune from civil liability only as to those judicial acts performed in exercise of his jurisdiction.

II. In the total absence of any judicial proceeding having been invoked or even contemplated, Judge Stump's secret approval of the permanent sterilization must be deemed a nonjudicial act as to which no judicial immunity attaches.

Although we might wish for some subheadings to further delineate the analysis, these headings enable us to understand the argument. When we confront a brief that states its argument simply, we find it attractive and are likely to find it more persuasive than its counterpart with eight headings.

C. Explain Technical Information

In today's world, the lawyer often must master the technology and vocabulary of such disciplines as engineering, medicine, economics, and the various sciences. Presenting technical arguments to a legal or lay audience is where the challenge lies. If you fail to provide a satisfactory explanation of technical terms and concepts, your audience may decide that your argument is just too complicated to grasp. To be an effective advocate, you must persuade your audience that it can understand your argument.

When you must use a technical word or phrase, define it first. Use as simple a definition as the circumstances permit. Include only those complexities that the reader must know to understand your argument and make a decision.

For example, suppose you are writing a brief that deals with waste from a nuclear power plant and requires you to refer to transuranic waste. You could define it as waste contaminated with alpha-emitting radionuclides of atomic number greater than 92 and half-lives greater than 20 years in concentrations greater than 100 nanocuries per gram. However, the judges may not need to have this level of understanding about transuranic waste. If not, your technical definition might put them in the wrong frame of mind to follow your argument. It might make them insecure about their ability to grasp your argument. It also might require them to spend so much time understanding the technicalities that they fail to follow the thrust of your argument.

To avoid the problem, you might define transuranic waste as waste that is not high-level waste but that still remains toxic for hundreds of years and requires long-term isolation. If you believe that it is advisable to include the technical definition, you might place it in a footnote and place the simple explanation in the text.

In explaining complicated material, you may find it helpful to use analogies. An excellent illustration appears in *Carolina Environmental Study Group v. United States.*[3] There, Judge McMillan explains how a nuclear reaction takes place in a nuclear power plant:

> The fuel rods in the reactor stand on end, with vacant spaces among them.
>
> Control rods, with some type of insulation or shielding function, are let down from above and occupy the spaces among the fuel rods and separate the fuel rods, thereby preventing atomic reaction. The physical layout is roughly similar to that which would obtain if one hair brush were laid on a table with its bristles (fuel rods) sticking up, and another hair brush were pressed down on it with its bristles (control rods) pointing down.
>
> When heat is desired, the control rods are lifted, the fuel in the fuel rods starts reacting, and atomic fission or atom-splitting takes place.[4]

Judge McMillan begins by defining two technical terms, fuel rods and control rods, and then explains how a reaction takes place by making an analogy that uses a common item, a hairbrush.

As you might guess, Judge McMillan's first career was as a trial lawyer. During the years spent persuading juries, he learned to explain complex material in simple terms. When he became a judge, he had to persuade

---

3. 431 F. Supp. 203 (W.D.N.C. 1977), *rev'd sub nom.* Duke Power Co. v. Carolina Envtl. Study Group, 438 U.S. 59 (1978).
4. *Id.* at 206-07.

members of the bench and bar that he had made correct decisions. His skills as a trial lawyer continued to come in handy.

II. WRITE IN A PERSUASIVE BUT CREDIBLE STYLE

Some lawyers try to be persuasive by overstating their cases and by using emotionally charged verbs, adjectives, and adverbs. However, writing with a purple pen inevitably marks the practitioner as an amateur. Other lawyers state their cases without adding a persuasive edge of any sort. Their style does the client a disservice. It is possible to put your best foot forward without stepping over the line into obvious exaggeration.

For our generation of lawyers at least, there is a preferred style. It is assertive, but reasoned and even a little understated. This approach respects the intelligence of the audience. It allows the reader to be persuaded to adopt the writer's conclusion rather than attempting to force the conclusion on the reader in a way that might cause the reader to become defensive and reach a contrary conclusion. Consider this excerpt from a brief:

> Grantly's claim of false imprisonment shows complete ignorance of elementary tort law. The railroad is not liable, because it had more than ample grounds to detain him. Grantly's conduct was so outrageous that it demanded action by the railroad. Not only did he curse the female security officer and the ticket officer, but he went further. When asked to leave, he engaged in unwarranted abusive behavior by starting a shoving match with the male security officer.

Compare it with this version:

> Grantly's claim of false imprisonment fails, because he gave the railroad ample grounds to justify detaining him. He cursed the female security officer and the ticket agent and, when asked to leave, started a shoving match with the male security officer.

The first version gives no more information than the second. The overwriting distracts the reader from the core argument and probably irritates the reader who has heard this sort of rhetoric too many times to be persuaded by it. Moreover, the first sentence unnecessarily alienates the opposing lawyer.

Here, the facts are what persuade. If you want to make your argument more persuasive, add more relevant facts. You might quote or paraphrase Grantly's offensive language. If the male security officer suffered any injuries, you might describe them. If these events went on over a few minutes, you might state the duration to indicate the seriousness of the disturbance. The key is to persuade not with purple prose, but with facts and arguments.

To be clear, we are not recommending that you never use a pejorative adjective. For example, these sentences would be perfectly acceptable:

> Grantly was loud, abusive, and disorderly. His behavior gave the railroad the right to detain him.

The adjectives offer a telling summary. They are not used as a substitute for facts or as an attempt to intensify the impact of a sentence that should focus on facts. Instead, they serve a legitimate persuasive purpose.

Here is another example. Your client is suing the railroad, because it failed to repair a bridge. Whenever it rained, the bridge leaked, and a puddle or ice patch formed on the road below. Your client drove under the bridge, hit an ice patch, and lost control of her car. You argue that the railroad had notice of the problem and therefore must pay your client for damages resulting from the accident. Here is a written argument that makes the point by relying on facts:

> The railroad had actual or constructive notice of this problem in at least two ways. First, it should have known that the spot was frequently the scene of accidents. Second, it had an engineering report giving notice of the bridge's condition.

If you wished to strengthen the argument, you would bolster it with facts. You might enumerate the number of reported accidents that occurred. You also might quote or refer to the critical language in the engineering reports. Your rewrite might read this way:

> The railroad had actual or constructive notice of this problem in at least two ways. First, it knew or should have known that the spot was frequently the scene of accidents — three serious accidents in the preceding five months. Second, it had an engineering report executed for it that placed the bridge on a list of bridges needing maintenance or repair.

Here is an overwritten version of the same argument. As you read it, you should recognize that the rhetoric fails to make the argument stronger and, by its distracting nature, probably weakens it.

> The railroad showed callous disregard for the public, because it had clear and unmistakable notice of this serious problem in at least two ways. First, the railroad would know that the spot was the scene of many tragic accidents. For it to deny such knowledge is inconceivable. Second, the railroad had in its possession its own internal engineering report that clearly reported the bridge's life-threatening condition.

An effort to avoid purple prose might lead some writers to underwrite and fill their sentences with unnecessary qualifiers. Here is an example:

> The plaintiff claims that the railroad should have had notice of the problem. There are two ways in which the railroad might have known. First, the fact that the spot was frequently the scene of accidents — for some of which the spot may have been a contributing factor — is knowledge that a competently run railroad or its supervisory administrators should have had. Second, the railroad had engineering reports executed for it indicating that the bridge was on a list of bridges in need of maintenance or repair.

This is not the prose of an advocate. If you did not know that this version was the product of the client's attorney, you would not guess it. This version has too many tentative verbs: "The plaintiff claims that"; "the railroad might have known"; and "the spot may have been a contributing factor." In addition, the part of the sentence beginning with "indicating" could be made stronger by using more concrete language: "placing the bridge on a list of bridges needing maintenance or repair."

The goal is to argue honestly, but still to put your best foot forward. The second version above meets these goals quite well. In contrast, the underwritten version bends over backwards not to overstate the client's case, and, therefore, does not advance it.

The rule about overwriting also applies to the way in which you characterize opposing counsel. Consider this paragraph from a court opinion:

> The English language, blending and building upon the vocabulary of its Latin and Germanic roots, is a marvelous and omnificient language, offering a rich variety of words and expressions to describe or explain a single thought. And so, in characterizing the complaint made in this appeal by Mr. David Bruce Baker, we have much to choose from — ludicrous, preposterous, silly, asinine, ridiculous, absurd, nonsensical, frivolous, outrageous, unreasonable, laughable, foolish, unsound, and incongruous come to mind, but there may be others. Meritless and erroneous are partly descriptive, but somehow they don't seem to capture the full flavor of the thought. In other words, we propose to affirm.[5]

Although a judge may be able to use this language to characterize an attorney's work — and we have reservations about whether that is appropriate — as an attorney, you should not. When you use such insulting words, you mark yourself as a bush-league lawyer. You may also find yourself the subject of censure from the court:

> Nevertheless, our review of the record indicates that defendants' briefing below relies on ad hominem attacks not relevant or helpful to the

---

5. Marquardt v. Papenfuse, 610 A.2d 325, 327 (Md. Ct. Spec. App. 1992).

court's expeditious resolution of the dispute, which attacks necessarily augmented the fee demand.[6] Accordingly, we vacate the portion of the district court's order finalizing the amount of the fee award and remand for the court to reduce the total fee by deleting amounts incurred in mounting ad hominem attacks.

In addition to paying a literal price in fines or loss of fees, you also may pay a price in the future. The next time you face the attorney that you have ridiculed, you may have a weak case and desperately want to settle. However, your opponent may be delighted to have the opportunity to repay your earlier compliments. In the end, your reputation and your client's case will suffer the repercussions.

III. DEAL WITH CONTRARY ARGUMENTS IN AN AFFIRMATIVE WAY

Some lawyers unwittingly put themselves on the defensive in the way in which they address the arguments of their opponents. Suppose you must refute the argument that a contract provision is unenforceable. Your client is a forty-year-old adult who recently sold an automobile to a sixteen-year-old minor. The minor wants to void the contract. The infancy doctrine

---

6. The record is replete with such attacks, particularly during discovery. We cite only a few examples:

- "Ms. Bauer's [May 21 letter to the court] is of a kind with her reckless initiation and malicious prosecution of her baseless lawsuit, namely it is tainted by her dishonesty, deviousness, and disingenuousness." — Def's Response to Ptf's Excuses for Disobedience of Court Orders (ROA Doc. # 18, at 2).
- "Ms. Bauer's shameless begging for the sympathy of the court on the grounds that she is a pro se litigant 'in over her head' is a devious attempt to avoid the consequences of her arrogant disregard of three unequivocal Orders of the Court." — Def's Response to Ptf's Excuses for Disobedience of Court Orders (ROA Doc. # 18, at 3).
- "Every minute this case remains undismissed by you is an affront to the legal system and due process. We insist on meeting face-to-face IMMEDIATELY, as ordered, to explain to you why you have no case, why you are likely to be assessed our client's attorneys' fees, and why you should be held in contempt. You ignore our demand and the Court Order at your great peril. You are right only about one thing, you are in 'way over your head.' " — May 21, 2007 E-mail from Def. Counsel to Bauer (ROA Doc. # 19, Ex. 1).
- "Your refusal to meet up to NOW after you have had the ample opportunity to confirm that you have NO CASE is a violation of the May 2 Order for which we will seek sanctions including DISMISSAL, CONTEMPT, and the AWARD OF DEFENDANTS' ATTORNEY'S FEES." — May 22, 2007 E-mail from Def. Counsel to Bauer (ROA Doc. # 19, Ex. 2).
- "Ms. Bauer has pursued this case blindly, recklessly, vindictively, maliciously and without a shred of evidence to support her wild and deluded claim of copyright infringement. . . . Ms. Bauer's opposition papers mirror the nasty, mean-spirited approach she has taken in prosecuting this matter." — Def's Reply on MSJ, at 8-9 (filed Nov. 9, 2007).

Bauer v. Yellen, 2010 WL 1740815, *2 (2d Cir. 2010).

allows a minor to repudiate a contract unless the transaction involves the purchase of a necessity. Here is the wrong way to start out:

> The defendant contends that the contractual provision transferring ownership rights to the car is invalid because the recipient is a minor. He relies on the infancy doctrine, which permits a minor to disaffirm a contract. Contrary to his argument, the infancy doctrine, which would otherwise enable the minor to void the contract, does not apply when a minor purchases a necessity. Here, the defendant needed the car to drive to work; therefore, it is a necessity. The defendant's argument, then, is not consistent with the case law.

In this paragraph, you begin by putting the opponent's argument first in a clear, succinct way. Then you state that the argument is wrong and begin to explain why.

The writing style is defensive. To be sure, you must deal with contrary arguments. To ignore them would be suicidal. However, you need not deal with them in a way that gives the reader the impression that the opponent is the assertive party. When you write this way, the reader may conclude that you are too overwhelmed by the opponent's arguments to formulate an affirmative argument of your own.

Here is a better way to address an opposing argument:

> The contract transferring the car to the defendant is valid. Here the defendant needed the car to drive to work. When a minor purchases a necessity, the minor must abide by the contract. Because the vehicle in this case is a necessity, the doctrine of infancy does not apply. Under that doctrine, a minor can disaffirm only a contract for an item that is not a necessity.

Here, we begin with an affirmative statement of our client's argument. Only then do we discuss the opponent's argument. Moreover, we deal with the issue in a way that emphasizes our affirmative argument: the contract is valid.

In this example, we do not directly state that the opponent has raised the issue of infancy. If we found it necessary to acknowledge that the opponent has made this argument, we would do so without overemphasizing the fact. We could revise the second sentence this way: "The vehicle is a necessity. Therefore, contrary to the opponent's contention, the doctrine of infancy does not apply."

Suppose that your client won in the trial court and now is defending that victory on appeal. You can make a particularly persuasive argument:

> As the trial court held, the contractual provision transferring the car's ownership rights to the minor is valid. Ruling against the appellant, that court correctly recognized that the vehicle was a necessity, and therefore

the doctrine of infancy did not apply. The court's position follows the case law.

With a lower court's decision in your client's favor, you can strengthen your argument by invoking that authority. If your client loses in an intermediate appellate court, you still could stress your victory at the trial level. If you had a supportive dissent written by a respected jurist, you would note it. If you have neither a favorable decision below nor a persuasive dissent, you might emphasize a similar favorable case in another jurisdiction. We will discuss dealing with adverse authority again in Chapter 7.

EXERCISES

1. Mary Lufton is suing United Motors for injuries that she suffered in an automobile accident. She was driving a car manufactured by United Motors and claims that a design defect caused the accident. Since the accident, United Motors has made a change in its design. Lufton seeks to introduce the design change as evidence that her car was defectively designed. United Motors objects, invoking the state's evidentiary Rules 403 and 407.

   Rule 403 states:

   > Although relevant, evidence may be excluded if its probative value is substantially outweighed by the danger of unfair prejudice, confusion of the issues, or misleading the jury, or by considerations of undue delay, waste of time, or needless presentation of cumulative evidence.

   In pertinent part, Rule 407 states:

   > Whenever, after an event, measures are taken which, if taken previously, would have made the event less likely to occur, evidence of the subsequent measures is not admissible to prove negligence or culpable conduct.

   In its memorandum to the court, United Motors outlines the argument this way:

   I. Because the plaintiff alleges culpable conduct, Rule 407 applies to this action in strict liability.
   II. Because the plaintiff alleges culpable conduct, Rule 407 excludes evidence of the design change.
   III. To succeed in this strict liability action, the plaintiff must prove that United Motors engaged in culpable conduct.
   IV. Therefore, plaintiff alleges culpable conduct by United Motors.
   V. Therefore, Rule 407 excludes plaintiff's evidence of subsequent design change.

VI. As a policy matter, excluding evidence of remedial measures encourages manufacturers to produce safer products.

VII. As a policy matter, excluding evidence of remedial measures prevents the jury from incorrectly finding an admission of fault.

VIII. Because the probative value of evidence of the design change is substantially outweighed by the danger of prejudicing the jury, Rule 403 bars this evidence.

Please revise this outline so that it presents the argument in a simple form that is easy to understand.

2. In the same case, Mary Lufton outlines her argument this way:

I. Because the plaintiff, Mary Lufton, does not allege culpable conduct, the evidence that United Motors took remedial measures is admissible

II. Because Rule 407 does not apply to this action in strict liability, the evidence that United Motors took remedial measures is admissible.

III. Because Lufton brings this action in strict liability, she is not alleging culpable conduct by United Motors.

IV. Although Lufton could have brought this action in negligence, she has brought it in strict liability.

V. Guided by proper instructions, the jury should be permitted to make an informed decision by fairly weighing all the relevant evidence.

VI. Whether or not the evidence is admitted, a manufacturer is motivated to take remedial steps to avoid the risks of more legal actions and bad publicity.

VII. Admitting evidence of remedial measures thus is supported by strong social policies.

VIII. Because the probative value of the evidence substantially outweighs the risk of prejudicing the jury, Rule 403 permits the jury to hear this evidence.

Please revise this outline so that it presents the argument in a simple form that is easy to understand.

3. Please revise this sentence to create one or more sentences that make your argument logical and easy to understand.

United Motors should not be granted a new trial where evidence of its subsequent design change would be excluded, because the trial court did not cause substantial prejudice to United Motors by admitting evidence of a subsequent design change.

4. You are describing to an educated, but nonscientific, audience the danger posed to the ozone layer in the stratosphere. You want to give your audience a general understanding of the role that industrial chemicals play in depleting the ozone layer. Here is a draft paragraph of your presentation. Please revise it so that it is not unnecessarily technical.

Human activity that depletes the ozone layer includes the use of industrial chemicals, most notably halocarbons and chlorofluorocarbons [CFCs]. The chemicals rise into the stratosphere where the sun's radiation breaks them down and causes them to release atoms of chlorine and bromine. These atoms react with the ozone molecules and destroy them. More specifically, the chlorine atoms attract ozone's third oxygen atom, and the ozone molecule decomposes into an oxygen molecule and a chlorine radical. When a chlorine monoxide molecule confronts a free oxygen atom, they form a new oxygen molecule and a chlorine radical. A free chlorine atom catalyzes numerous reactions that destroy more ozone molecules. Like chlorine, bromine atoms also destroy the ozone.

5. You represent Madeline Neroni, the plaintiff in a personal injury accident. While crossing at the intersection of two streets, Neroni was hit by a car that the defendant, Thomas Towers, was driving. Instead of crossing at the crosswalk, Neroni entered the street by passing between two cars parked south of the crosswalk. Towers argues that he is not liable, because Neroni assumed the risk. According to Towers, when Neroni exposed herself to danger by stepping out behind two parked cars, she fully appreciated the risk and exposed herself to it.

Here is a paragraph that you might include in your argument:

Towers argues that he is not liable, because Neroni assumed the risk. According to Towers, assumption of the risk arises here, because Neroni knew and appreciated the risk. However, even if the danger was obvious or discoverable by the exercise of reasonable care, a plaintiff who appreciates the danger does not assume the risk unless the plaintiff appreciates it fully. A full appreciation is not present here. If Neroni's conduct shows that she failed to appreciate the danger fully, she is, at best, contributorily negligent. Neroni's conduct falls short of assumption of the risk.

Please rewrite the paragraph so that it sounds less defensive and more affirmative.

CHAPTER 5

Write a Well-Organized Argument

I. STRUCTURE YOUR ARGUMENT

The hallmark of many an unpersuasive argument is poor organization. A badly structured brief or report is a tremendous imposition on the reader. The reader must expend so much energy determining the organization of the argument that he or she has no energy with which to consider the argument itself. In addition, the reader may not know which arguments the writer is stressing.

The lesson is clear: Do not waste the reader's energy. To be persuasive, make the argument's organization easy to understand and encourage the reader to focus on the important points.

A. Make Your Organization Readily Apparent

An important key to persuasive writing is producing a well-organized document with a structure that the reader can follow easily. An obvious structure permits the reader to understand your argument as effortlessly as possible. Pass up stream-of-consciousness writing in favor of organization.

The way to organize is to write according to an outline and to put your conclusions first. Although legal education allegedly teaches students to "think like an outline," you still may not be the type of writer who is comfortable outlining before you write. In that case, write first and then reorganize so that your written product fits an outline. That is, write the outline after you have finished and then, where necessary, reorganize according to the outline.

Here is an example. Suppose that the government wins a conviction against the defendant for possessing cocaine, and now the defendant moves for a new trial in the interests of justice. The defendant argues that he received an unfair trial, because the court admitted as evidence a package of cocaine. According to the defendant, the police's chain of custody arguably had discrepancies. At various times, different officers were in charge of the evidence, and, in their reports, they described it slightly differently.

The chain of custody documents how the evidence (here, the cocaine) passed from one hand to the next until it got to court. By having a record of the possession, handling, and locations of the evidence, the prosecution can show that there was no tampering or misconduct concerning the evidence, and therefore, it is authentic. If the chain of evidence is defective, a court may not admit the evidence. If there are some discrepancies, the prosecution must show that there is a reasonable probability that the evidence has not been changed in important respects.

You are the government's attorney. In drafting a response, you might begin by writing a summary of the argument. It might look like this:

> The evidence meets the "reasonable probability" test for admitting physical evidence, because a reasonable probability exists that the article has not been changed in important respects. There was no evidence of tampering; the procedures followed in handling the cocaine have been found adequate in the past. Additional evidence on the chain of custody would have been cumulative at best. The defendant's argument that further testimony might raise and answer questions is only conjectural. Three different police officers testified that the evidence was recovered from the defendant. Any discrepancies in the officer's testimony are insignificant, as the jury reasonably concluded. Moreover, at trial, the defendant had ample opportunity to bring out any inconsistencies in the testimony.

Your next step is to use this summary to write an outline of the argument. A natural part of devising the outline is to restructure the argument to make it clear and compelling. You must decide what arguments and information to emphasize and in what order to place them. In making these decisions, you should recall one of the lessons in Chapter 4: Make your argument as simple as possible.

You might begin by drafting a sentence that states your thesis and then decide on your major headings. After some thought, you might decide on this thesis sentence and two major headings:

> The evidence meets the test for admissibility, because a reasonable probability exists that it was not changed while in custody.
>
> I. The test for admitting physical evidence is that, in reasonable probability, the article has not been changed in important respects.
> II. The evidence here meets the reasonable probability test.

You then would decide on subheadings. Your final outline might look like this:

> The evidence meets the test for admissibility, because a reasonable probability exists that it was not changed while in custody.

I. The test for admitting physical evidence is that, in reasonable probability, the article has not been changed in important respects.

II. The evidence here meets the reasonable probability test.

A. Three different police officers testified that the evidence was recovered from the defendant.

B. There is no evidence of tampering: In the past, the procedures followed in handling the cocaine have been found adequate.

C. Additional evidence on the chain of custody would be cumulative at best.

1. It would be purely speculative to argue that further testimony might raise and answer questions.

2. At trial, the defendant had ample opportunity to bring out any inconsistencies in the testimony.

3. As the jury reasonably concluded, any discrepancies in the officers' testimony are insignificant.

If you follow this outline and make most of the heading topic sentences for your paragraphs, the structure of your argument will be readily apparent and persuasive. To illustrate the effectiveness of outlining, let us use the outline to construct a summary of the argument. It would look like this:

The evidence meets the test for admissibility, because a reasonable probability exists that it was not changed while in custody. The test for admitting physical evidence is that, in reasonable probability, the article has not been changed in important respects. Here, the package of cocaine was not changed in important respects.

The package of cocaine meets the reasonable probability test for two reasons. First, three different police officers testified that the evidence was recovered from the defendant. Second, there is no evidence of tampering. In handling the cocaine, the officers used procedures that have been found adequate in the past.

At the trial, sufficient evidence existed to establish the chain of custody; any new evidence would be cumulative at best. Therefore, a new trial to seek new evidence is unnecessary. It would be purely speculative to argue that further testimony might raise and answer questions. At the trial, the defendant had ample opportunity to bring out any inconsistencies in the testimony. As the jury reasonably concluded, any discrepancies in the officers' testimony are insignificant.

By comparing this summary with the initial version, we can see the difference that outlining makes. Although the initial version makes the same arguments, it requires the reader to engage in some effort to fully piece them together. In contrast, the revised version flows easily and, therefore, is more persuasive.

B. State Your Argument at the End of the Introductory Paragraph

As we discuss later in this chapter, you usually will begin a paragraph with a topic sentence in which you state the paragraph's major idea. However, when you are beginning a document or a large section of a document, you normally should state your argument in a topic sentence at the end of the introductory paragraph or paragraphs. With this technique, you begin the paragraph by laying some groundwork for your argument and then build to a conclusion. In this way, you give some context for your argument and then let the reader know exactly what the argument is before he or she faces the task of digesting it in full.

To be an effective advocate, you need to place yourself in the shoes of your reader. The best way to start is to remember your experiences as a reader. Think of the times that you have read briefs, reports, or court opinions that did not state the argument or conclusion until the end of the document. You undoubtedly did not enjoy the suspense. In an effort to discover the conclusion, you probably peeked ahead. As a reader, you wanted to know right away where the argument was going. Your reader will have the same need to know that you had.

Here is an example. On September 18, 2001, Congress authorized the President to "use all necessary and appropriate force against those nations, organizations, or persons he determines planned, authorized, committed or aided" the attacks of September 11, 2001. During the American invasion of Afghanistan, Salim Ahmed Hamdan was captured and detained at the Guantanamo Bay Naval Base in Cuba, where he was charged with conspiracy to commit terrorism. Instead of facing a civilian court, Hamdan discovered that the Executive convened a military commission to try him; Hamdan then challenged the authority of the commission. On this jurisdictional issue, the district court found in favor of Hamdan, only to face reversal before the circuit court. The Supreme Court eventually ruled in Hamdan's favor. *Hamdan v. Rumsfeld*, 548 U.S. 557 (2006). Before the Court, the Solicitor General argued the government's position. In its brief, the Solicitor General could have included this opening paragraph:

> The court of appeals properly held that petitioner's pre-trial challenge to his military commission is without merit and that the district court's unprecedented injunction against that proceeding should be set aside. For centuries, this Nation has invoked military commissions to try and punish captured enemy combatants for offenses against the law of war. Petitioner is a confirmed enemy combatant—indeed, an admitted personal assistant to Osama bin Laden—who was captured in Afghanistan in connection with ongoing hostilities and has been charged with violating the law of war.

This paragraph is a perfectly acceptable way to start out. It satisfies the most important requirement, stating your argument at the beginning.

However, a more effective way would be to place the topic sentence at the end of the paragraph:

> For centuries, this Nation has invoked military commissions to try and punish captured enemy combatants for offenses against the law of war. Petitioner is a confirmed enemy combatant — indeed, an admitted personal assistant to Osama bin Laden — who was captured in Afghanistan in connection with ongoing hostilities and has been charged with violating the law of war. The court of appeals properly held that petitioner's pre-trial challenge to his military commission is without merit and that the district court's unprecedented injunction against that proceeding should be set aside.

In fact, this is the paragraph that the Solicitor General employed.

The revised paragraph builds to its conclusion. It begins by discussing the general legal principle. It then becomes more specific and states the legal argument. Because the paragraph ends with the legal argument, the reader naturally expects the subsequent paragraphs to explain that argument more fully. The last sentence thus provides a transition to what follows.

The principle governing the introductory paragraph has a corollary respecting the concluding paragraph. When possible, the concluding paragraph should parallel the introductory paragraph. Write a concluding paragraph that builds to a conclusion and ends with the topic sentence. The topic sentence should be your conclusion. In this way, you reinforce the point you are arguing.

The corollary on concluding paragraphs is flexible. It works best in briefs. In other documents, other formats also can be effective. For example, here is the conclusion section of a law review article. The section begins with the article's conclusion, the results of an empirical study. It then places the results in context and ends with a very general conclusion to which the study results point.

> Our study clearly shows that federal courts of appeals infrequently cite legal periodicals. Furthermore, most citations are to recent articles from a small group of elite journals.
>
> This paucity of citations demonstrates the continuing tension in legal education resulting from two conflicting definitions of the enterprise. One definition identifies legal education as professional training. The other identifies it as an academic endeavor. Yet, citation studies demonstrate that legal scholarship makes only a modest direct contribution to the daily practice of law. Thus, the time has come to acknowledge that legal scholarship is overwhelmingly an academic endeavor of little immediate perceived value to the rest of the profession.[1]

---

1. Louis J. Sirico, Jr. & Beth R. Drew, *The Citing of Law Reviews by the United States Courts of Appeals: An Empirical Analysis*, 45 U. Miami L. Rev. 1051, 1056-57 (1991).

C. Give the Reader a Road Map

When you are setting out on a trip, you want to know your destination and how to get there. A road map helps. It identifies the roads on which you will travel, perhaps points out some landmarks, and shows you the location of your destination.

The reader is also setting out on a journey. At the outset, you can help orient him or her by supplying a road map paragraph. In it, you tell the reader your conclusion, your argument, and the order in which you will present it. Without the road map paragraph, the reader may get lost and fail to learn what your conclusion is, much less your argument.

Here is an example. Crawley discovered that someone had fraudulently cashed a check of his and subtracted the amount from his bank account. Crawley now sues the bank, which you represent. You move to dismiss the complaint, arguing that Crawley waited too long to sue, and now two separate statutes of limitations preclude his lawsuit. In your motion, you might include this roadmap paragraph:

> State statutes bar Crawley from bringing this action for two reasons. First, he failed to comply with the three-year statute of limitations for notifying a bank of an unauthorized endorsement. Second, he failed to comply with the four-year statute of limitations for bringing an action for conversion.

With this introduction, the reader knows that you will be making two arguments invoking two statutes of limitations, one for notifying the bank of an unauthorized endorsement and one for bringing a conversion action. The reader also expects you first to argue that Crawley waited too long to notify the bank of the unauthorized endorsement. Without the road map paragraph, the reader would not know what to expect next. The easier you make it for the reader to follow your argument, the more persuasive you will be.

Here is a more formal road map paragraph. It appears near the end of Part I, the introductory section of the Report of the Association of American Law Schools Special Committee on Problems of Substance Abuse in the Law Schools:

> The report is intended to provide both information and advice. Part II reports information concerning the nature and extent of the substance abuse problem in the legal profession and in the law schools. Part III describes efforts outside the law schools to deal with substance abuse — particularly the extensive initiatives undertaken by the legal profession and by the medical profession to attack similar problems. One of the lessons to be learned from the experience of the bar and the medical colleges is the overriding importance of confidentiality in substance abuse programs. For that reason, Part IV examines the need to assure students of the confidentiality of substance abuse counseling

and treatment and to inform them about the use of that information in the bar admission process. Part V briefly reviews federal legislation applicable to the problem of substance abuse in the law schools. Part VI reports on existing law school policies and practices concerning substance abuse in general, and specifically on substance abuse by law students. Part VII discusses the problem of substance abuse by law faculty. Finally, Part VIII contains a set of recommended policies and programs that law schools should consider in order to deal more effectively with the problem of substance abuse.[2]

With so detailed a road map, the reader is very unlikely to get lost. However, the report's authors could have helped the reader further by better describing the destination, that is, including a brief summary of the committee's recommendations.

D. Use Topic Sentences

As an advocate, you want to make certain that the reader understands every building block of your argument. The building blocks are the paragraphs. To construct sound building blocks, use topic sentences.

As you recall, a topic sentence states the main idea of a paragraph. It provides the topic of the discussion that goes on in the paragraph. Although most paragraphs have one topic sentence, some paragraphs may begin with two or three. In these cases, the topic sentences collectively state the one main idea of the paragraph, and the precise point of the paragraph appears in the final topic sentence before the discussion part of the paragraph begins. (If you have more than one point to make in a paragraph, you need more paragraphs. In each paragraph, you make only one point.)

In most paragraphs, the topic sentence is at the beginning. However, it sometimes appears at the end. As we discussed earlier in this chapter, you will want to place the topic sentence at the end of the introductory paragraph of your argument and of any major section of your argument.[3]

Consider this example. A criminal defendant has lost at trial. On appeal, he argues that his attorney failed to properly represent him. You represent the attorney. In particular, the defendant argues that the attorney failed to present an "alibi defense"; that is, the attorney should have put on the stand two witnesses who would have testified that the defendant was elsewhere at the time of the crime. If you were not conscious of the power of the topic sentence, you might write this paragraph:

Two weeks before the defendant's trial, his attorney had used these two witnesses to present an alibi defense in the trial of co-defendant

---

2. 44 J. Legal Educ. 35, 37 (1994).

3. You may decide not to use a topic sentence when the general idea of the paragraph is clear, for example, in a narrative of the facts. However, when you are making this decision, exercise caution. By omitting a topic sentence, you risk making the theme of the paragraph unclear.

Thurman Carlton. The defense failed. The jury rejected the argument and convicted Carlton of first degree murder. However, at the defendant's trial, his attorney did not present the alibi defense. Nonetheless, despite ample evidence to convict him of other, more serious offenses, the defendant was convicted of only aggravated assault.

Without a topic sentence to give the paragraph unity and direction, the reader must figure out the point of the paragraph: Presenting these witnesses would have been detrimental to the defendant. Even if the reader manages to correctly identify the point, you have weakened your argument in two ways. First, you have made the reader waste energy deciphering the paragraph so that he or she has less energy to focus on its argument. Second, you have deprived the paragraph of a sentence that could give your argument greater intensity.

Suppose that you decide to revise the paragraph and include a topic sentence. If you fail to place it at the beginning, you could end up with this result:

Two weeks before the defendant's trial, his attorney had used these witnesses to present an alibi defense in the trial of co-defendant Thurman Carlton. The defense failed. The jury rejected the argument and convicted Carlton of first degree murder. Presenting the testimony of these alibi witnesses would have been detrimental to the defendant. At the defendant's trial, his attorney did not present the alibi defense. Nonetheless, despite ample evidence to convict him of other, more serious offenses, the defendant was convicted of only aggravated assault.

Here, the topic sentence is the third to last sentence. Until the reader reaches it, he or she does not know what you are arguing. Again, the reader is spending disproportionate energy determining the structure of the paragraph and has less energy to spend understanding your argument.

Suppose that this time, you revise and place the topic sentence first:

Presenting the testimony of these alibi witnesses would have been detrimental to the defendant. Two weeks before the defendant's trial, his attorney had used these witnesses to present an alibi defense in the trial of co-defendant Thurman Carlton. The defense failed. The jury rejected the argument and convicted Carlton of first degree murder. However, at the defendant's trial, his attorney did not present the alibi defense. Nonetheless, despite ample evidence to convict him of other, more serious offenses, the defendant was convicted of only aggravated assault.

Now you've got it right. By placing the topic sentence at the beginning, before the discussion part of the paragraph, you give the paragraph unity and direction. The paragraph becomes an effective building block of your argument.

As we discussed earlier, sometimes you need a group of topic sentences to state the point of the paragraph. In our example, suppose that you decide to include the defendant's argument in the paragraph. In that case, you will want to begin with an affirmative statement of your client's argument, raise the defendant's argument, and then refute it. (See Chapter 4, Part III.) This strategy requires using three topic sentences:

> In a singularly brutal rape-murder case, defendant's counsel employed effective vigorous strategies that resulted in only a fifteen-year sentence. The defendant argues that his counsel should have pursued an alibi strategy and placed two alibi witnesses on the stand. However, presenting the testimony of these witnesses would have been detrimental to the defendant. Two weeks before the defendant's trial, his attorney had used these witnesses to present an alibi defense in the trial of co-defendant Thurman Carlton. The defense failed. The jury rejected the argument and convicted Carlton of first degree murder. However, at the defendant's trial, his attorney did not present the alibi defense. Nonetheless, despite ample evidence to convict him of other, more serious offenses, the defendant was convicted of only aggravated assault.

As you can see, the point of the paragraph appears where it should be: just before the discussion begins, in the final topic sentence.

E. When Appropriate, Recapitulate Your Point at the End of the Paragraph

Sometimes, you will find it effective to recapitulate your point at the end of the paragraph, particularly if you can do so with some flair. For instance, in the last example, you might decide to end the paragraph with this additional sentence:

> Had his attorney pursued the alibi strategy, the defendant might now be serving a life sentence.

Even if you are not creative enough to construct so appealing an ending, you may decide that you need a concluding sentence. An ending like this would be perfectly satisfactory:

> If his attorney had pursued the alibi strategy, the defendant might have been convicted of a more serious offense.

II. PUT YOUR BEST ARGUMENTS FIRST AND DEVELOP THEM MORE FULLY

When we read a brief, report, court opinion, or other document, we usually pay more attention at the beginning. After a while, our interest wanes. In addition, we expect the important arguments to come first and to be developed in proportion to their importance. We can use this information to improve our advocacy. It tells us to place the most important arguments first and allocate more space to them.

To a great degree, which arguments are the most important depends on the facts of the case and the statutes and case law in your jurisdiction. However, there are some general principles that you can use. The most important is to emphasize your least radical arguments. A radical argument is one that requires a court to make new law or reject precedent. A court is far more comfortable ruling in your favor if you can persuade it that your argument is a generally accepted one and actually quite conservative.

Here is an example. Your client suffered injuries when she slipped and fell on worn stairs in her apartment building. When she demanded that the landlord pay her resulting expenses, the landlord refused, relying on this clause in the lease: "The landlord shall not be liable for damage or injury to person or property."

As her lawyer, you can make two counterarguments. First, any attempt to contract away responsibility for negligence is contrary to public policy; therefore, the clause is invalid. Second, although the clause may protect the landlord from liability when the injury is caused by a tenant's negligence, it should be interpreted not to apply when the injury is caused by the landlord's negligence. Here, the injury resulted from the landlord's negligence; therefore, the landlord is liable.

If we assume that both arguments might succeed, which one should you argue first and develop more fully? You should begin with the argument based on the interpretation of the lease clause. That argument is stronger, because it is the least radical. Courts are hesitant to invalidate an entire lease or lease provision or to decide a major social issue. They much prefer to rely on a less momentous decision like interpreting a clause rather than invalidating it. Therefore, you should offer the court the argument based on interpreting the clause, a reasonable, conservative way to decide the case.

The principle favoring nonradical arguments has numerous applications. Most notably, it leads you to prefer arguments that raise nonconstitutional issues over ones that raise constitutional issues. Whenever possible, courts try to avoid deciding cases on constitutional grounds.

As with all rules, sometimes, you will decide to break this one. Sometimes, the nature of the arguments and their relation to one another dictates the order in which you should present them.

For example, suppose your client is a defendant in an action for libel. You have two defenses. First, the statements are not libelous. Second, even if they are libelous, they are true. Your second argument is the strongest. However, if you place it first, your argument will not flow. If you begin with your first argument, you can start by explaining the law of libel and set the stage for the second argument. The solution: Place your first defense first and your second defense second. Nonetheless, develop your second defense as fully as if it were your first defense.

EXERCISES

1. Here are eight sentences. Please rearrange them to create two paragraphs. Make the first paragraph an introductory one that ends with a topic sentence. Make the second paragraph one that begins with a topic sentence. At the beginnings of some of the sentences, you may add introductory phrases and transitional words, for example, "According to the court," and "Therefore."

   a. Butterwell cannot gain relief from the Equine Corporation simply because the assault he suffered took place on the sidewalk bordering Equine's building.

   b. In this city, landowners do not control sidewalks; the city owns them.

   c. A landowner has no duty to protect an invitee from incurring injury on property that it does not control.

   d. An invitee died after being assaulted in a nearby parking lot that the defendant Chamber of Commerce did not own.

   e. The decedent was not on property that the Chamber controlled, and, therefore, the Chamber owed him no duty of care.

   f. In *Steinmetz v. Stockton City Chamber of Commerce*, the Court of Appeals confirmed that a tenant or landowner like Equine has a duty of care that extends only to the property it controls.

   g. A defendant like the Chamber or Equine cannot be responsible for criminal conduct that takes place on property it does not control.

   h. The Chamber had no right to station security guards on property it did not control, no right to place lighting in a parking lot other than its own, and no right to control the activities of its invitees or third parties occurring off the property that it controlled.

2. Here is a paragraph from a brief arguing that a state should adopt the rule that a majority of states follow. Please add a concluding sentence that will serve as a topic sentence for the paragraph.

   > This appeal requires the court to decide whether an injury to an allegedly defective product, here, a truck, is compensable in tort. The majority rule rejects the tort remedy and permits the plaintiff to seek relief under contract law. The minority rule holds that a manufacturer's duty to make nondefective products requires a tort remedy to the purchaser of the product for damage to the product itself when the defect creates an unreasonable risk of harm.

3. When your client took a shower at his apartment, he was scalded. The poorly maintained hot water heater had raised the water temperature excessively high. The lessor points to an exculpatory clause

freeing her from all liability, even in cases of negligence. You have two possible arguments. First, the clause can be interpreted to hold the lessor liable. Second, the clause is unconscionable and, therefore, void. A clause that is unconscionable is invalid, because the terms of the agreement are extremely unfair to one party. All things being equal, which argument should be your primary one?

4. Your grandparents gave land to the city so long as the city used it for a park. If the land were to be used for another purpose, it would immediately revert to the grantors. Four years ago, the city turned the park into a parking lot. Now that your grandparents have passed away, you are their successor with respect to the land in question. You demand that the city return the land to you. However, the city points to a state statute of limitations that would require you to demand the land back in a legal action within two years of the breaking of the condition.

   You have two possible arguments. First, the statute constitutes an unconstitutional taking of property. Second, the statute does not apply to the facts of your case. Assuming that you could make either argument with some degree of success, on which argument should you rely most heavily?

CHAPTER 6

Adopt a Persuasive Writing Style

Thus far, we have discussed a general theory of writing persuasively and an approach to structuring your argument. With this chapter, we move on to specific techniques for making your substantive arguments strong. In this chapter, we present the three most powerful techniques for writing persuasive sentences and paragraphs:

1. Be concrete.
2. When you want to emphasize a word or idea, place it at the end of the sentence.
3. When appropriate, use the same subject for a series of sentences.

I. BE CONCRETE

Suppose that you represent Proudie, the plaintiff in a personal injury case. In your argument, you might write this sentence:

> Proudie has established that his emotional injuries manifested themselves physically.

After some reflection, you might decide to rewrite it this way:

> Proudie has proven that his emotional injuries caused coronary artery disease and a heart attack.

The rewrite permits you to make a more compelling case for your client. Consider the words that you changed. Instead of the abstract word "established," you used "proven," a concrete word with a connotation of activity. Instead of the abstract word "manifested," you used the concrete word "caused." Instead of describing the critical injuries with the vague and abstract word "physically," you identified them concretely as "coronary artery disease and a heart attack." The lesson: Write in concrete terms.

When you argue for a client, you are not arguing for an abstract legal principle. You are arguing for a decision that has practical consequences. In the same manner, judges are not interested in debating legal abstractions; they are interested in resolving specific disputes. When you write concretely, you drive home the fact that your case is not an academic debate, but a conflict involving real people.

Some lawyers use abstract words in the mistaken belief that they are achieving a lofty tone. However, the goal of persuasive writing should be a different one: to paint a graphic picture in the reader's mind. To achieve this goal, use the simplest language possible, use words that the reader is least likely to have to look up in the dictionary, and use words that describe things in concrete terms.

Here is another example. The Rocky Hill News, a weekly newspaper, incorrectly stated that your client, Nally, sold contaminated vegetables at his store. On Nally's behalf, you are suing the newspaper for false light invasion of privacy; that is, the newspaper placed Nally in a false light in the public eye. The News argues that it is not liable, because it did not know it was making a false statement and that it did not act in reckless disregard of the truth. On behalf of your client, you argue that for the News to be liable, you need prove only that it acted negligently.

Here is a sentence that might appear in your argument:

> For a private individual to recover compensatory damages in a false light invasion of privacy action against a media defendant, he or she should need to prove only that the publisher printed the statement negligently.

The sentence is unnecessarily abstract. See what happens when we revise it by merely including the names of the litigants.

> For a private individual like Nally to recover compensatory damages in a false light invasion of privacy action against a media defendant like the Rocky Hill News, he should need to prove only that the News printed the statement negligently.

Even this small a change makes the sentence far more concrete and more likely to hold the reader's attention. By being more concrete, we can make the sentence even more persuasive:

> For a private individual like Nally to win compensatory damages in a false light invasion of privacy action against a media defendant like the Rocky Hill News, he should need to prove only that the News acted negligently in stating that he sold contaminated vegetables.

In this rewrite, we made changes designed to make the sentence easier to understand and to create a feeling that Nally deserves compensation. We changed "recover" to "win" and "asserting" to "stating." We retained "compensatory damages," because it is a legal term of art for which there is not a better substitute. We used "contaminated" instead of "poisoned," because most readers use "contaminated" in everyday conversation, and some readers might find "poisoned" to overstate the facts and lose faith in our honesty. Most significantly, we included specific information about what the newspaper did. It made a damaging charge against a merchant that was bound to ruin his business.

You could make this sentence even more understandable by breaking it into two sentences:

> Here, Nally, a private individual, seeks compensatory damages against the Rocky Hill News, a media defendant, for placing him in a false light in the public eye. To prevail, Nally need prove only that the News acted negligently in stating that he sold contaminated vegetables.

Here is a final example. You represent Trinkets, a small store in a mall. Suburban Realty, the lessor, is demanding that Trinkets relocate to a part of the mall that will attract fewer customers. It argues that the lease gives it this authority. In your argument, you might include this sentence:

> Accepting the lessor's construction of the lease would mean that the lessor has the right to move the lessee to a less desirable part of the mall.

Because the sentence is abstract, the argument is not as persuasive as it could be. The argument becomes stronger when we make the sentence more concrete:

> Accepting Suburban Realty's interpretation of the lease would mean that it has the right to move its lessee, Trinkets, from a prime location to a part of the mall that would attract fewer customers.

We can make the sentence even more persuasive by making it even more concrete:

> Accepting Suburban Realty's interpretation of the lease would mean that it has the right to move its lessee, Trinkets, from a prime location at the mall's entrance to the basement, where it would attract fewer customers.

II. WHEN YOU WANT TO EMPHASIZE A WORD OR IDEA, PLACE IT AT THE END OF THE SENTENCE

A. To Emphasize Information, Use the End of the Sentence

In a sentence, the beginning and the end are the best places to put information on which you want the reader to focus. Use the beginning of the sentence for information that is already familiar to the reader. This information is usually the subject of the sentence. Also use the beginning for information that the reader expects or can understand easily. Use the end of the sentence for new information that you want to emphasize.

Using the end of the sentence for emphasis is almost intuitive. Jokes have their punch lines at the end. In mystery stories, we discover the culprit at the end. We like closure. For example, if you were organizing the American Revolution, which rallying cry would you pick?

It is tyranny to tax citizens who are unrepresented!

or

Taxation without representation is tyranny!

If you were Winston Churchill assuming the position of prime minister in war-time England, which would you say?

Blood, toil, tears, and sweat are all that I have to offer you.

or

I have nothing to offer but blood, toil, tears, and sweat.

If you were Oliver Wendell Holmes, which would you write?

Experience, not logic, has been the life of the law.

or

The life of the law has not been logic: it has been experience.

To use a more conventional example, you might write:

It was an impermissible conflict of interest for the attorney to represent both defendants.

However, if you wished to emphasize that the attorney had a conflict of interest, you would do better to write the sentence this way:

For the attorney to represent both defendants was an impermissible conflict of interest.

You can extend this principle to clauses. The last clause in a sentence gets emphasis. For example:

The defendant failed to meet her burden, as the trial court held.

In this sentence, you emphasize that the trial court agreed with your assertion. However, you probably want to emphasize that the defendant had failed to meet her burden. If so, you would revise the sentence to end with the clause you wish to stress and with the word "burden":

> As the trial court held, the defendant failed to meet her burden.

Even if you are writing a sentence in which you are not making a dramatic point, do not let it trail off. Instead, end it with a strong word. You want the reader to see you as confident and assertive. Sentences that trail off are not assertive.

B. If Necessary to Make Use of the End of the Sentence, Forgo the Active Voice

Sometimes the only way to place the appropriate word at the end of the sentence is to pass up a strong active-voice verb in favor of a weak active-voice verb or the passive voice. Using the end of the sentence is such a powerful tool that most of the time you will decide to forgo the strong active-voice verb. Consider this example:

> Assumption of the risk must be proven by the defendant.

To eliminate the passive voice, you might revise the sentence this way:

> The defendant must prove assumption of the risk.

Although the second version may have a strong active verb, the sentence may not suit your purposes. If you wish to emphasize that the burden of proof is on the defendant, then the first version is more effective. Thus, you may decide to sacrifice the active voice to write more persuasively.

Here is another example:

> The psychotherapist–patient privilege protects confidential communications between a psychotherapist and the patient. Although the Commonwealth has an interest in preserving the confidential relationship between a victim and her psychotherapist, that interest is overridden by the defendant's right to confront and cross-examine a hostile witness.

This sentence ends by emphasizing the defendant's right to confront and cross-examine. To keep that idea at the end of the sentence, you must use the passive-voice verb "is overridden." Replacing it with some active-voice verb like "must submit to" or "must succumb to" would leave you with a verb that fits less well in the sentence or possibly changes its meaning.

C. To Emphasize More Than One Word or Idea, Use a Semicolon or More Sentences

Suppose you find that you have too many words or ideas that you want to emphasize. You can accommodate them by creating more positions in your sentences that give emphasis. Use a semicolon or create more than one sentence.

Use a semicolon to connect two independent clauses that are so intimately related that they belong in the same sentence. The word before the semicolon and the word before the period will receive emphasis. Here is an example from Justice Harlan's dissent in *Poe v. Ullman*:

> Due process has not been reduced to any formula; its contents cannot be determined by reference to any code.[1]

By using a semicolon, Justice Harlan was able to emphasize two words: "formula" and "code." He also constructed a sentence that emphasizes the substantive parallelism of the clauses.

Creating more than one sentence is any easy way to emphasize more words or ideas. Suppose you are arguing that a court-appointed guardian should not have the right to terminate life-sustaining medical treatment. As a first draft, you might write this sentence:

> If there is a right to forgo medical treatment, the anomaly of vesting it in a third person should be avoided and the patient should exercise that right.

After thinking about your draft, you decide that you want to stress two points. First, the right to end medical treatment is the patient's. Second, to permit a guardian to make the decision would be anomalous. To emphasize both points, you must use two sentences.

> If there is a right to forgo medical treatment, the only person who may exercise that right is the patient. To vest the decision in a third person would be anomalous.

In the rewrite, you end one sentence with "patient" and one with "anomalous." Thus, you stress both your points.

D. To Emphasize Information, Place It at the End of the Main Clause and Place the Main Clause at the End of the Sentence

By a main clause, we mean an independent clause, that is, a clause that could stand by itself as a complete sentence. For readers, the main clause

---

1. 367 U.S. 497, 542 (1961).

is the one that receives the most attention. If you place the information you want to stress at the end of the main clause, you give it great prominence.

Suppose you are arguing that an expert witness's testimony is inadmissible. In your first draft, you might write this sentence:

> Her expert testimony is inadmissible, because her opinion is based on her expertise in philosophy as opposed to psychology.

If you wanted to emphasize the reasons for the testimony's inadmissibility, you might be satisfied with this sentence. However, if you want to emphasize that the testimony was inadmissible, you might revise the sentence this way:

> Because the expert has credentials in philosophy as opposed to psychology, her testimony is inadmissible.

In this version, you emphasize "inadmissible" by placing it at the end of the sentence. In addition, you enhance the emphasis by keeping that idea in the main, independent clause and placing that clause at the end of the sentence.

E. To Deemphasize Information, Place It in a Dependent Clause That Is Not at the End of the Sentence

This lesson on emphasizing arguments has a corollary. Sometimes you want to downplay adverse information. To do so, do not place the information at the end of the sentence and do not place it in the main clause. Instead, place it in a dependent clause that is not at the end of the sentence. Consider this example:

> The driver was responsible for his decision to drive drunk, although the passenger had purchased beer for him.

Suppose that you represent the passenger. You do not want to emphasize that the passenger bought beer for the driver. Nonetheless, it is a fact and it would be suicidal to ignore it and permit your opponent to point out your omission. Therefore, you need to include it, but deemphasize it. Keep the information in the dependent clause and place the main clause at the end of the sentence:

> Although the passenger had purchased beer for the driver, the driver was responsible for his decision to drive while drunk.

With this rewrite, you include the damaging information. However, you still emphasize to the reader that the driver bears the responsibility for driving drunk.

III. WHEN APPROPRIATE, USE THE SAME SUBJECT FOR A SERIES OF SENTENCES

By using the same subject for a series of sentences, you make it clear that you are telling the story of the subject. As a result, you give a series of sentences unity and direction and reinforce your argument.

Suppose that your client is bringing an action for employment discrimination against her former employer, the Omega Corporation. She is bringing her action under the Employment Discrimination Act, which prohibits racial discrimination in the workplace. Once harassment occurs, the statute requires the employer to eliminate the misconduct by taking prompt remedial action. Your client argues that Omega failed to take this action. Her argument might include this paragraph:

> The inadequate response by Omega violates the Act. Although a prompt investigation is the first step an employer should take, Omega did not investigate the claims of harassment at the time of the first complaint. Omega's mere verbal reprimands were insufficient to stop the discrimination. Stronger steps were within Omega's power. Suspending, demoting, transferring, or firing the supervisor were possibilities. Moreover, Omega's corrective steps were so tardy that they did not take place until after the employer had been forced to leave the company. Omega thus failed to meet its statutory obligation.

Although you have made an accurate argument, you can make it far more persuasive. You need to paint an unfavorable picture of Omega. To achieve this goal, transform the argument into a story about Omega and its neglect:

> The Employment Discrimination Act prohibits racial harassment in the workplace. Once harassment occurs, the Act requires an employer to take prompt remedial action to eliminate the misconduct. Here, Omega failed to take this step.
>
> With its inadequate response, Omega violated the Act. Although an employer should initially respond by promptly investigating the complaint, Omega failed to take this first step. When its verbal reprimands proved insufficient to stop the discrimination, it failed to take stronger steps. Although it could have suspended, demoted, transferred, or fired the supervisor, it failed to exercise any of these options. When Omega finally took corrective steps, it acted so tardily that the employee had already been forced to leave the company. Omega thus failed to meet its statutory obligation.

In this rewrite, whenever possible, the subject of each sentence and clause is either "Omega" or "employer." The rewrite makes it clear that you are discussing Omega's misconduct and detailing how it failed to comply with the statute. In this way, you present a compelling argument for employment discrimination.

This lesson may lead you to wonder if using the same subject prevents you from adding variety to sentences. Many of us were taught to vary the subject of the sentence to keep the reader from becoming bored. You might have been tempted to use various synonyms for Omega, for example, "the corporation," "the employer," and "the defendant."

This concern for variety is misplaced. You probably were not bored when you read the rewrite. If you had used synonyms for Omega, you might have confused the reader, who could wonder whether "Omega," "the corporation," "the employer," and "the defendant" all referred to the same entity. Because legal writing often requires the reader to struggle with difficult analysis, you want to make your sentences as unconfusing as possible. Do not sacrifice understandability for variety.

How do you add variety to your sentences? There are two effective methods. The first is to vary the length of your sentences. (You will find it particularly effective to end some paragraphs with a short sentence that has a punch line.) The second is to begin some sentences with phrases or dependent clauses.

For an illustration, look again at the second paragraph in the last example. In the six sentences, the main clauses all have the same subject. However, four begin with dependent clauses, and one begins with an introductory phrase. The first and last sentences are short; the rest are medium to long. These differences give the paragraph more than enough variety.

Sometimes the lack of variety adds to your effectiveness. For example, here is a perfectly acceptable paragraph:

> On September 18, the eleven plaintiffs walked in front of a group of houses on Laurel Road. The signs they carried bore their message and were carried on the public sidewalk. They sang softly together, and no one was accosted, blocked, or touched. Nonetheless, they were jailed.

Here is a rewrite in which every sentence has the same subject, every sentence is short, and, with one exception, the first word of every sentence is the subject:

> On September 18, the eleven plaintiffs walked in front of a group of houses on Laurel Road. They walked on the public sidewalk. They carried signs bearing their message. They softly sang together. They accosted no one. They blocked no one. They touched no one. They were jailed.

The parallel construction of each sentence makes this paragraph particularly compelling. Of course, if you were to write every paragraph this way, you would lose your effectiveness quickly. However, an occasional paragraph like this one is very striking.

You can gain the benefit of using the same subject for a series of sentences in a more "toned down" way by introducing some or all of the sentences with an introductory clause or phrase. Here is an example dealing with ineffective assistance of counsel where you want to emphasize the failings of the lawyer:

> Until one hour before trial, the defense counsel had never met with the defendant and thus never had the personal exchange so necessary to a strong defense. Because she never had the opportunity to observe her client, she could not judge his mannerisms and overall appearance. Therefore she did not know that her client was somewhat shy and, at trial, would not come across well to the jury. By placing her client on the stand, the defense counsel made a tactical error that she could have avoided by taking the time to conduct a personal interview.

In this example, the first sentence begins with a dependent clause. The second sentence begins with the word "therefore," and the third sentence begins with a phrase. Yet, each sentence has the same subject, which gives the paragraph cohesion and direction.

EXERCISES

1. Please assume these facts:
   (a) Conway was an employee at a building site. At the time of the accident, he was standing on the steel frame of the building.
   (b) A crane unloaded building supplies on the building frame, and the frame collapsed.
   (c) Conway fell between nineteen and twenty feet. As a result of the fall, Conway fractured a vertebra.
   (d) As a result of the fall, Conway had three reconstructive surgeries. During one of the surgeries, a rod was implanted to support his backbone.

   You represent Conway. Please rewrite this passage to make it more concrete and, therefore, more compelling:

   > While Conway was executing his employment obligation on the frame of the building, a crane deposited materials on the frame for use in constructing the building. The frame collapsed, and Conway fell and incurred a fracture of his vertebra. Because of this event, he has been compelled to undergo reconstructive surgical procedures, including rod implant surgery.

2. Please rewrite this sentence to emphasize that the landlord violated its obligations:

   > The landlord violated its obligations, according to the trial court.

3. Please rewrite this sentence to emphasize that the roadways in question are private and that the financial responsibilities of the lot

owners will be allocated on a proportionate basis. Hint: You may wish to use more than one sentence:

> The private roadways on this subdivision will not be serviced by the municipality, but on a proportionate basis by the lot owners with respect to future costs of care, maintenance repair, and snow removal.

4. Using the lessons in this chapter, please rewrite this paragraph to make it more effective. Please explain what changes you made and why.

> The ordinance is invalid as it applies to land in this town. Although some land in the town is authorized to permit hosting a waste dump, that property is unsuitable for this purpose. The town thus has made it impossible for the town to receive a permit from state authority, namely the state Department of Environmental Resources, to dispose of this commodity on property zoned for this purpose.

CHAPTER 7

Write Compelling Introductions

In *City of Ladue v. Gilleo*, 512 U.S. 43 (1993), Margaret Gilleo protested the first Gulf War by placing signs in her window and on her lawn. The city of Ladue brought legal action arguing that Gilleo had violated the local ordinance forbidding most signs in residential areas. Gilleo responded by arguing that the ordinance infringed on her First Amendment rights. In its brief to the United States Supreme Court, the city introduced its case this way:

> The question presented in this case is whether the City of Ladue, a small and principally residential community, has the right to protect the quality of life of its residents by prohibiting noncommercial and commercial signs that proliferate, cause visual blight, diminish the value of real estate, or create safety hazards.

Thus, the city's lawyers framed the case as one dealing with a good faith effort to protect the quality of life in a small town. In contrast, the lawyers for Margaret Gilleo framed the case as one dealing with an infringement of First Amendment rights:

> This case concerns a citizen's First Amendment right to display a small unobtrusive sign at her home, expressing her views on an important public issue, notwithstanding a municipal government's asserted aesthetic interests disfavoring such signs.

Gilleo's lawyers thus asked the court to balance core First Amendment rights against a minor violation of aesthetic regulations "disfavoring such signs."

In this case, the lawyers on both sides used introductions that would succinctly state their central arguments in an appealing way. They understood the purpose and value of an introduction.

Here is another example. Suppose you represent plaintiff Fred Trollo, who was injured in a car accident. When you draft your complaint, you might decide to preface it with a brief introduction telling the court what the case is about:

This complaint results from a car accident on London Highway. While defendant Frank Loppe was driving north, he struck the rear of plaintiff Fred Trollo's car. Because of Loppe's negligent driving, Trollo suffered severe injuries. The injuries were new and exacerbated injuries that Trollo had suffered in an accident one year previously.

If you were representing the defendant, Frank Loppe, you might preface your answer with this introductory paragraph:

In this case, defendant Frank Loppe bumped plaintiff Fred Trollo's car. One year previously, Trollo had been in another car accident and had suffered serious injuries. Loppe denies that the recent incident resulted in new injuries. Trollo has not clearly documented any new injuries.

Both these examples illustrate the power of a good introduction. An introduction is what the reader encounters when his or her attention is at its most intense. It sets the stage for the rest of the argument. Even if the reader's attention flags when perusing the last half of your document, he or she will still remember how your introduction summarized your argument. As you have seen, you can use an introduction to provide a factual context for the issues and to offer an overview of your argument. You can also use an introduction to put a favorable "spin" on the case and to spark the reader's interest.

Lawyers are using introductions more often and in more places than in the past. Some lawyers begin a set of pleadings or a motion with a short introduction that explains the issue and prepares the court for the argument. Given how difficult the format of most pleadings makes it for the reader to comprehend what the case is about and what you are seeking, introductions are of vital importance. In briefs, lawyers sometimes begin with an introduction or start the Statement of Facts, Summary of Argument, or Argument with an introduction. Perhaps we have learned the lesson from the business world where the opening pages of a lengthy report are almost always an executive summary.

In this chapter, we discuss introductions by offering a large number of examples, all from the same case. In *U.S. Term Limits v. Thornton*, 514 U.S. 779 (1995), the issue was whether a state could impose term limits on members of Congress.

Article I, §§ 2 & 3 of the United States Constitution lists certain requirements that individuals must meet in order to become members of Congress. For example, a member of the House of Representatives must be at least 25 years old, be a citizen of the United States for at least seven years, and be an inhabitant of the state in which he or she has been elected.

In *U.S. Term Limits, Inc. v. Thornton*, the issue was whether a state could impose additional requirements, Here, Arkansas voters had amended their state constitution with "Amendment 73," which prohibited a congressional candidate's name from appearing on the general election ballot if the candidate had already served three terms in the House of Representatives or two terms in the Senate. (The Supreme Court held that the amendment was invalid, because a state cannot impose qualifications for congressional service in addition to the qualifications that the Constitution already imposes.)

There is not one correct way to write an introduction. What you write depends on what will appeal to your audience, how complex the issue is, and how much of a "spin" you think you can effectively put on the introduction. By examining a variety of introductions, we can explore different ways to use an introduction to inform and to persuade.

I. USE INTRODUCTIONS TO EXPLAIN THE ISSUE AND YOUR ARGUMENT

One way to write an introduction is to state your argument in a simple and straightforward way. Here is the opening paragraph of an amicus brief filed by the Solicitor General on behalf of the United States:

> This case involves the interpretation of federal constitutional provisions that address the composition of the national legislature. The provision under challenge, Amendment 73 to the Arkansas Constitution, attempts to impose term limits on the service of Members of the United States House of Representatives and the United States Senate by prohibiting the names of long-term incumbent Members from appearing on the ballot. Amendment 73 is inconsistent with the structure of the federal system in that it effectively makes eligibility for membership in the Congress dependent on regulation by a State. Amendment 73 also impairs the right of voters freely to choose their federal representatives. For these reasons, the United States has a substantial interest in this case.

This introduction sets out the structure of the argument in the brief in a fairly dispassionate way. Perhaps the writers believed that in the role of an amicus with an obvious stake in the outcome, the United States government would sound authoritative and somewhat above the fray if it adopted this tone.

Here is the first paragraph of the Summary of Argument of an amicus brief favoring term limits. It was filed by pro-term limits organizations in five states:

> The Constitution does not prohibit the enactment of further qualifications imposed by states upon their Congressional candidates. Sections 2 and 3 of Article I do not prohibit the states from imposing further qualifications from those listed, and the 10th Amendment authorizes state action where the Constitution does not prohibit it. This comports with the framers' and ratifiers' understanding of the Constitution. To prohibit imposition of such

qualifications would frustrate sound public policy. Finally, Arkansas term limits meet the requirements states must meet when imposing additional qualifications upon Congressional candidates.

Compared to the introduction to the United States' brief, this introduction places a greater emphasis on the history and policy concerns that the brief stresses. Moreover, the organization of the introduction permits the reader to anticipate the order in which the brief presents its arguments.

II. USE INTRODUCTIONS TO EMPHASIZE YOUR ARGUMENT

In addition to using an introduction to state the issue and your argument, you can also use it to emphasize how compelling your argument is. Again, how subtly or how directly you present your argument depends on your audience and the context. Because courts are usually conservative and formal in style, you probably will opt for subtlety. In the following examples, the introductions offer arguments that highlight law, history, public policy, and democratic values.

The following introduction comes from the brief filed by respondent Bobbie Hill on behalf of the League of Women Voters of Arkansas and another voter. Hill was formerly president of the League. The introduction places an emphasis on the legal argument against term limits by setting forth the relevant federal constitutional provisions.

> The Constitution deals comprehensively with elections to Congress. With respect to the House of Representatives, it provides that: (1) "Members [shall be] chosen every second Year" (Art. I §2, cl. 1); (2) the choice shall be made "by the People of the several States" (*id.*); (3) Members must meet three specified qualifications (*id.*, cl. 2); (4) a vacancy is to be filled by the "Executive Authority" of the state (*id.*, cl. 4); (5) the state shall prescribe the "Times, Places and Manner" of holding elections, but Congress may at any time "make or alter" such regulations (*id.*, §4, cl. 1); (6) the House shall be the "Judge of the Elections, Returns and Qualifications of its own Members" (*id.*, §5, cl. 1); and (7) the House may "with the Concurrence of two thirds, expel a Member" (*id.*, §5, cl. 2). Similar provisions govern elections to the Senate.

By stating the provisions in such detail and in a logical order, the introduction strongly argues that these rules present a comprehensive scheme that allows for no additions by state governments. Although the numerous citations to the Constitution add authority to the argument, they interrupt the flow of the sentences. In this situation, the writers might have considered declining the standard advice encouraging us to minimize footnotes and instead placed the citations in footnotes.

In the brief for Congressman Ray Thornton, the introduction sets out a detailed historical argument explaining why term limits are invalid:

> During the debates over the ratification of the proposed Constitution, opponents mounted unsuccessful efforts in several states to amend the document in order to provide for term limits for members of Congress — a limitation the Framers had eliminated during the Constitutional Convention. More than 200 years later, petitioners and their supporters contend that the Framers' rejection of term limits was meaningless and that anti-Federalist efforts to amend the Constitution to provide for rotation were entirely superfluous. According to petitioners, States have always possessed the authority to impose additional qualifications for membership in Congress without following the process for constitutional amendment specified in Article V. Thus, they maintain that an amendment to the Arkansas constitution expressly designed to "disqualify congressional incumbents from further service" . . . is constitutionally permissible.

This argument relies on the intent of the Framers to dispute the assertion that states can impose term limits. The argument, however, goes one step further. It states that by trying to impose term limits, Arkansas is attempting to alter a fundamental decision that the Framers made in structuring the political system. Thus, the debate over term limits is not only about a close parsing of the Constitution, it is about overriding the intent of the Framers.

In the next illustration, the brief of the Allied Educational Association uses a historical perspective to make a policy argument in favor of term limits. It argues that the modern political system lacks a vital element: the citizen legislator. Therefore, the argument goes, the political system requires a major change to restore it to the system the Framers constructed:

> The Framers of the United States Constitution intended that the people of the respective States have the power to pursue such courses as are necessary to elect to the United States Congress individuals who truly represent the will of the people. Yet, the concept of the "citizen legislator" has, to a great extent, been lost in the modern phenomenon of legislatures being essentially controlled by a self-perpetuating, professional aristocracy.

In support of term limits, the brief for the State of Arkansas also contrasts how the Framers envisioned the working of the political system with how it currently operates:

> At issue in this case is whether the Constitution allows the States to structure their electoral procedures for the offices of the United States Representative and Senator in order to ensure that the institutional advantages of incumbency (particularly long-term incumbency) neither create nor perpetuate modern-day legislative fiefdoms that, by crippling the

ability of challengers to unseat office-holders, render the political process unresponsive to the electorate. The Framers of the Constitution envisioned frequent turnover for legislative offices, especially for the House of Representatives, whose members must stand for re-election biennially. For most of our history, the Framers' prediction was correct. But in recent decades, incumbents in the federal, state, and local political systems have been re-elected at an unprecedented — and, to some, alarming — rate.

This introduction makes essentially the same argument as the previous example, but uses more sentences and includes a more complex statement of the argument. Perhaps, then, the previous example is easier for the reader to grasp and, therefore, is more persuasive.

An appendix to the brief includes charts depicting the trend toward re-election in Arkansas and the nation. Perhaps the brief's drafters could have made their introduction more persuasive by including some statistics.

Several briefs supporting term limits infuse their introductions with the theme that the movement favoring term limits is democracy in action. For example, the first paragraph of the Summary of Argument of this brief for several pro-term limits groups forcefully points out that the Arkansas amendment resulted from a popular vote:

> The people of Arkansas are authorized to enact Amendment 73, the challenged term limit, pursuant to Article I, 2 and the Seventeenth Amendment of the United States Constitution. Because Amendment 73, Arkansas' term limit, was enacted through a plebiscite by a majority vote of the people of Arkansas, it constitutes a decision by the people pursuant to Article I, § 2 and the Seventeenth Amendment as to who shall represent the Arkansas electorate in Congress.

The brief for U.S. Term Limits, the petitioners, highlights the same theme:

> On November 3, 1992, 60% of the voters of Arkansas adopted the Arkansas Constitution's Amendment 73, declaring:
>
>> The People of Arkansas find and declare that elected officials who remain in office too long become pre-occupied with reelection and ignore their duties as representatives of the people. Entrenched incumbency has reduced voter participation and has led to an electoral system that is less free, less competitive, and less representative than the system established by the Founding Fathers.

Thus, this introduction fortifies the democratic theme by noting the impressive numerical percentage of voters who endorsed term limits (60%). It therefore shows that the actual amendment was successful, because it stems from a widespread concern that the existing electoral system is less democratic.

The brief of Citizens for Term Limits and the Pacific Legal Foundation takes the democratic theme beyond Arkansas to argue that there is a "national groundswell of support" for term limits.

> Without question, the issue of congressional "term limits" is the single most important governance issue to come before the Court in decades. In 1992, no less than 14 states voted (by margins ranging from 52% to 77%) to enact some form of ballot access restriction to the long-term incumbents in Congress. The national groundswell of support for this method of reining in unaccountable political careerists shows the mandate of the People for change in the halls of Congress.

Note how the use of statistics strengthens the introduction's assertion that a national groundswell calls for term limits. However, the brief fails to identify the fourteen states or describe more fully the types of restrictions that they placed on voting for incumbents. Such a striking statistic calls for documentation.

In this brief submitted by two Arkansas members of Congress, the writers use legal references to bolster their argument that the Arkansas voters had the power to turn their support of term limits into binding law:

> Exercising the powers retained by them under the Arkansas Constitution (Ark. Const. Amend. 7) and the Constitution of the United States (U.S. Const., art I, §4, cl. 1; *id.*, amend. IX and X), the people of the State of Arkansas have chosen to exclude the names of multi-term congressional incumbents from ballots for election to the offices previously held by those individuals. Ark. Const., amend. 73, §3. . . . Nothing about that choice contravenes the requirements of the federal Constitution.

Here, the brief also makes an indirect argument that the Arkansas amendment does not forbid multiterm congressional incumbents to run. Although incumbents cannot place their names on the ballot, they can still run as write-in candidates. Thus, the amendment does not impose term limits, but only makes it harder for incumbents to win.

Is it possible for opponents of term limits to make an argument that the ban on term limits is undemocratic? Consider this introduction in the brief of the American Civil Liberties Union:

> This case concerns issues of fundamental importance in any constitutional democracy. As Chief Justice Warren wrote, "[t]he right to vote freely for the candidate of one's choice is of the essence of a democratic society, and any restrictions on that right strike at the heart of representative government." *Reynolds v. Sims*, 377 U.S. 533, 555 (1964). Because of their unique perspective and history of defense of voting rights and constitutional liberties, these amici respectfully submit this brief in support of respondents on the merits.

Reynolds v. Sims is the leading case requiring states to reapportion their legislatures on the principle of "one person, one vote." The briefs supporting term limits focus on democracy as the collective voice of all voters and argue that democracy therefore demands term limits. In contrast, this brief focuses on democracy as guaranteeing rights to individual voters, in this case, the right to vote for incumbents.

It is possible to overwrite an introduction. For example, in this brief, filed by the Republican Party of Arkansas, the writers may have taken an approach that is too strident:

> The implausible reading of the Constitution's Article I §2, c1.2 and §3 adopted below is indefensible. It conflicts with the Constitution's text, structure, and history. It ignores the theoretical foundations of the American government. And if such a strained interpretation was ever necessary to protect the Republic against possible anti-republican assault, as some have claimed, that day is now long past. The decision below must be overturned.

Although this introduction claims to rely on the Constitution's text, structure, and history to support its position favoring term limits, it fails to give us even a general idea how these authorities support its argument. Only the last sentence indirectly tells us that the brief supports term limits. Thus, the introduction fails to support its conclusions with any specific arguments that we might find persuasive.

These introductions show that a capable writer can make a wide variety of arguments in support of his or her client. Choosing the best argument is often a skill that results from good intuition and extensive practical experience. And, of course, experienced writers will always disagree over what the best choice is. In any case, the aspiring writer will make it a point to read the opening paragraphs of many legal documents to master the craft of writing compelling introductions.

EXERCISES

1. This chapter includes a number of introductions from briefs in *U.S. Term Limits*. Of the introductions that argue for the constitutionality of term limits, which one do you find most persuasive? Why? Of the introductions arguing against the constitutionality of term limits, which do you find most persuasive? Why?

2. You are writing a brief arguing for the constitutionality of term limits. Please write a persuasive introductory paragraph and explain why you wrote it as you did.

3. You are writing a brief arguing against the constitutionality of term limits. Please write a persuasive introductory paragraph and explain why you wrote it as you did.

4. Here is a set of facts recounting a case. The case is now on appeal. Please draft introductory paragraphs for the briefs of each party.

   a. This is a commercial landlord–tenant dispute. The plaintiff, Angel Realty, is the landlord, and the defendant, Two Brothers Corp., is the tenant.

   b. Two Brothers operates a restaurant in a strip mall. The store next door is vacant and is also owned by Angel Realty.

   c. Section 1.04(B) of the lease states in pertinent part:

   > Landlord, at its option, reserves the right at any time during the term of this lease to reconfigure the premises by either increasing or decreasing the size of the premises. Tenant agrees to cooperate with the Landlord in all matters relating to reconfiguration of the premises at all times for the performance of Landlord's reconfigured space work.

   d. Angel proposed to exercise this right under the lease to take away some space from the restaurant to accommodate a prospective tenant next door. Angel proposed to give the restaurant additional space extending into vacant space on the other side of the restaurant and also to give the restaurant a concomitant reduction in rent.

   e. Negotiations between the parties failed, and Two Brothers refused to cooperate with Angel.

   f. Angel served a notice of default upon Two Brothers. The notice set forth the relevant terms of lease section 1.04(B) and asserted "you are in default of this provision of your lease in that you have failed to cooperate with the landlord and provide the landlord access to the premises to begin reconfiguring your premises."

   g. Angel later served notice of cancellation and terminated the lease. Angel then brought this action seeking an award of judgment of possession and a warrant of eviction.

   h. As a defense, Two Brothers argued that the notice of default was insufficiently particular in describing how Two Brothers defaulted.

   i. According to the jurisdiction's case law, notice must (1) be sufficiently particular to demonstrate what remedial action is demanded of the tenant, and (2) state which lease provision requires this action. Here, the court found notice sufficient, particularly given its commercial context.

   j. According to the court, even if the notice itself was not fully sufficient, the correspondence and communication between the parties prior to notice allowed Two Brothers to fully appreciate the nature of the breach with which it was charged. Here, in light of the extrinsic evidence, the notice was sufficient.

   k. Two Brothers also argued that the lease provision did not permit Angel to add more space to the restaurant's premises to mitigate the effect of the loss of space. According to Two Brothers, Angel's conduct breached the lease.

l. The court rejected this interpretation of the lease provision. It held that Angel's proposal was reasonable and in good faith.

m. According to the court, a reasonable person would be justified in believing that the lease provision permitted Angel's proposal.

n. The court awarded Angel a judgment of possession and a warrant of eviction.

CHAPTER 8

State Your Facts Persuasively

"The facts speak for themselves," wrote Demosthenes,[1] Euripides,[2] Plautus,[3] and Terence.[4] "Fools must be rejected not by argument, but by facts," wrote Flavius Josephus, the Judean general and historian.[5] "Facts are ventriloquists' dummies Sitting on a wise man's knee, they may be made to utter words of wisdom; elsewhere they say nothing or talk nonsense," wrote British author Aldous Huxley.[6] According to a commonplace among lawyers, cases are decided on the facts. Therefore, the lawyer should write the underlying factual narrative with a view toward persuading the reader to find for the client.

Despite the wisdom of the ages, a surprising number of lawyers have no idea how to make the facts of their case part of a persuasive argument. If you followed the example of many lawyers, you would present the facts in a neutral and tedious manner. If you followed the example of others, you would attempt to make the facts a part of your advocacy. However, you would do it in the wrong way. You would write in a flamboyantly opinionated style and frequently ignore adverse facts that your opponents were bound to point out.

Instead of imitating these bad examples, you should use your common sense: State the facts in objective language, but, nevertheless, put your best foot forward.

To illustrate the principles in this chapter, we use excerpts from the briefs submitted to the United States Supreme Court in *Hazelwood School District v. Kuhlmeier*.[7] In that case, students at Hazelwood East High School brought an action against the principal, the school district, and other individuals affiliated with the school system. The principal had censored

---

1. *The Great Thoughts* 104 (George Seldes ed., 1985) (De Falsa Legatione).
2. *Id.* at 134 (Fragments).
3. *Id.* at 338 (Aulularia).
4. *Id.* at 410 (The Eunuch).
5. *Id.* at 215 (Against Apion).
6. *Time Must Have a Stop* 301 (1944).
7. 484 U.S. 260 (1988).

articles in Spectrum, the school newspaper. The articles dealt with pregnant students and the divorces of the parents of students. In this litigation, the plaintiff-students argued that, for First Amendment purposes, Spectrum was a public forum. In a public forum, the First Amendment applies, and, under the facts of this case, the students argued that it forbids censorship. Ultimately, the United States Supreme Court ruled against the students.

I. WRITE OBJECTIVELY, BUT PERSUASIVELY

Although the rules for presenting the facts in a case require avoiding value-laden words and opinionated writing, you still can use objective statements to advance your client's position. Here is an example.

In *Kuhlmeier,* the school board's attorneys argued that the board and the principal acted reasonably to protect the privacy of students and their families and to ensure fairness to the divorced parents who were discussed in an article. Because of the rule about objective writing in the Statement of the Case (also called the Statement of Facts), the attorneys could not include in the Statement their opinion that the principal acted correctly in censoring statements that arguably violated the privacy of the parents. However, they made the point by objectively asserting facts. They employed this strategy by reproducing the words of students that appeared in the censored articles. For example:

> My dad didn't make any money, so my mother divorced him.
> My father was an alcoholic and he always came home drunk and my mom really couldn't stand it any longer.
> My dad wasn't spending enough time with my mom, my sister and I. He was always out of town on business or out late playing cards with the guys. My parents always argued about everything.

A less astute lawyer might have omitted the examples and written only a general sentence like this:

> The newspaper included articles in which students discussed their parents' divorces.

Although this sentence conveys the same facts as the original, it does not send the same strong message: The student writers were invading the privacy of families and perhaps making untrue or unfair accusations.

The factual reporting in the original version is far more persuasive than rhetoric would have been. Even if the conventions of legal discourse permitted using rhetoric in the Statement of the Case, the school board's attorneys would have been wise to stick with the facts. If they had included the facts and then added a paragraph of rhetoric, they would have indulged in an extravagance that would have weakened the impact of the facts.

II. STRESS FAVORABLE FACTS AND DEEMPHASIZE UNFAVORABLE FACTS

You must state all critical facts, whether they help or hurt your case. If facts are helpful, you want to make sure that they stand out for the reader. If they are adverse, you want to make sure that they do not dominate your narrative.

For example, in *Kuhlmeier*, the school board's attorneys wanted to stress that the district court found in the board's favor. Of course, the attorneys could have merely mentioned the fact as they chronicled the case's procedural history:

> The United States District Court for the Eastern District of Missouri denied declaratory relief to the plaintiffs.

However, this sentence would have had no persuasive impact. It is a sentence that the opposing litigants might have used.

Instead, the school board's attorneys emphasized the district court's opinion in the second paragraph of the Statement of the Case:

> On May 9, 1985, after a three-day trial to the court, the Honorable John F. Nangle, Chief Judge, United States District Court for the Eastern District of Missouri, held respondent's First Amendment rights were not violated when petitioners prohibited publication of articles containing "personal accounts" of pregnant high school students and students' explanations of why their parents divorced. He found that petitioners reasonably acted to protect the privacy of the students and their families, to avoid the appearance of official endorsement of the sexual norms of the pregnant students, to ensure fairness to the divorced parents whose actions were characterized, and to limit the school-sponsored newspaper to materials appropriate for high school age readers.

Throughout the Statement of the Case, the board's attorneys quoted the district court's opinion extensively. By pursuing this strategy, they achieved three goals. First, they emphasized an important fact. Second, they made an appeal to authority — the opinion of the judge who was closest to the evidence in the case. Third, they permitted the judge's words to make the school board's argument for it.

An additional goal is to deemphasize adverse information. The school board's attorneys presumably wanted to downplay the fact that the controverted articles did not include the names of the students who were quoted. At the same time, they could not omit the fact. Their opponent surely would include it and possibly claim that the school board misled the court by ignoring it. Therefore, they buried this fact in a paragraph containing information damaging to the student plaintiffs:

> The student authors of the pregnancy profiles and "Divorce's Impact" story used questionnaires to research their articles. Each subject was

told the information would be used in Spectrum. The three pregnant girls were told their names would not be used. They were not given, however, any instructions regarding parental consent, and there was no evidence such consent was obtained. The parents of the students quoted in the "Divorce's Impact" article were not "contacted to explain or rebut the quoted statements of their children." App. A-39.

They could have buried the adverse information more deeply by rewriting the paragraph this way:

The student authors of the pregnancy profiles and "Divorce's Impact" story used questionnaires to research their articles. The student subjects were not given any instructions regarding parental consent, and there was no evidence such consent was obtained. Each subject was told the information would be used in Spectrum. The three pregnant girls were told their names would not be used. The parents of the students quoted in the "Divorce's Impact" article were not "contacted to explain or rebut the quoted statements of their children." App. A-39.

To appreciate this strategy, consider how they might have written the paragraph:

Each student quoted in the story was told the information would be used in Spectrum. Their parents were not contacted. However, the three pregnant girls were told their names would not be used.

This version contains the same information as the original. However, it leads off with damaging information and does not develop information favorable to the board as completely as it could have. As a result, the writer runs the risk that the reader will focus on the steps the students took to avoid any breaches of privacy.

III. TO MAKE FACTS MORE GRAPHIC,
STATE THEM IN DETAIL

As the previous examples suggest, a way to emphasize a fact is to state it in detail. As readers, we assume that information receiving more space is more important than information receiving less space.

For example, the school board's attorneys argued that the newspaper was a classroom project completely under the school's control. To provide a factual basis for their argument, they might have written:

The teacher selected the newspaper's staff, made decisions on such matters as publication dates, and worked closely with the students writing articles and laying out the paper.

Instead of settling for these generalizations, they adopted a more persuasive tack. To emphasize the degree of control, they quoted the district
court's opinion, which set out the teacher's authority in great detail:

> [The teacher] selected the editor, assistant editor, layout editor and layout
> staff of the newspaper. He scheduled publication dates, decided the
> number of pages for each issue, assigned story ideas to class members,
> counseled students on the development of stories, reviewed the use of
> quotations, edited stories, adjusted layouts, selected the letters to the edi-
> tor, edited the letters to the editor, called in corrections to the printer, and
> sold papers from the Journalism II classroom.
>
> [After a draft was completed, the teacher] would review the article,
> make comments, and return it to the students to be rewritten or researched
> further. Articles commonly went through this review and revision process
> three or four times.

In contrast, the students' attorney had to argue that the students enjoyed
considerable independence in running the newspaper. Therefore, their
brief should have detailed different facts. The brief might have included
this passage:

> The newspaper's chief editors made decisions on such matters as what
> articles to publish, when to publish, and when an article was ready for
> publication.

However, the brief draws greater attention to the critical facts by stating
them in detail. Because the lower court's opinion was adverse, it cites
alternative authority, the trial transcript:

> The editor-in-chief and assistant editor made the decisions on what
> articles would be included in the paper, according to the advisor's
> testimony.
>
> The student editors scheduled the publication dates, the number of
> pages and the number of issues, according to the advisor. The editor-in-
> chief would check an article ready for publication to see if it had sufficient
> facts and research.
>
> Cathy Kuhlmeier testified that as the layout editor, she wrote no
> stories, and her work for the paper consisted of selecting which stories
> would be included (along with her three staff members), what parts of
> articles would fit into the available space, and positioning them into the
> page size. She also indicated that the copy editors changed article content
> and the editor-in-chief and assistant editor told the staff members what
> an article should cover. There was no testimony that the advisor decided,
> changed or controlled content in any way. (References to transcript
> omitted.)

Another use for detail is to emphasize the actions that someone failed to take. For example, in the amicus brief of the American Civil Liberties Union, the attorneys wanted to emphasize that the principal's decision to censor the newspaper was an automatic, unreasoned response. They made the point by noting the steps that a reflective decision maker might have taken:

> The principal's decision to censor the six articles was made unilaterally and without any articulated reasons. He did not discuss his objections with the students or raise the possibility of editorial revisions. Indeed, he did not even inform them of his actions. The students first learned that two full pages of their newspaper had been cut when the paper was released.
>
> Subsequently, the principal indicated that his concerns were limited to two articles. . . . Specifically, the principal feared that. . . . He also objected to. . . .

In these paragraphs, the attorneys listed sins of omission to subtly argue that the principal acted arbitrarily and only later invented rationales for his action.

IV. INCLUDE STATEMENTS OF OPINION BY REPORTING THE OPINIONS OF OTHERS

In stating the facts of your case, you cannot assert your opinion about those facts. However, you can insert opinions favorable to your client: Instead of stating your own opinion, report that someone else offered that opinion. In this way, you are stating a fact — what someone else stated — not your opinion. This technique is called "masked editorializing."

Kuhlmeier offers several illustrations. For example, the school board's attorneys wanted to argue that the teacher of the Journalism class had virtually complete control over the newspaper. Therefore, they quoted the words of the trial court:

> The district court found that the teacher of Journalism II "both had the authority to exercise and in fact exercised a great deal of control over Spectrum," and "was the final authority with respect to almost every aspect of the production and publication of Spectrum, including its content."

Later on in the Statement of the Case, the attorneys reiterate the point, again by quoting the trial court:

> The district court found "the most telling facts are the nature and extent of the Journalism II teacher's control and final authority with respect to almost every aspect of producing Spectrum, as well as the control or pre-publication review exercised by Hazelwood officials in the past."

The students' attorney might have countered these arguments by quoting the words of the opinion of the Eighth Circuit, which held in their favor.

In these examples, the attorneys make the essential points without rhetoric or value-laden adjectives and adverbs. Moreover, they do not berate the opposing party. Instead, they report the assertions of the court below. In this way, they state facts in an objective manner and still write as advocates. By placing their respective opinions in the mouths of authoritative third parties, they also make their arguments far more persuasive.

When you engage in masked editorializing, you are not limited to quoting the opinion of the court below. You might quote the testimony of a litigant, an expert witness, or other witness.

V. PRESENT YOUR STATEMENT OF FACTS IN AN ORDERLY AND EFFECTIVE MANNER

When you draft a Statement of Facts, think about how to gain and keep the reader's attention. If the initial paragraphs do not interest the reader, he or she may read the remaining paragraphs only casually and thus disregard an important part of your argument.

The typical lawyer begins the Statement of Facts by dryly reciting the case's procedural history. If you start with this introduction, you will have to work hard to gain the reader's interest. If you then unfold your narrative in chronological order, you will ensure that the reader cannot identify the central issue until he or she has digested several paragraphs or pages. To improve your effectiveness, you need a better way to organize the Statement of Facts.

Begin your Statement of Facts with a single sentence that identifies the central issue and captures the reader's attention. In *Kuhlmeier*, if you were writing the school board's brief, you might begin your Statement of Facts with this sentence:

> This case concerns the right of a school system to exercise control over a school-sponsored newspaper to protect the privacy of students and their parents and to teach responsible journalism.

If you were writing for the student plaintiffs, you might begin with this sentence:

> This case concerns the constitutional right of students to publish a newspaper without censorship by school officials.

As you can see, each opening sentence identifies the issue from the viewpoint of the respective party. Although each sentence is ostensibly objective, each includes a strong element of advocacy.

Unless the case's procedural history is important to your case, it should not comprise the second paragraph. Because the procedural history usually is tedious and not critical, do not permit it to become a boring introduction to your narrative. Instead, present parts of it when they naturally arise in the course of your narrative, usually toward the end.

If you believe it important to present the procedural history at the beginning of the narrative, create a subheading entitled "Procedural History" and place the history under it. Then create a second subheading entitled "Facts" and proceed with your narrative. In this way, you present the procedural history at the beginning, but invite the reader to pass over it, if he or she wishes.

When you begin the narrative, you should consider leading off with an introductory paragraph or two that summarize the facts and intrigue the reader. If you were writing this sort of paragraph for the school board in *Kuhlmeier*, you might write it this way:

> At the Hazelwood East High School, the Hazelwood School district authorizes a course entitled Journalism II in which students learn to publish a newspaper and become responsible journalists. In May 1983, students in that class attempted to publish articles containing personal accounts of pregnant high school students and student explanations of why their parents divorced. The high school principal believed that these articles invaded the privacy of students and their parents and might be unfair to the divorced parents. Therefore, he refused to permit their publication. As a result, he faced litigation by certain disgruntled students in the Journalism II class.

If you were writing a similar paragraph for the plaintiff students, you might write it this way:

> For many years, students at Hazelwood East High School have published a newspaper, Spectrum. In May 1983, the principal disapproved of proposed articles on controversial subjects in the lives of contemporary teens, namely, divorce and teenage pregnancy. Therefore, he censored the newspaper. The student journalists brought this action and argue that the school has violated their First Amendment rights.

In both examples, the writers prepared the reader for what would follow so that the reader would be able to digest the narrative more easily. In addition, the writers summarized the facts from their respective client's viewpoint and thus contributed to the briefs' persuasive power.

As you can see, with minimal effort, you can organize your Statement of Facts so that it is highly accessible to the reader. If you write factually, but still write as an advocate, the accessibility of your narrative will make it a compelling part of your argument.

1. Here are the facts of an automobile negligence case. Jack Chadwick struck and injured John Bunce, a six-year-old boy. John and his mother are bringing an action for personal injuries and medical expenses. They argue that Chadwick failed to keep a proper lookout and should have either stopped driving or driven more slowly when he had extreme difficulty seeing the street in front of him You represent John. Please use this information to write a statement of facts favorable to him.

   a. At 7:30 p.m., daylight saving time, on July 8, John Chadwick was driving along Hogglestock Road at approximately 20 to 25 miles per hour.

   b. At 7:30 p.m., it was still daylight. Sunset was at 7:40 p.m.

   c. The police report states that no improper driving was indicated, that Chadwick had been driving at approximately 20 to 25 miles per hour, and that 25 miles per hour was the maximum safe speed under prevailing conditions.

   d. On Chadwick's right side, the south side of the road, was a row of commercial buildings with diagonal parking. On the left side was a residential area. There was no cross street or pedestrian crosswalk in the vicinity.

   e. John Bunce, a six-year-old boy, was playing with other children near the curb on the left hand side and ran into the path of Chadwick's car.

   f. According to the police report, the car's skidmarks were 38 feet long, and the impact could have occurred anywhere within the 38 feet. At the end of the skid, the left wheel marks were 20 feet from where the south curbline would have been if there had been no parking area.

   g. The impact broke the glass of the vehicle's left headlights and caused a dent in the front of its left front fender.

   h. The only eyewitnesses were Chadwick, John, and Harry, John's eight-and-one-half-year old brother, who was one of the children playing there.

   i. Harry testified that while he was watching another boy, who had fallen off his bicycle, he noticed that John had left and "he was about more than halfway across the street and I said 'John, watch out.' He started to turn around, but he didn't get all the way turned around and the car hit him."

   j. John testified: "I didn't see the car before I started across the street. Then I heard my brother calling me and yelling 'Watch out!' I started to turn around, but it was too late. I saw the car coming at me."

k. Chadwick testified:

> I didn't see him until after I hit him, because the sun was glaring off the cars that were parked on the side of the road there and it was hard to see. The glare came from the cars parked in the shopping center and from the cars coming toward me and anything that would glare. When I struck the boy, I was driving where I should have been, near the middle of the road. When I hit the brakes, it was the same time that I hit him. I couldn't see the other side of the street, because there were so many cars backing in and out of the shopping center there and cars coming from the opposite direction. I was trying to look in all directions to make sure there was nothing there. Then I heard a thud and saw the kid rolling down the street. When I heard the thud, I guess simultaneously I hit the brakes and turned to the right. That was it.

2. You are Jack Chadwick's lawyer, from Exercise 1. Please write a statement of facts favorable to him.

CHAPTER 9

Use Authority Persuasively

When making legal arguments, you are typically trying to persuade an audience that will not be swayed by the originality of your argument, but rather by the strength of the authority that supports your argument. The more directly your authority supports the proposition you are arguing for, the more persuasive your argument will be. The more powerful the source of your authority, the more your audience will generally respect it.

To a large degree in our common law system, the strength of your authority depends on how well you present it, and how well you make analogies between existing authority and the ruling you seek. There are three primary sources of authority in our system — constitutions, statutes and accompanying regulations, and case law. All can be used well and persuasively, or not. This chapter gives you some guidelines for using authority persuasively.

I. USE STATUTES AND CONSTITUTIONAL PROVISIONS EFFECTIVELY

A. Focus on the Relevant Language

When making arguments for which you have statutory or constitutional authority, you must begin with the plain language of the provision at issue, for that is where courts look first in analyzing such authority. This typically means that you should quote the language to be applied early in your argument. You should not indiscriminately quote extensive portions of a statute, but only those portions that must be interpreted to reach a result in your case. For example, if you are making an argument that your client has been stalked by another individual, you might use this statute:

§ 1708.7. Stalking; tort action; damages and equitable remedies

(a) A person is liable for the tort of stalking when the plaintiff proves all of the following elements of the tort:

(1) The defendant engaged in a pattern of conduct the intent of which was to follow, alarm, or harass the plaintiff. In order to

establish this element, the plaintiff shall be required to support his or her allegations with independent corroborating evidence.

(2) As a result of that pattern of conduct, the plaintiff reasonably feared for his or her safety, or the safety of an immediate family member. For purposes of this paragraph, "immediate family" means a spouse, parent, child, any person related by consanguinity or affinity within the second degree, or any person who regularly resides, or, within the six months preceding any portion of the pattern of conduct, regularly resided, in the plaintiff's household.

(3) One of the following:

(A) The defendant, as a part of the pattern of conduct specified in paragraph (1), made a credible threat with the intent to place the plaintiff in reasonable fear for his or her safety, or the safety of an immediate family member and, on at least one occasion, the plaintiff clearly and definitively demanded that the defendant cease and abate his or her pattern of conduct and the defendant persisted in his or her pattern of conduct.

(B) The defendant violated a restraining order, including, but not limited to, any order issued pursuant to Section 527.6 of the Code of Civil Procedure, prohibiting any act described in subdivision (a).

(b) For the purposes of this section:

(1) "Pattern of conduct" means conduct composed of a series of acts over a period of time, however short, evidencing a continuity of purpose. Constitutionally protected activity is not included within the meaning of "pattern of conduct."

(2) "Credible threat" means a verbal or written threat, including that communicated by means of an electronic communication device, or a threat implied by a pattern of conduct or a combination of verbal, written, or electronically communicated statements and conduct, made with the intent and apparent ability to carry out the threat so as to cause the person who is the target of the threat to reasonably fear for his or her safety or the safety of his or her immediate family.

(3) "Electronic communication device" includes, but is not limited to, telephones, cellular telephones, computers, video recorders, fax machines, or pagers. "Electronic communication" has the same meaning as the term defined in Subsection 12 of Section 2510 of Title 18 of the United States Code.

(4) "Harass" means a knowing and willful course of conduct directed at a specific person which seriously alarms, annoys, torments, or terrorizes the person, and which serves no legitimate purpose. The course of conduct must be such as would cause a reasonable person to suffer substantial emotional distress, and must actually cause substantial emotional distress to the person.

(c) A person who commits the tort of stalking upon another is liable to that person for damages, including, but not limited to, general damages, special damages, and punitive damages pursuant to Section 3294.

(d) In an action pursuant to this section, the court may grant equitable relief, including, but not limited to, an injunction.

(e) The rights and remedies provided in this section are cumulative and in addition to any other rights and remedies provided by law.

(f) This section shall not be construed to impair any constitutionally protected activity, including, but not limited to, speech, protest, and assembly.

You would not, however, want to quote the entire statute at the beginning of your argument. It would be distracting, and might leave the court wondering which parts of the statute are important to the case. Thus, you should quote only the important language, and omit the rest. In your case, the court will have to interpret the following language, so you should probably quote it:

§ 1708.7. Stalking; tort action; damages and equitable remedies

(a)(1)   The defendant engaged in a pattern of conduct the intent of which was to follow, alarm, or harass the plaintiff. . . .

(a)(2)   As a result of that pattern of conduct, the plaintiff reasonably feared for his or her safety, or the safety of an immediate family member. . . .

(3)(A)   The defendant, as a part of the pattern of conduct specified in paragraph (1), made a credible threat with the intent to place the plaintiff in reasonable fear for his or her safety, or the safety of an immediate family member and, on at least one occasion, the plaintiff clearly and definitively demanded that the defendant cease and abate his or her pattern of conduct and the defendant persisted in his or her pattern of conduct. . . .

You can probably think of ways to edit this language further; for example, you can quote only the specific phrase(s) the court will have to focus on. If the issue in dispute in your case is whether the requisite reasonable fear was present, you might simply quote the language about "reasonable fear for his or her safety." The choice of language to quote will necessarily depend on the issues actually in controversy in your case.

If any of the definitions in the statute are important to your argument, you might want to quote those, too. You should save such quotes until you get to the part of the argument in which the defined term becomes important.

B. Use Predictable, Clear Organization

You should organize your arguments according to the organizational scheme of the statute. Typically, statutes are organized into elements that must be satisfied for the statute to apply. Your argument should be structured accordingly. For example, if you were making an argument based on the preceding stalking statute, your argument headings could appear as follows:

I. The defendant engaged in a pattern of conduct intending to follow, harass, or alarm the plaintiff.

II. As a result of the defendant's pattern of conduct, the plaintiff reasonably feared for her safety and the safety of her family.

III. The defendant made a credible threat to the safety of the plaintiff and her family.

IV. The plaintiff clearly and definitively demanded that the defendant cease his pattern of conduct, but the defendant persisted.

You will notice that the suggested argument structure includes four headings, while the statute seems to contain only three elements. In reality, the credible threat and demand to desist elements are separate, and your analysis will be clearer if you treat them as such.

You should do the same thing with statutes that are not explicitly divided into elements: Identify the requirements to be met, and set them out as elements in your analysis. For example, you may be arguing a case involving this statute:

Every teacher in the public schools shall hold pupils to a strict account for their conduct on the way to and from school, on the playgrounds, or during recess. A teacher, vice principal, principal, or any other certificated employee of a school district, shall not be subject to criminal prosecution or criminal penalties for the exercise, during the performance of his duties, of the same degree of physical control over a pupil that a parent would be legally privileged to exercise but which in no event shall exceed the amount of physical control reasonably necessary to maintain order, protect property, or protect the health and safety of pupils, or to maintain proper and appropriate conditions conducive to learning.

The statute identifies the elements that must be present for a teacher to avoid criminal penalties:

1. Action must be in performance of the teacher's duties.

2. Physical control must be equivalent to that which a parent could legally exercise.

3. Physical control must be no more than necessary to:

   a. Maintain order,

   b. Protect property,

   c. Protect the health and safety of pupils, or

   d. Maintain proper and appropriate conditions conducive to learning.

Again, you should create headings that identify these points of analysis, so the court can more easily follow your argument.

You may find that previous court decisions interpreting your provision have already identified elements for analysis. If so, follow the structure they have created.

By following the structure of the statute or of previous decisions, you make your arguments in a predictable way, and you use the language the court will have to apply in evaluating your client's case. Courts have a much easier time understanding, and therefore being persuaded by, your arguments if they present information in a familiar and organized way.

II. USE CASE LAW EFFECTIVELY

Although Oscar Wilde declared that "consistency is to the life of the intellect . . . a confession of failure,"[1] most of us, including judges, like the stability and predictability that consistency offers. Judges like their decisions to be consistent with past decisions of their court. They also must be persuaded that their decisions are consistent with those of any higher court. In legal analysis and argument, being consistent means following precedent. Justice Oliver Wendell Holmes once wrote: "We believe the weight attached to [precedent] is about the best thing in our whole system of law."[2] Invoking precedent is a powerful tool of persuasion.

The difficulty with invoking precedent arises when the earlier case does not support your position or a court cannot clearly determine whether it supports your position. You might argue that the earlier case was wrongly decided. However, this tactic would work at cross purposes with your desire to claim that you are arguing consistently with existing case law. Therefore, an argument rejecting precedent should be an argument of last resort. Your first argument should be that existing law supports your position or, at least, is consistent with it.

In this chapter, we first review ways to select the most favorable precedent. We then discuss two ways to deal with seemingly adverse precedent: interpreting case holdings broadly or narrowly, as appropriate, and distinguishing cases on their facts. Finally, we explain how to deal with adverse precedent without sounding defensive.

A. Rely on Favorable Precedent

The rules for invoking favorable precedent are easy enough. Give the most attention to cases in your jurisdiction with fact patterns similar to

---

1. Hesketh Pearson, *Oscar Wilde: His Life and Wit* 171 (1946).
2. *Summary of Events*, 7 Am. L. Rev. 558, 559 (1873); *Value of Precedent*, in *Justice Oliver Wendell Holmes: His Book Notices and Uncollected Letters and Papers* 34-35 (Harry C. Schriver ed., 1936).

yours. If you cannot find these cases, find others with parallels to your case, preferably in your jurisdiction. Here are some general rules:

1. Rely most heavily on cases from higher courts in your jurisdiction dealing with issues and facts closest to those in your case. Discuss those cases fully.
2. Rely on cases with facts and issues close to yours that come from the court to which you are arguing. Discuss those cases fully.
3. Discuss cases in your jurisdiction with issues and facts related to yours. The more that a case parallels yours, the more you should discuss it.
4. Discuss cases from other jurisdictions that are parallel to your case. If most jurisdictions follow the rule or application you advocate, label it the majority position. If most courts or many prestigious courts have adopted your position in the recent past, label it the trend of law. If there is a leading case, discuss it fully.
5. When you are documenting a majority position or trend of law, you may use long string citations. In other situations, you should avoid them and generally stick to the most recent leading cases. When you use string citations, consider following each cite with a parenthetical that briefly describes the case. For example: *Union County v. Hoffman*, 512 N.W.2d 168 (S.D. 1994) (permitting the abatement of a nonconforming use — here, a trailer park — that is a public nuisance).
6. If no direct precedent addresses your case and the law is unsettled, support your argument with the cases and other authorities that seem most relevant. Cases from your jurisdiction should receive the most discussion. You probably will need to cite many cases and authorities and give them careful attention.

These rules would gain the agreement of most skilled legal writers. However, the difficult problems arise when precedent does not support your argument — either the earlier cases are ambiguous or they appear to go against you. To these troublesome matters we next turn our attention.

B. Interpret Precedent Narrowly or Broadly, as Appropriate

Most holdings are open to more than one interpretation. When dealing with precedent, select the interpretation that furthers your case. Depending on the facts of your case, you will choose to interpret the holding narrowly or broadly.

Here is an example of how to interpret a holding narrowly. A lease states that the tenant has no duty "to restore any damage caused by fire, windstorm or any other casualty beyond his control." In the case, Alford leased a store from Majestic, Inc., and through their negligence, Alford's employees started a fire that burned down the building. The court held that Alford's employees were in his control and therefore ordered Alford to pay damages. Your client is a tenant who rented a store under a lease with the same clause as in *Majestic, Inc. v. Alford.* One of your client's employees who was angry at your client intentionally started a fire and burned down the store.

The landlord argues that under *Majestic,* your client is liable for the wrongful act of the employee. In response, you argue that the case does not establish liability for all conduct by an employee. You argue that your client is not liable, because *Majestic* held only that a tenant is liable for the acts of a negligent employee and not an employee who acts intentionally in a manner that the tenant would not authorize. Thus, you interpret the holding in the prior case narrowly.

In interpreting the holding narrowly, please note that you are not relying on an arbitrary rationale for the way that you read the case. A rationale for distinguishing a case must make sense. Here, you focused on a factual difference in the cases. You might also back up your argument by noting that the landlord could have protected himself by purchasing fire insurance.

Here is an example of how to interpret a holding broadly. Our client is Lilian, a five-year-old. When Bernard, an eight-year-old, continually rode his bicycle close to Lilian in a threatening way, Lilian threw a rock at the bicycle and unintentionally hit Bernard in the eye. Bernard brought an action for battery. In your jurisdiction, the case of *Gresham v. Courcy* found a battery when a five-year-old boy punched another boy in the eye.

We could try to distinguish *Gresham* on the facts by arguing that Lilian is a girl and the defendant there was a boy. However, the distinction is not a persuasive one, particularly because of the general belief that girls mature more quickly than boys. We could distinguish the facts by noting that the *Gresham* defendant aimed the punch at the plaintiff, while Lilian aimed it at the bicycle and missed. Unfortunately, standard tort law would not recognize this distinction and would hold Lilian liable.[3] Therefore, this argument would require us to seek a change in very traditional law.

The better approach is to read the *Gresham* holding broadly to require determining on an individual basis whether a child can form the requisite intent to commit a battery. Our argument might read this way:

> As the *Gresham* court held, tort liability arises when a child realizes the injurious consequences of his or her conduct. Following *Gresham* requires determining a child's mental capacity on an individual basis. In *Gresham,* the court upheld a finding that a five-year-old boy was liable, because he realized the injurious consequences of punching another boy in the eye. However, here, Lilian, the young girl, lacked the maturity to understand the consequences of throwing a rock at a bicycle. Moreover, at her age, she could not understand that in aiming a rock at a bicycle, she might hit its rider in the eye.

With this argument, we reject the narrow holding that *Gresham* found five-year-olds to have the mental capacity to commit battery. Instead, we

---

3. See W. Page Keeton et al., *Prosser and Keeton on the Law of Torts* §9, at 39-40 (5th ed. 1984).

argue for the broad holding that, although a five-year-old may have the capacity, a court must make an individual determination about each child. In our argument, we argue that having this capacity requires the ability to understand the consequences of one's action. Because the argument sounds sensible, it has a chance of succeeding.

Here is another example. In July, our client, Eames, stopped paying his monthly rent when the air conditioning unit in his apartment broke and Framley, the landlord, failed to repair it.

In *Thorne v. Barchester*, our state's supreme court found an implied warranty of habitability in residential leases. An implied warranty of habitability is a guarantee implied by law that when a landlord leases residential property, the landlord promises that the property is and will remain suitable for living until the lease ends. In *Thorne*, the tenant did not have to pay the rent, because the landlord had implicitly warranted that the apartment would meet the standards of the city housing code and then failed to repair conditions that violated the code.

In that case, the tenant did not have to pay rent, because the landlord failed to repair conditions that violated the local housing code. In our case, however, the housing code does not require a landlord to provide air conditioning.

The landlord's lawyer will argue that *Thorne* applies only when the landlord violates the housing code. To succeed, we must counter this narrow reading with a broad one. We might introduce our argument like this:

> As the *Thorne* court held, a landlord implicitly warrants that the leased premises pose no threat to a tenant's health and safety. Just as the housing code violations in *Thorne* threatened the health and safety of the tenant, the lack of air conditioning during a hot urban summer threatens the well-being of tenants like Eames.

In this example, we cited *Thorne* for a very general holding. We treated the precise holding—the landlord has a duty to ensure that residential property will satisfy housing code standards—as only an example of the general duty that a landlord owes a tenant. We then argued that maintaining an air conditioning unit is so similar to meeting housing code standards that it also falls within the landlord's general duty.

C. Argue That Adverse Precedent Is Distinguishable on the Facts

One way to harmonize adverse precedent is to argue that the contrary case is distinguishable from your case on its facts. If possible, go one step further and argue that the case really supports your position: Argue that the policy underlying the case is the one you are advancing.

Here is an example. Under common law, one type of tenancy is called a "tenancy at will." A landlord can end a tenancy at will immediately, without giving the tenant any notice. However, §1.202, a state statute, requires a landlord to give a tenant at will thirty days' notice before ending the tenancy. Our client is a hotel that is trying to end the stay of one of its guests without having to wait thirty days. The counterargument is that the guest is a tenant at will and must receive thirty days' notice before termination. In *Griselda v. Alexandrina*, a court has held that residents of a rooming house are tenants at will and are entitled to thirty days' notice. We must distinguish that case from our client's case. We might phrase our argument this way:

> A hotel guest is a licensee, that is, a person who has permission to remain on another's property without gaining any ownership rights in the property. Because a hotel guest is not a tenant at will, a hotel can remove a nonpaying hotel guest at any time. As the *Griselda* court noted, the statute balances the landlord's rights as a property owner with the tenant's expectation of some degree of permanency. Roomers legitimately expect to enjoy a certain permanency of occupancy. Hotel guests do not. Although *Griselda* interpreted §1.202 to require a rooming house to give a guest thirty days' notice, that holding does not reach hotels and their licensees.

As you can see, this paragraph distinguishes *Griselda* on its facts by differentiating between a rooming house and a hotel. Moreover, it offers a legitimate reason why the distinction should make a difference here: Roomers have an expectation of staying longer than do hotel guests. By looking to the legitimate expectations of the defendants in each case, it argues that the same policy rationale should underlie both cases.

D. Deal with Adverse Precedent in a Positive Way

As we have emphasized, to be persuasive, you must present your arguments in an affirmative way. This principle applies when you are dealing with adverse precedent. If you deal with contrary arguments in a defensive way, the theme of your opponent's argument will dominate. If you want your theme to dominate, you must take an assertive stance.

For example, consider the last illustration, which distinguished rooming houses from hotels. Note that the sample paragraph makes the argument by presenting it in a positive way and not seeming to be on the defensive. However, suppose the preceding paragraph read this way:

> In *Griselda v. Alexandrina*, the court interpreted §1.202 to require giving thirty days' notice to the resident of a rooming house. The court noted that the statute balances the landlord's rights as a property owner with the tenant's expectation of some degree of permanency. According to the court, its interpretation of the statute was proper, because roomers legitimately expect some degree of permanency. However, *Griselda* is distinguishable from the present case, because a hotel guest is a licensee and not

a tenant. Moreover, unlike roomers, hotel guests do not enjoy an expectation of permanency. Therefore the notice requirement should not apply to hotels and their licensees.

Although this paragraph makes the same argument as the preceding one, it is not as persuasive. It leads off by presenting the opposing arguments and only then does it try to distinguish the hotel's case. As you can see, it is better to present your argument in an affirmative way and then introduce and deal with any contrary argument.

To further examine the principle of writing in a positive way, look at the other examples in this chapter. In each, the passage begins by emphasizing the writer's argument and only then taking on the opponent's argument.

Here are the first two sentences of each of the first four examples in this chapter. After each, we have placed a revision showing what the first two sentences might have looked like if the writer had adopted a defensive posture. The originals begin by stating the writer's theme and only then analyze the adverse precedent. As you will see, they illustrate the better way to present a persuasive argument.

> **Assertive:** Under the lease provision, when a tenant's employee intentionally damages the premises, the risk of loss is on the landlord. The landlord can protect itself by carrying insurance to cover the loss. Although *Majestic, Inc. v. Alford* holds the tenant liable for damages that an employee causes through negligence, it does not extend liability to damages that an employee intentionally causes.
>
> **Defensive:** As *Majestic, Inc. v. Alford* holds, under this lease provision, a tenant is liable for the negligent acts of its employee. We do not question that holding. However, in the present case, the tenant's employee intentionally caused the damage. The holding in *Majestic* does not apply to this situation.

> **Assertive:** As the *Gresham* court held, tort liability arises when a child realizes the injurious consequences of his or her conduct. Following *Gresham* requires determining a child's mental capacity on an individual basis.
>
> **Defensive:** As the plaintiff argues, *Gresham v. Courcy* found a battery when a five-year-old child punched another child in the eye. According to the plaintiff, the defendant here, like the defendant in *Gresham*, is liable, because a five-year-old realizes the injurious consequences of her conduct.

> **Assertive:** As the *Thorne* court held, a landlord implicitly warrants that the leased premises pose no threat to a tenant's health and safety. Just as the housing code violations in *Thorne* threatened the health and safety of the tenant, the lack of air conditioning during a hot urban summer threatens the well being of tenants like Eames.
>
> **Defensive:** In *Thorne v. Barchester*, this state's supreme court found that a landlord implicitly warrants that the rental property meets housing code standards and agrees to repair conditions that violate the code. As the

landlord here maintains, the housing code does not require air conditioning; nevertheless, the *Thorne* holding should be extended to cover air conditioning and any other conditions that pose a threat to the tenant's health and safety.

EXERCISES

1. George Walker saw a car accident in which Phil Smith hit Matthew, George's son-in-law. As a result of seeing the accident, George suffered severe mental anguish and brought an action in tort for negligent infliction of emotional distress. In his defense, Smith argues that George cannot bring this action, because George is only a bystander, and only an immediate family member can sue for this tort.

   Your jurisdiction has two relevant cases. In *Blanyar v. Pagnotti*, a child witnessed his cousin drown on a neighboring property due to the neighbor's negligence. The court held that a person who suffers mental anguish after witnessing his or her cousin sustain injuries cannot obtain relief for negligent infliction of emotional distress, because he or she is not a member of the cousin's immediate family. In *Sinn v. Burd*, the court held that a parent who suffers emotional distress after witnessing his or her child injured after an auto accident has a sufficiently close relationship to the victim to obtain relief for negligent infliction of emotional distress.

   Here is one way to write Walker's argument:

   > As Smith argues, *Blanyar v. Pagnotti* makes clear that not all affected individuals can seek relief for negligent infliction of emotional distress. There, the court held that a bystander could not recover damages after witnessing another person's injuries, because the bystander was the victim's cousin and not a member of the victim's immediate family. Smith argues that *Blanyar*'s logic requires rejecting Walker's claim for relief. However, the close relationship between a parent and child, which necessitates recovery, is supported by *Sinn v. Burd*. There the court found that a bystander could recover for negligent infliction of emotional distress because the bystander was the parent of the victim. The logic of *Sinn v. Burd* should apply here, despite the *Blanyar* holding.

   Please rewrite this paragraph to make it more persuasive.

2. Please refer to the facts in the first question. Here is one way to write Smith's argument:

   > In *Sinn v. Burd*, the court found that a parent could recover for negligent infliction of emotional distress after witnessing his or her child injured by a negligent third party. Underlying the *Sinn* decision was the rationale that parents could recover damages for mental anguish,

because parents are so closely related to their children that they should be able to recover damages for mental anguish. Walker would extend this rationale to apply to the relationship between a father-in-law and a son-in-law. However, here, the father-in-law is not actually a true parent. As *Blanyar v. Pagnotti* holds, a person who is not an immediate family member, like George Walker, is not entitled to relief, because there is not sufficient evidence to find that the bystander and the victim were close enough to allow recovery. Therefore, Smith should not be liable to George Walker for negligent infliction of emotional distress.

Please rewrite this paragraph to make it more persuasive.

3. Please assume these facts:
   a. Scatcherd is president of the Sowerby Corporation.
   b. Sowerby furnished Scatcherd with an automobile to use for business, pleasure, or convenience.
   c. Sowerby paid for all the gasoline used in the automobile.
   d. On June 1, Scatcherd was driving the automobile on a personal errand and hit Fillgrave, a pedestrian.
   e. Fillgrave has brought a negligence action against Sowerby. Fillgrave argues that Sowerby is liable under the doctrine of respondeat superior: When a servant operates a master's vehicle with the master's permission, the master is liable.
   f. In *Moffat v. Greshamsbury*, Greshamsbury was the vice-treasurer of Desmolines, Inc.
   g. Desmolines furnished Greshamsbury with an automobile to use for business, pleasure, and convenience.
   h. The cost of gasoline was allocated between Greshamsbury and Desmolines so that Desmolines paid for only the gasoline used on business.
   i. Greshamsbury was driving the automobile on a personal errand and hit Moffat, a pedestrian.
   j. Moffat brought a negligence action against Desmolines under the doctrine of respondeat superior.
   k. The court found that although Greshamsbury was liable, Desmolines was not.

You represent Fillgrave. You argue that the Sowerby Corporation should be liable. Please write a brief summary of your argument and deal with the adverse precedent of *Moffat v. Greshamsbury*.

CHAPTER 10

Make Equity and Policy Arguments

I. ARGUE MORE THAN THE LAW

In most cases that go to trial, and certainly in most cases on appeal, both parties have sound legal arguments. Therefore, if you argue only the law, you run a strong risk of losing. If you want to improve your odds, you must argue more than the law. You must argue the equities and social policy.

To argue the equities means to argue that your client is the most sympathetic litigant and should win as a matter of justice. For example, your client parks her car in a large parking lot and returns later only to discover that her car has been stolen. On her behalf, you sue the parking lot and probably argue that it breached its duty to you. To argue the equities, you would emphasize that your client was a captive customer of the parking lot; she had no other safe place to leave her car. She thus was forced to entrust her car to the defendant and ultimately found that the trust was betrayed.

If you represent the parking lot, you also should make an argument on the equities. You would argue that your client makes a good faith effort to run a secure parking facility. However, your client knows that complete security is not possible. Therefore, it posts large signs and prints on its tickets a notice that disclaims liability and instructs its customers to lock their cars.

As the example illustrates, arguing the equities does not necessarily require making an impassioned plea for justice. In fact, these sorts of pleas can work against you if they sound exaggerated. Here, as in other types of persuasive writing, the best strategy is a slightly understated argument backed by compelling facts. Make the court aware of your client's plight. However, avoid the heavy rhetoric.

To argue policy means to argue that the holding you seek has beneficial consequences for society and the holding that your opponent seeks does not. For an example, we can return to the case in which your client's car was stolen from the parking lot. To bolster your legal argument with a policy argument, you might state that a parking lot has a duty to meet the legitimate expectations of customers that their cars will be safe. A decision favoring your client will send an important message to parking lot owners.

If you represent the parking lot, you might argue that requiring parking lots to guarantee fail-safe security would make their insurance costs prohibitive or make insurance unavailable. As a result, public parking could become exorbitantly expensive or even nonexistent.

As you can see, the equity argument focuses on the particulars of a case and attaining a fair result for your client. In contrast, the policy argument generalizes about what the case's outcome might mean for society. In our example, the equity arguments of the competing litigants pit fairness to the car owner against fairness to the parking lot. The policy arguments pit encouraging the parking lot industry to be more responsible against saddling that industry with a debilitating financial burden.

Of the two types of arguments, we believe that equity arguments are more persuasive, especially in the lower courts. However, your best strategy is to use both equity and policy arguments. It will be difficult for a court to reject your position if you can show that it not only has the backing of the law, but it also accords with fundamental notions of fairness and benefits society.

Now that we have introduced equity and policy arguments, we will use more examples to gain experience with them. Most of our examples will come from the illustrative case we used in Chapter 8, *Hazelwood School District v. Kuhlmeier*.[1] In that case, students in a high school journalism class produced Spectrum, the school newspaper. When the principal censored controversial articles, the students brought a legal action. They argued that Spectrum was a published forum in which the First Amendment forbade the principal's censorship.

II. MAKE EQUITY ARGUMENTS

In *Kuhlmeier*, the students' advocates could have focused exclusively on the legal argument. They could have referred to leading cases to define a public forum and then argued that cases finding a public forum had facts similar to the facts here. They could have argued that cases not finding a public forum were distinguishable.

Of course, the opposing lawyers would present their own legal argument. They would conclude that the case law did not support classifying a high school newspaper as a public forum. As for cases supporting the students, they would distinguish them on the facts.

To increase the odds of prevailing, the attorneys should introduce equity arguments favoring their respective clients. For example, the school board's attorneys might have stressed that treating the newspaper as a public forum would interfere with their efforts to teach students to be

---

1. 484 U.S. 260 (1988).

responsible journalists and adults. They might have included a passage like this one:

> The school created the newspaper not as a public forum, but as a teaching vehicle. Instead of adopting a hands-off policy toward the newspaper, the school used it to instruct students in responsible journalism and citizenship. In the current controversy, the school was teaching students not to invade the privacy of others, not to risk charges of defamation, and to avoid hurting others for the sake of cheap sensationalism. To achieve these goals, they necessarily had to exercise some content control.

As for the plaintiff-students' equity argument, the attorneys filing an amicus brief for People for the American Way argued that the school created a limited public forum for expressive activity. Therefore, they emphasized the extensive freedom that the student editors and writers enjoyed. To make the argument stronger, the attorneys created empathy for the students by showing how much they were benefiting from publishing the newspaper. As part of this equity argument, they quoted the Eighth Circuit's opinion:

> Spectrum was not just a class exercise in which students learned to prepare papers and hone writing skills, it was a public forum established to give students an opportunity to express their views while gaining an appreciation of their rights and responsibilities under the First Amendment to the United States Constitution and their state constitution.[2]

In both examples, the equity arguments are not merely general appeals for empathy. Both examples refer to the legal issue: whether the newspaper is a public forum. By tying the equity argument to the legal argument, they make the legal argument more persuasive.

III. MAKE NEGATIVE EQUITY ARGUMENTS

So far, we have discussed using equity arguments to create empathy for your client. However, you also can make a "negative equity" argument in which you portray the opposing litigant or some third party in an unfavorable light.

In *Kuhlmeier*, the students' attorney used this technique in describing the conduct of the principal. In the next paragraph, the attorneys portrayed the

---

2. Kuhlmeier v. Hazelwood School District, 795 F.2d 1368, 1373 (8th Cir. 1986), *rev'd*, 484 U.S. 260 (1988).

principal as intruding in a setting in which he did not belong, dispossessing the teacher, and violating curricular rules:

> Until this case arose, [the] . . . journalism curriculum did not include the principal. One day he usurped the teacher's role, replaced himself as advisor and changed the teacher-advisor position into that of editor. He then directed that only four pages of the students' work be distributed at school. These actions were not consistent with the Curriculum Guide, were not inherent in the previous pattern of classroom activity and were contrary to the purpose of journalism education as adopted by Hazelwood.

Be careful not to overemphasize the opposing party's shortcomings. The negative strategy can backfire by leading the reader to dismiss your characterization as overblown and therefore unreliable. After losing faith in your credibility on the equities argument, the reader may lose confidence in the credibility of your legal analysis.

Although the negative equity strategy can be effective, you usually will have more success with emphasizing the equities that favor your client. Accentuating the positive is more persuasive than emphasizing the negative.

IV. MAKE POLICY ARGUMENTS

Although policy arguments work at a more abstract level than equity arguments, they still should relate to the facts of the case. The facts should provide an example of how the holding you seek would advance sound policy.

For example, in *Kuhlmeier*, the school board's attorneys had to counter the student argument that the newspaper was a public forum. To bolster their legal argument, they made the policy argument that a public forum is inconsistent with the pedagogical function of a school. More specifically, they argued that the court should not interfere with the running of a high school:

> The public secondary school classroom is not a competitive market of ideas wherein diverse thoughts compete for the allegiance of a discriminating audience. The secondary school classroom involves a highly selective presentation of ideas and expression as dictated by the course curriculum. The purpose is to convey information to, and inculcate societal values in, minors. The state as teacher must have the authority to select what information is conveyed and by whom.

The students' attorney might have written a corresponding paragraph like this one:

> As a public forum, a high school newspaper plays an important educational role. The classroom is a place for conveying information and ideas in

accordance with a course curriculum. However, the larger educational experience exposes students to a competitive market of ideas and teaches them to make discriminating choices. For this educational mission, a newspaper is a potent teaching tool. As a forum for diverse ideas and opinions, it challenges students to make the sorts of evaluations we expect of responsible citizens.

In each example, when the reader considers the policy argument, he or she thinks of it in the context of Hazelwood East High School. Because the reader ties the policy argument to the specifics of the case, the argument makes the litigant's position more persuasive.

V. COMBINE EQUITY AND POLICY ARGUMENTS

If an equity or policy argument can increase your persuasiveness, imagine how you can strengthen your argument by combining equity and policy arguments.

Combining the two is not difficult. As we have seen, equity and policy arguments have much in common. Equity arguments necessarily deal with the facts of the case, and, to be effective, policy arguments must relate to the facts. Because the arguments share this quality, you can easily use both in the same paragraph.

For example, in its amicus brief supporting the students in *Kuhlmeier*, the People for the American Way argued that the school officials violated the First Amendment by interfering with the right to receive information. In making the argument, its attorneys combined equity and policy arguments:

> Although only the putative speakers are before the court, broader interests are at stake. In silencing respondents — student journalists who sought to address important social issues in the pages of Spectrum — petitioners placed an obstacle in the road to knowledge for members of the larger high school community, impermissibly contracting the spectrum of available knowledge.

In this passage, the attorneys appealed to the equities by making the student journalists attractive: The students tried to do something that was beneficial, and they were silenced. At the same time, the attorneys integrated the policy argument: Censorship is wrong, because it impermissibly contracts the spectrum of available knowledge.

The format of the paragraph is not the only one that the attorneys could have used. Here is another possible way to present the equity and policy arguments:

> Censorship of a student newspaper impermissibly contracts the spectrum of knowledge available to a high school community. This nation's

constitutional commitment to freedom of speech and the press militates in favor of declaring a newspaper to be a public forum. Otherwise, at schools like Hazelwood East High School, administrators preferring conformity to informed debate will ban newspapers like Spectrum when student journalists seek to address important social issues.

In this version, the paragraph begins with a policy argument, the importance of free expression. It then concludes with an equities argument that serves as an example of why the policy argument is so important.

Here is another example, this time from *Boos v. Barry*.[3] In that case, the petitioners challenged a District of Columbia statute forbidding critical political demonstrations near the official buildings of foreign governments. In their brief, their attorneys argued that the statute violates the First Amendment, because it failed to leave open alternative channels of communication for the petitioners' message:

> The First Amendment also requires that restrictions of public forum speech "leave open ample alternative channels for communication of the information." *Clark v. Community for Creative Non-Violence*, 468 U.S. 288, 293 (1984).

The attorneys then supported this legal argument with a policy argument that quoted an earlier United States Supreme Court case:

> As explained in *Young v. American Mini-Theatres, Inc.*, 427 U.S. 50, 76 (1976) (Powell, J., concurring):
>
>> The primary concern of the free speech guarantee is that there be full opportunity for expression in all of its varied forms to convey a desired message.

To further bolster the legal argument, the attorneys introduced an equities argument to demonstrate how important this requirement is to individuals like their clients:

> Petitioners are individuals of no great means. They are not supported by political action committees and cannot afford to buy radio or television time or pay for newspaper ads. Their ability to communicate depends largely upon effective picketing — a unique mode of communication. The anti-picketing provisions of §1115 apply everywhere within 500 feet of the perimeter of any official foreign building. . . . If Petitioner Waller is allowed to protest against the backdrop of the Nicaraguan Embassy, his message will be conveyed effectively and likely will attract attention. But if he is relegated to holding his "STOP THE KILLING" sign in front of a Burger King restaurant

---

3. 485 U.S. 312 (1988).

some 500 feet away, he may be perceived as either a vegetarian or an eccentric; and the effectiveness of his message will be severely impaired.

The attorneys thus strengthened the legal argument by beginning with a very general policy argument concerning free speech. They then added an illustrative equity argument showing why the legal and policy arguments were particularly significant to citizens of limited financial means. By combining these different types of arguments, they permitted a synergism that strengthened their persuasiveness.

VI. DO NOT SEPARATE THE EQUITY AND POLICY ARGUMENTS FROM THE LEGAL ARGUMENTS

A common error by lawyers is to place the legal arguments in one section of a document and the equity and policy arguments in other sections. For example, in all too many briefs, the writer develops the various legal arguments and then tacks on an additional section that states the policy arguments. The attorney apparently expects the readers to remember the legal arguments and later to link them up with the respective policy arguments. Alternatively, the attorney assumes that a single all-purpose policy argument is sufficient to support the various legal arguments.

When you make a legal argument, integrate the equity and policy arguments. In this way, you ensure that the reader will make the connections among the arguments. In addition, instead of offering one very general equity argument and one very general policy argument for the entire document, you can tailor these arguments to the specific legal argument you are making. Many of the examples in this chapter serve as illustrations.

EXERCISES

1. Please assume these facts: The plaintiff, Martha Dunstable, sustained injuries after Clara Van Siever hit her while driving under the influence of alcohol. Before the accident, Dunstable and Van Siever, both minors, attended a party, which was the scene of intoxication and underaged drinking. During the course of the party, Allingtown police answered two calls in response to neighborhood complaints about the party. However, they took no corrective action. Sometime later, an intoxicated Van Siever entered her car parked along the street, backed it up, and hit Dunstable, who was standing in the street behind it.

   Dunstable brought a tort action against the Borough of Allingtown under the state's Municipal Tort Claims Act. The Act waives governmental immunity for "a dangerous condition of streets" when the condition "created a reasonably foreseeable risk of the kind of injury that was incurred." For there to be a waiver, the government must have had actual or constructive notice of the dangerous condition "at a sufficient time before the event to have taken measures to protect against the dangerous condition."

Dunstable argues that, under the Act, the borough is liable, because it created a dangerous condition when its police failed to stop under-aged drinking and failed to stop individuals from driving while intoxicated. The borough responds that "dangerous condition" refers to conditions like potholes and not the circumstances in this case. Therefore, the borough argues, sovereign immunity protects it from liability.

You represent Martha Dunstable. Please list the persuasive equity and policy arguments you could make.

2. Please refer to the facts in the first question. You represent the Borough of Allingtown. Please list the persuasive equity and policy arguments you could make.

3. Until recently, Alexandra Repolsky lawfully resided in the United States as an alien. She came to this country to escape political and economic upheaval in her native country of Bohemia. Repolsky's elderly parents remain in Bohemia; however, her three sisters live in the United States as lawful permanent residents.

When Repolsky first came to the United States, she tried to find a job as an accountant, a field in which she had worked in Bohemia. Unable to find a position, Repolsky decided to borrow money from a loan shark, a common practice in Bohemia. The loan shark, Tobias Makker, was rumored to be a member of an organized crime family.

When Repolsky was unable to earn enough money to pay back the loan shark, Makker threatened her life. Repolsky offered to work as an accountant for Makker if he would forgive her loan. Makker agreed. While working for Makker, Repolsky discovered that he was not paying income taxes on all his annual income. However, because she was concerned that he might harm her, she continued to work for Makker even though she was aware that she might also be charged with tax evasion.

Eventually, Makker and Repolsky were charged with tax evasion and were convicted. Repolsky was sentenced to serve a one-year term in a minimum-security prison. However, her sentence was later reduced to 500 hours of community service providing free tax advice to low-income individuals. After Repolsky completed her required community service, she continued to provide these services. In the meantime, Repolsky met and married a United States citizen. They now have two young children, both born in the United States.

The United States Immigration and Naturalization Service (INS) has issued an order of deportation against Repolsky, because she committed a "crime involving moral turpitude." However, under applicable law, the INS will consider equitable and policy factors to determine whether it might be in the best interest of the United States to grant her a waiver of deportation.

You represent Repolsky. Please list equity and policy arguments that favor your client.

4. Please refer to the facts in the last question. You represent the INS. Please list equity and policy arguments that favor your client.

5. In violation of federal criminal law, your client Diane Shouldan presented false information in a report to the Environmental Protection Agency. She originally submitted the incorrect information at her employer's instruction, but later expressed concern about it to him. Two weeks later, she was fired for "lack of loyalty."

You argue that the dismissal was a wrongful discharge. Ordinarily, employment is "at will"; that is, an employer can fire an employee for any reason or no reason. However, there is an exception to the "at will" doctrine: a discharge is unlawful when it violates an express public policy. You argue that the express public policy here is in a federal criminal statute prohibiting making the false statement to the EPA. As part of your brief to the trial court, you draft these paragraphs:

> An at-will employee cannot be terminated for refusing to violate a public policy stated in a statute. *Adams v. Cochran & Co.* In *Adams*, an employee lost his job because he refused to drive a company truck that did not conform to safety regulations. The court found that the exception to at-will employment applied when an employee was "forced to choose between risking criminal liability [and] being discharged from his livelihood."
>
> The *Adams* court held that the exception must involve a "statutorily declared public policy." The facts as presented do not indicate a clear situation in which Shouldan was given a choice of complying with orders that would require violating a statute or discharge. The fact pattern might suggest more a situation in which she was terminated in retaliation for expressing reluctance to continue to obey such instructions in the future.
>
> The primary strength of Shouldan's case is the weight of the circumstances leading toward a holding by the court that a favorable finding would comply with the policy advocated in *Adams*. The gravamen of *Adams* is to alleviate danger to employees put in a position of either violating the law (and public welfare) or losing their livelihood, and Shouldan's complaint clearly falls under this policy.
>
> A growing body of persuasive scholarly opinion supports finding the wrongful termination exception under at-will employment. Professor Blades examines the issues involved in the coercive power

employers might wield and how that power can potentially lead to abuse. The "prime source" of this power, Blades states, is the absolute right of discharge found under the at-will doctrine. This right of discharge can be used to terminate for any cause, including "for cause morally wrong." Blades finds that the scope of the employer's appropriate control over the employee is impossible to define with precision.

When this control involves violation of statute or public policy this is perhaps of most immediate concern to the judiciary. An employer imposing a course of action upon an employee that constitutes potentially criminal behavior threatens basic social goals and values. Many of our rights and privileges are vulnerable to abuse through an employer's power.

A note in the Harvard Law Review also looks at tort cases finding that the defendant employer's conduct toward the employee undermines some important public policy. Cases of this type extend back to as early as 1959. *Peterman v. Teamsters Local 396*. In *Peterman*, plaintiff/ employee allegedly lost his job for refusing to commit perjury. The California Court of Appeals reasoned that the employer's conduct jeopardized the policy of encouraging full and honest testimony. Though they have construed it very narrowly, a number of other courts have recognized the existence of the public policy exception.

The Harvard note states that "these decisions indicate an increasing dissatisfaction with the at-will doctrine. The policy and doctrinal basis of the original common law rule has been superseded by modern contract and tort principles that require revision of the doctrine."

Please rewrite this passage to strengthen and better integrate your equity and policy arguments. You may need to restructure the original substantially to achieve an appropriate level of integration and make the argument persuasive.

CHAPTER 11

Writing for Nonlegal Audiences

The two most important things to keep in mind as you contemplate any form of communication are audience and purpose. In their eagerness to get their thoughts onto the page, even experienced writers, and those who carefully prepare for oral advocacy by writing out their arguments, sometimes forget precisely what their goal is when they sit down to write a persuasive document. If you are trying to persuade a nonlegal audience, you may be hoping to persuade a client to retain your services, a jury to decide in favor of your client, or a lawmaking body to adopt or reject a specific proposal. To accomplish this goal, you must use the tools discussed in this book in ways that will be most effective with your particular audience.

I. WRITING FOR CLIENTS

For purposes of this discussion, assume that the clients you need to persuade are lay clients, unsophisticated in legal processes and analysis. If your clients are sophisticated general counsel or corporate officers who have extensive experience with lawyers, your approach should more nearly approximate that suggested in the next chapter for communicating with other lawyers.

When you communicate with lay clients, consider the expectations and hopes those clients probably have for communications from their lawyers. Several likely expectations come to mind.

- Reassurance
- Demonstration of competence
- Clarification of the procedural status of the matter, and explanation of what happens next
- Clear explanation of applicable law
- Presentation of available options and consequences
- Predictions about how matters are likely to be resolved
- Demonstration of concern for the client as a person
- Clear explanation of fees and costs
- Respect for the intelligence and contributions of the client

This list demonstrates the complexity of the client's needs and expectations and the difficulty of meeting them all. Whether you are trying to persuade a client to accept a settlement, adopt some other specific course of action, or merely trying to persuade the client that you know what you are doing and are taking good care of the client's matter, every communication with a client has persuasion as a goal. How do we accomplish this difficult task? Here are three suggestions:

- Use appropriate language
- Provide useful information
- Inspire confidence

A. Use Appropriate Language and Provide Useful Information

Use language the client will understand and provide only details that will have significance to lay clients. Although technical legal language and the details of legal processes and authorities may be necessary to persuade other lawyers or judges, they will only confuse and frustrate your clients. For example, suppose you are writing to your client about the possibility of entering into a plea bargain. You wish to explain the process thoroughly, and thus your first draft might look like this:

> Before you plead guilty to a lesser charge, you should be aware of what exactly plea bargaining means; the nature of the crimes with which you were charged; the nature of the lesser offenses with which you could be charged; and the consequences of plea bargaining. Plea bargaining is the process whereby the accused and the prosecution negotiate a mutually satisfactory disposition of the case. Before a court can accept a guilty plea, it must first make sure that you enter the plea with a complete understanding of the nature of the charge and the consequences of your plea. There are basically four kinds of pleas. You can plead not guilty to the entire indictment; you can plead guilty to the entire indictment; where two or more offenses are charged, you can plead guilty to one or more, but not all, of the offenses charged or guilty to a lesser offense with respect to any or all of the offenses charged (providing that there is a factual basis for the crime); or you can plead not responsible by reason of mental disease or defect. In plea bargaining, you should be prepared to concede some or all of your guilt in exchange for certain sentencing concessions. However, you must be advised that the prosecutor may recommend a specific sentence. This, however, does not cabin the judge's discretion, unless he or she previously agreed to the proposed plea. Plea bargaining is not a constitutional right. Thus, as I stated earlier, it is my best judgment based on the history of prosecutors, the nature of the offense, and your background, that the prosecutor will plea bargain.

This example uses terminology the average client will find difficult to understand, and it provides far more detail than the client really needs or can process at this point. If the client has specific questions, you can address them in a subsequent letter or in a personal conversation. With this in mind, you might revise your draft to read this way:

> Before we begin discussions with the prosecutor, I would like to offer a brief explanation of what plea bargaining means and what its consequences are. Plea bargaining is a negotiation between the prosecutor and the accused. The goal is to reach a mutually satisfactory agreement that resolves the charges without the need for a trial. Before a court can accept a guilty plea that results from plea bargaining, it must first make sure that the accused completely understands the nature of the charge and the consequences of the plea.
>
> When we talk to the prosecutor, we will discuss both the charges to which you may plead and the appropriate sentence. If you decide to plead guilty, you may plead guilty to some or all of the offenses charged or to a lesser offense that may be included. In plea bargaining, you should be prepared to concede some guilt in exchange for sentencing concessions. The prosecutor may recommend a specific sentence or the judge may use his or her own discretion.

Here is another example of a letter that is almost guaranteed to leave the client with more questions than it answers. It casually tosses around legal jargon and concepts without explanation and has a stream of consciousness flow that suggests the writer was thinking the problem through for the first time as the letter was being written. These characteristics are highly unlikely to encourage client comprehension or create trust in the lawyer.

> Once again, to address recovery against Mr. Walker, there is still the issue of his negligence. Negligence is a cause of action that will allow a victim to recover against an individual who has committed a legally recognized wrong. If you would like me to continue with your case, I will send you another letter that goes into more detail about following this theory for recovery. I must tell you though that because you were not wearing your seat belt, you may be regarded as being contributorily negligent in causing your own injuries. I must research that issue to find out if our state is a comparative negligence jurisdiction. If it is, your amount of recovery will be reduced or barred based on how much you contributed to your own injuries. In light of this issue, you may want to consider whether it is worth going ahead with this claim or seeking an alternative recourse with Mr. Walker.

Here is a rewrite that the client should have a better chance of understanding. It simplifies the language, does not throw around concepts the client may or may not be familiar with (or that the client may not even need to understand), and clearly lets the client know what the lawyer is thinking and intends to do next.

We may sue Mr. Walker on the basis of his negligence. A victim of negligence may recover against an individual who committed a legally recognized wrong. Thus, we must show that Mr. Walker caused the accident by doing something careless or illegal. Because you were not wearing your seat belt, a court may decide that you had a role in causing your own injuries. I must research that issue to find out whether a court in this state might decide that you should receive less money or no money because you were not wearing your seat belt.

B. Inspire Confidence

The client needs to believe that you are competent and that you have the client's best interests at heart. If you cannot convey these messages, you may not have many clients to represent. For example, suppose you are explaining to a potential client how you will handle the client's problem and what your services will cost. Feeling a little uncertain because of your inexperience, you might draft this paragraph:

> At this point I have tried to give you a general idea of where you are with regard to the law and the penalties you face. Considering the severity of the charges levied against you, it is inappropriate at this time for me to advise you as to a definite course of action. As we discussed at our meeting, if you wish to obtain my services, I will need an $8,500 retainer check before I proceed. This check will be deposited in an escrow account and drawn upon at a rate of $100/hour. Please be aware that a case of this magnitude will probably be time consuming. However, realizing that you are not a wealthy woman, I will see to it that the initial $500 covers you at least up to the point where I can advise you as to a definite course of action.

There is no reason to rewrite this paragraph — it should never have been written in the first place. While you must discuss fees with a prospective client, you should not ask a client to part with $500 when you seem to be saying that the case may be too complex and serious for you to handle with any degree of assurance.

Tell your client what $500 will buy. Presumably, you will use the initial five hours to conduct research and perhaps begin negotiations with opposing counsel. Then you will be ready to advise your client on a course of action. If this is your plan, state it in your letter. By presenting a concrete plan, you will promote confidence in your abilities.

Here is another example. Suppose you represent a client charged with embezzlement. You are advising him that a defense he has suggested will fail. You might draft this paragraph:

> You have expressed what you consider may be a viable defense to these charges. You stated that you originally began stealing the money as an act of retaliation against the bank, because bank officers ignored some alleged

sexual harassment charges you asserted against a female executive vice president. Unfortunately, my research did not uncover any evidence that retaliation for ignored sexual harassment charges is a viable defense to any of your criminal charges. Although you felt that it would be your way of compensating yourself for the alleged abuse, there is no guarantee that a court would have believed your story and awarded you any compensation. Thus, I disagree that this is a viable defense and may only be considered by the judge as being a reason for your actions.

After reading your draft, you would recognize its shortcomings. Although it explains that the law does not support the client's proposed defense, it does not demonstrate an understanding of the client's perspective. Therefore, it will not contribute to a good rapport with the client. You might revise the letter this way:

> You have offered a defense to these charges. You stated that you originally began stealing the money as an act of retaliation against the bank because bank officers ignored sexual harassment charges you asserted against a female executive vice president.
>
> Unfortunately, the law does not recognize retaliation for ignored sexual harassment charges as a justification for committing criminal acts. Although you felt that you were compensating yourself for the alleged abuse, the law requires that you pursue legal action to receive compensation. We can still pursue such an action if you would like to.
>
> In addition, even though the sexual harassment will not be a defense to the criminal charges, the judge or the prosecutor may consider it in imposing a sentence or negotiating a plea bargain. I will certainly raise the sexual harassment issue with the prosecutor and the judge.

Here is a final example. In this letter, the lawyer seems to think the client can handle his own case.

> First, your concern about the robbery is understandable. However, under the circumstances and without more information, I cannot in good conscience advise you as to the relative strength of your position. Your possible legal vulnerability notwithstanding, a minimum showing of four basic elements would be required for Ms. Graves to be successful against you. A successful demonstration of negligence on your part by Ms. Graves requires that (1) you had a clearly identifiable duty to protect tenants from harm outside of your building; (2) you breached (failed to fulfill) your duty to protect; (3) she suffered actual harm or damage; and (4) your failure to protect was the causal link to her suffering harm.

What is the client likely to think upon receiving this letter? "Am I liable or not? What was I going to pay this lawyer for anyway?" After reading this letter, the client will not have much confidence in the lawyer. You should not give clients definite answers when you do not have them; however, at least you should explain how the elements of the law might apply to the client's situation.

Clients are a crucial audience. You must persuade your clients that you are the kind of lawyer they can trust to handle some of the most difficult and significant events of their lives. An essential part of a successful legal career is learning to communicate with clients in a way that they can understand and that inspires their confidence.

II. WRITING FOR JURIES

The concept of "writing" for juries may seem a little strange at first, as you will be dealing with them only in making oral presentations during a trial. Nevertheless, if you do not write out your thoughts in some organized, coherent manner before you walk into a courtroom, you are unlikely to be very effective or persuasive. The importance of persuading juries cannot be overstated, yet such communication is not something we do well: "[A] jury trial is very often much like watching a foreign movie without subtitles," observes Wall Street Journal legal editor Steven Adler. "If there's a lot of action, you have a general idea what's going on. If there isn't a lot of action, you're in trouble."[1]

Trials are often conducted in a language that is needlessly alien to the jury. According to Adler, who has observed trials and talked with jurors, jurors often have difficulty with such words as "ambiguously," "representation," "conversion," "tacitly," "nucleus," "executing," "artifice," and "immaterial," words with which lawyers are comfortable and that they use regularly. "Sometimes [jurors] ask for dictionaries, and usually the judge does not permit them to have a dictionary. They are simply seeking a definition of the word that they can understand so they can make use of it."[2] Because the judicial system has failed to remedy the communications chasm between the jury on the one hand and the judge and attorneys on the other, it continues to impair the jury's ability to do justice.[3]

This section of the chapter is intended to help you formulate the written notes that will guide your oral presentations to juries. As we did when thinking about writing for clients, let us identify some expectations juries are likely to have. They expect lawyers to:

- clearly explain the facts and the law
- offer a comprehensible theory of the case
- make the case interesting

---

1. *Panel One: Judge-Jury Communications: Improving Communications and Understanding Bias*, 68 Ind. L.J. 1037, 1038 (1993) (reprinting Proceedings of the Annenberg Washington Program Conference, April 10, 1992: Communicating with Juries).
2. *Id.* at 1039.
3. See Fred H. Cate & Newton H. Minow, *Communicating with Juries*, 68 Ind. L.J. 1101, 1118 (1992).

- respect the intelligence of the jurors and the importance of their function
- make jurors want to return a verdict in favor of your client

To help fulfill these expectations, use appropriate language and explain concepts clearly and concretely.

A. Use Appropriate Language

As when writing for lay clients, you must communicate with juries using language that simply and clearly communicates the concepts you are trying to convey and not lapse into excessive legal jargon. Clear language is particularly important for juries, because they have to process what you are saying by listening to it. They do not have the opportunity to go back for a second look at a passage they found particularly difficult or troubling.

Consider this portion of the prosecutor's opening statement in the trial of a legislator charged with corruption. It might work well in a hornbook or treatise. How would you communicate the same information to a jury?

> The crime of embezzlement is committed when a person comes lawfully into the possession of property, and afterwards and while it is in his possession forms and carries out the purpose of taking it for his own use. The evidence will show that the defendant:
>
> - knowingly and willfully stole, embezzled, and converted to his own use and to the use of others
> - without authority
> - funds of the United States well in excess of $100
> - which had come under his control because of his position as a member of Congress.
>
> Further, in embezzling the items and funds, the government will show that the defendant committed other crimes. The evidence will show that the actions of the defendant constituted the following additional crimes: mail and wire fraud, conspiracy, concealing material facts, and obstruction of justice.

You need to simplify the language and thus increase the likelihood that the message will be received. Here is one possible rewrite that avoids legal jargon and explains in plain English what the government intends to prove:

> The crime of embezzlement is committed when a person gets property legally, and afterward decides to take it for his own use. The government will show that the defendant knowingly and willfully embezzled funds of the United States well in excess of $100, which came under his control because of his position as a member of Congress.
>
> Further, the government will show that the defendant committed other crimes, including mail and wire fraud, conspiracy, concealing material facts, and obstruction of justice.

B. Explain Concepts Clearly and Concretely

If a jury is to understand and remember a point, the lawyer must make the point simply and, if possible, in a way the jury can actually "see." Using concrete language and images allows the jury to organize information in a way that makes it easier to retain and use when the time comes to evaluate the evidence.

In an opening statement, a lawyer must "package" the case so the jury can understand the significance of the evidence that is about to be presented. The lawyer also should provide an idea of the roles of the various participants in the trial, including the jury. Put yourself on the jury that hears this portion of an opening statement.

> Ladies and gentlemen, my job is to present evidence, in the form of both documentation and live testimony, before you. My opposing counsel will do the same. Your job is to listen to all the evidence, from both sides, and weigh the credibility of each document and witness. In other words, my job is to put the pieces of the puzzle in front of you, piece by piece, sometimes bigger ones. Your job is to decide what pieces you believe and disbelieve from each side's case. At the conclusion of my case in chief, the defendant will present evidence. Once again, your job will be the same. You must choose Cain from Abel. At the end of these presentations, I will come forward again, and attempt to explain how all these pieces fit together. My opposing counsel will explain what puzzle or lack thereof she believes is formed. Ladies and gentlemen, the evidence will develop over these next few weeks, and, at the conclusion, I will ask you to think about everything and return verdicts against the defendant of guilty as charged on all the counts alleged.

Confused? What images played through your mind as you read this statement: weighing evidence? doing a puzzle? reflecting on biblical characters? Were they helpful or distracting? Did you understand what your role was or what the roles of counsel were? Compare this opening in the same case.

> Your Honor, Counsel, ladies and gentlemen of the jury. My name is _____. I work for the United States Department of Justice. I am a prosecutor. This trial will unfold today like the pages of a book. Consider my remarks here as the table of contents. The book has characters — the defendant, his family, his colleagues. Many of these characters will testify for you today. This testimony makes the pages of the book — and the facts of this case. The book has a story. A real life story. A story about crime. A course of criminal conduct, spanning not one year, not five or even ten years, but twenty years. Twenty years of conspiracy and theft . . .
>
> Ladies and gentlemen, the facts of the case will be painfully clear. It is my sad duty to present the government's case, chapter by chapter. It is for

you, the jury, to do the much more important task, the writing of the final page and, as the defendant's secrets are revealed, line by line, you will see that this book can have only one ending. The final paragraph must mark the conviction of the defendant.

The second example is much clearer; it evokes only one image — reading a book — and it carries that image throughout the discussion. The language is clear, simple, and concrete. The image is not distracting; it helps you visualize how the parts of a trial fit together and what functions the prosecutor and the jury serve.

What image(s) do you get from this passage?

In terms of sheer magnitude, the hiring of ghost employees was the defendant's most egregious act. The defendant, on a regular basis, would turn in to his payroll officer a payroll sheet that did not describe the duties performed by his employees.

So, what did the sheet describe, you might ask. Does this version seem clearer?

The hiring of numerous ghost employees was the defendant's most offensive act. The defendant, on a regular basis, turned in to his payroll officer payroll sheets for these employees. On the sheets, the spaces for describing the employees' duties were blank.

This version does not require that the jury already have the lawyer's knowledge about how the payroll sheets were designed, and what information they were supposed to contain. The jury gets a much clearer picture of a deliberate effort on the part of the defendant to conceal the fact that his "employees" were doing no work.

III. WRITING FOR LAWMAKING BODIES

Lawmaking bodies — including legislatures and administrative agencies — may be particularly difficult audiences to write for. You are likely to be facing individuals with a wide variety of experience and expertise and the possibility of private or political agendas that you must consider. How do you persuade such a diverse group to do something? You must be clear, you must rely on arguments that are likely to have broad rather than partisan appeal, and you must convince the group that your proposal deserves to be given priority when there are likely to be many ideas competing for the lawmakers' time and attention. Often you must make appeals that will build a coalition of groups with varied and even competing agendas; you cannot afford to alienate too many members of your audience when you need a majority to support your proposal.

Do you think this passage is likely to convince the British Parliament that it should overturn a century-old law requiring a six-month quarantine of all animals entering the country?

> In effect, there is a vicious cycle in which the British government helps to inspire terror of rabies in the British public, and the public in turn demands that the government maintain the highest possible level of rabies protection, whatever the cost. It is difficult not to conclude that neither side has stopped to take a look at the facts and actually weigh all the pros and cons of the rabies law.

This simple paragraph manages first to remind members of the audience that the constituency they serve is strongly against the writer's proposal, and then to insult both the audience and the public by accusing them of acting (or not acting) without thinking. This approach is not likely to persuade the audience to change a long-standing, popular policy. Might this approach work better?

> The United Kingdom's law requiring a six-month quarantine of all pets that are brought into the country violates the plain meaning of the Treaty of Rome. The law is no longer necessary in light of the minimal threat that rabies poses to residents of medically advanced nations. The quarantine law is a financial and emotional burden on all European Union citizens who wish to bring pets into Britain, unnecessarily restricts the freedom of movement of pet-owning EU citizens, and results in the suffering of the thousands of animals per year who are confined in kennels during the quarantine process. Ladies and gentlemen of Parliament, I ask you to vote for the abolition of this unnecessary and anachronistic law.

This version offers fact-based arguments that undermine the stated logic behind the law and refrains from judging the audience for .previously enacting or supporting the law. By also suggesting that circumstances have changed, it takes an approach that is much better designed to get the audience to take a fresh look at a century-old law.

Put yourself in Congress and think about whether you are likely to find this argument for health care reform persuasive:

> The current system is dominated by the powerful and rich insurance companies and health care providers, which have fought so hard to maintain the status quo. This should surprise no one. These companies have become fat charging exorbitant rates for their services, and often refusing to insure those with the greatest needs.
>
> As has been readily apparent in the past weeks, change will not be easy. The powerful lobbies hired by the insurance companies have sent their minions to Capitol Hill to fan the flames of fear while spreading misinformation and lies about the plan.

Too many times I have seen that money can buy influence and votes in this body. However, I should remind you that with an issue such as this, which touches so many Americans, your vote on this bill will be scrutinized. Should you choose to serve the powerful interests desperate to maintain the status quo instead of your constituents, I promise you that you will be held accountable.

If you have worked with lobbyists in the past, are you likely to feel that your vote was purchased, or that you were simply persuaded to do the right thing? While an audience composed of members of the general public might react very well to these arguments, a substantial number of congressional representatives might be annoyed or even offended by the implications of the argument. The writer is using scare tactics to persuade. Open contempt for the audience is far more likely to produce rationalization and retrenchment than change. Compare this argument:

But far too many Americans have been left out in the cold wondering what will happen to them or a loved one. For too many Americans who cannot afford insurance, poverty is only an aging parent in need of care or a sick child away. This is unacceptable and we can do better! Families fortunate enough to afford coverage often find, after years of paying premiums, that when they need insurance their benefits are capped by so-called lifetime insurance limits, which are used up long before their condition improves. This is unacceptable and we must do better. Other Americans suffering illnesses find that in their time of greatest need they are simply dropped and find it virtually impossible to find coverage elsewhere. The crisis is one of affordability and availability. As an example of how much health care costs have skyrocketed: In 1981, the average American family paid about $145 a month for health care while today that same family is likely to pay more than $1,000 a month for the same coverage. We can and must do something to reform this system.

This argument offers supporting facts and gives the legislators an idea of how their constituents are being hurt by the current system. Focusing on constituents rather than the legislators themselves appeals to the legislators' better instincts and reminds them why they are in office. Empirical data and the needs of constituents should be much more useful persuasive tools for lawmakers than personal attacks and threats, although in recent years some legislators seem to have ignored that reality.

Arguments that are excessively dry and legalistic are equally unlikely to persuade lawmakers. Although lawmakers make the laws, they are not all trained in the law. For example, the following argument to a city council might work reasonably well in an appellate brief, but it is likely to lose the intended audience pretty quickly:

Obviously, an important factor is how Bill 10-8 would affect existing case law. The case that governs this issue is *IbnTamas v. United States*. In 1979, the court of appeals reviewed a homicide case in which the trial court had excluded expert testimony about battered women. The court of appeals remanded the case, ruling that expert testimony about battered women can be admitted under current law, if the trial court found the expert had sufficient skill, knowledge, or experience in the field, and if the methodology used in the expert's study on battered women had been generally accepted by the scientific community. This ruling restates the second and third prongs of the *Dyas* test for the admissibility of expert testimony. On remand, the trial court concluded that the defendant failed to establish that the expert's methodology for studying battered women had been generally accepted by the expert's colleagues. The court of appeals upheld the trial court's finding on the ground that it was not clearly erroneous.

This decision goes against the trend today, which points toward admitting expert testimony on domestic abuse when it is possibly relevant. The increasing acceptance of domestic abuse testimony is partly due to the American Psychological Association's endorsement of its use beginning in 1984. Furthermore, in 1991, the United States Congress passed a resolution stating that "specialized knowledge of the nature and effect of domestic violence is sufficiently established to have gained general acceptance," and that expert testimony "concerning the nature and effect of domestic violence, including descriptions of the experience of battered women, should be admissible when offered in a state court."

The following approach is much clearer and more concrete, and more likely to give the lawmakers positive and comprehensible reasons to support the proposal:

Expert testimony helps explain to a trier of fact that a lay person's perceptions of what would be a "normal" or reasonable reaction to a batterer are different from the actual behavior and mentality of a battered woman. For example, experts can testify how battered women may reasonably believe that calling the police is futile because, even when called, the authorities frequently fail to respond to "domestic" incidents. Experts can explain that a battered woman's inability to leave her batterer may be due to social and economic reasons, such as that the victim's family does not accept a woman leaving a marriage or the victim simply cannot afford to leave because she and her children are financially dependent on the batterer. In addition, the expert can explain that the victim had a reasonable fear that her batterer would follow her if she left and inflict greater injury as punishment for leaving. Testimony that explains why it was reasonable for a battered woman to stay with her batterer helps to bolster the defendant-battered woman's credibility and helps to show that the woman's belief in the necessity of force was reasonable as well.

Expert testimony can also help to explain why resorting to deadly force against a weaponless assailant may have been reasonable. A battered woman may reasonably come to believe that her companion is capable of killing or seriously injuring without the use of a weapon. Very often, the woman will have experienced first-hand how near-death she could be, solely from her partner's weaponless hands and fists.

Any time you write to persuade audiences who have not been trained in the law, be especially sensitive to the need to use simple, concrete language and to explain technical concepts clearly. Put yourself in the audience's position and think about the expectations you would have and the arguments that would make you want to take the proposed action. Then do your best to meet those expectations and make those persuasive arguments.

EXERCISES

1. Your client is a landlord who wants to evict a tenant. The tenant has been paying only part of the rent, because the landlord has not made requested repairs. Also, the tenant is not the sort of upscale individual the landlord would like to attract to the building.
   a. Please rewrite this letter to a client. Explain the concepts in terms a lay client could understand and omit any information the client is unlikely to need.

   > As a factual predicate, you indicated that you recently acquired an apartment complex. You are the sole proprietor and your intentions are to renovate the building into an upscale development that will attract higher-income tenants — "yuppies." Your primary reason for seeking my advice, however, is that you anticipate difficulties with one of your tenants, Ms. Graves. As a legal introduction, let me interject that state law is embodied in the orders of the state legislature as well as in the decisions of the state courts. Therefore, some of the answers I will provide may stem from the state legislature — a statute, and others may stem from court decisions — case law.
   >
   > Fortunately, this state does not appear to require that a landlord pay the relocation costs of its tenants. A court decision that helps arrive at this conclusion is *Rockville Grovesnor, Inc. v. Montgomery County*. In 1980, in Montgomery County, the issue came up of whether a landlord was required to pay the relocation costs of tenants where an apartment building was undergoing conversion into condos. In that case, Montgomery County had a local ordinance that required that the landlord pay relocation costs. That ordinance was held invalid by the court. As a corollary of this decision, it would appear that a court would not require that you pay relocation costs to your present tenants in order for

you to renovate your building. Nevertheless, more research is needed. Also, your willingness to allow Ms. Graves to credit the $300 that she owes toward the storage of her belongings during the renovation period is probably a prudent tactical decision.

In the event Ms. Graves institutes a rent escrow action and you decide to institute eviction proceedings against her, we must guard against having that action perceived as retaliatory. An eviction or arbitrary increase in rent solely because the tenant filed a suit against the landlord is prohibited unless it occurs six months after the determination of the initial court case. Thus, rather than an eviction proceeding, you may want to consider filing an action seeking to obtain only the rent itself. Such an action or suit is called "distress for rent." In general, if the lease contains no provision as to repairs, the landlord may not be bound to make repairs. Therefore, an action to obtain the rent instead of an eviction is not prohibited and will not be viewed as retaliatory. Obviously, facts pertaining to the lease and the provisions contained therein will be important.

b. Please rewrite the following paragraph so the client could retain you to represent him with some degree of confidence. This letter is to the same client as in the previous exercise; the tenant who had not been paying rent was also mugged on the grounds of the apartment building.

Assuming that all of the facts that I received from you are one hundred percent accurate, I think you are limited in terms of the options that are available to you at this time. Your situation with Ms. Graves is a very tricky one. A landlord has a duty to exercise reasonable care for tenants' safety by keeping common areas in a reasonably safe condition. When no duty exists, a landlord who voluntarily provides security measures can constitute a breach of duty. With respect to the mugging, you are willing to work something out with Ms. Graves to ease the transition period at Shady Nook. However, she has not yet made any efforts to take any action against you. It is possible that she does not intend to do so. If so, you will be taking steps to prevent a problem that you have yet to be faced with. It looks as though you might be liable for Ms. Graves' attack to a certain extent. My suggestion on this particular point would be to wait until Ms. Graves takes legal action against Shady Nook before attempting to reach an agreement with her about some type of compensation for the attack. If she does take legal action, we will address a settlement at that time.

2. Please rewrite this argument to Congress so that it is less likely to offend members of the audience. Suggest ways the writer could

strengthen the appeal to give the legislators positive reasons to support the proposal.

Groups such as the National Rifleman's Society have successfully intimidated members of Congress from voting against laws as innocuous as preventing dangerous felons from buying handguns or preventing the sale of assault weapons. Business lobbies such as the Banking Lobby and the Insurance Lobby have spent their money to ensure favorable treatment under the federal tax laws that keeps them exempt from taxation of certain transactions while other businesses are not. The list goes on and on. These are just a few examples of the abuses and inequitable outcomes of our current lobbying system. Those who have the most money to spend wield the most influence on those who make the laws. This bill would help prevent that. This bill will help ensure that House members will respond more to their constituents back in their districts, by limiting the power and the influence of the money-wielding lobbyists. After all, what is it that "representatives" are supposed to do? They are supposed to represent the people from their districts and the interests of those people from their districts, not the interests of the cash wielding political action committees who lurk in the shadows of the lobbies of Congress. This bill will curtail the "fourth" branch of the United States government: the lobbyists who intimidate our congressional members by threats of supporting their opponents with big campaign bucks if they dare oppose them.

CHAPTER 12

Writing for Legal Audiences

When you write for audiences who have been trained in the law, primarily judges and lawyers, you still need to consider the particular needs of each audience. Although you can use more technical terminology and assume more familiarity with legal concepts, you must present your arguments in a way that makes each audience more receptive to adopting the course of action you advocate.

I. WRITING FOR JUDGES

Many lawyers frustrate judges by not adequately considering their needs and limitations. Judges are busy people who need lawyers to give them clear, succinct, well-supported, and well-thought-out reasons for deciding a case in a particular way. They need lawyers to ask for specific remedies and to justify the remedies in ways the judges can accept. Many of the chapters in this book offer ways to present arguments so they will be easier to comprehend, more interesting, and more persuasive. We do not intend to rehash that advice here. Instead, we focus on one specific aspect of thinking of judges as audiences: identifying the types of arguments and language most likely to persuade particular types of judges.

A. Writing for Trial Judges

Whether you are writing a trial brief, or drafting opening statements or closing arguments to be delivered to a trial judge, consider the judge's function and what he or she needs to perform that function effectively. The trial judge's function is to evaluate the evidence, determine the facts, and then apply the law to the facts. Thus, you must present the facts logically and efficiently and in a manner that leaves the judge with no choice but to conclude that governing law requires a judgment in your client's favor. You must also state the law succinctly and explain how the facts of the case fit into existing law. You must perform these tasks using appropriate language that is clear and concrete. You should also maintain a formal and respectful tone that acknowledges the significance of the occasion.

1. Make Appropriate Arguments

If you make presentations that are overly convoluted or that focus on facts or arguments that a trial judge is likely to consider irrelevant or unpersuasive, you will only frustrate the judge and increase the likelihood that the judge will find for your opponent. If you were a judge, trying to figure out exactly what happened, and what the law should do about it, how would you react to an opening statement containing this language?

> Good afternoon. May it please the court, my name is _____ and I represent the defendant in this case. The government alleges that my client engaged in a scheme to defraud the United States that lasted since the early 1970s. But there is one thing the government has overlooked — my client's forty years of exemplary public service. The accusations raised against my client are simply incompatible with his distinguished and dedicated public service. In an era of "Congress-bashing" and in a time when the sentiment of "throw the old guy out" is preached with almost religious zeal and fervor, my client has become merely the latest victim of the anti-Congress vultures circling the Capitol's rotunda.
>
>   In short, Your Honor, the prosecution will not be able to show beyond a reasonable doubt that my client is guilty of a scheme to defraud the government. The last thing my client would want to do is tarnish his reputation and his place in history — two things for which he has worked a lifetime. My client has faithfully served his constituents and his country for over 40 years; these charges and allegations are simply incompatible with his record. Accordingly, at the close of all the evidence, we will ask that Your Honor return the only possible verdict, a verdict of not guilty.

Is the judge likely to conclude that because the defendant has been in public service for many years, he could not have committed a crime? Or that the prosecution should be dismissed because it may have some political consequences? It is barely possible that such arguments may have an impact on a jury; the judge, however, is much more likely to be persuaded by a presentation suggesting that the prosecution cannot prove all of the required elements of the crimes charged. Here is a defense presentation that is better designed to meet the judge's needs, because it focuses on the facts and identifies the key weakness in the prosecution's case.

> The stationery store is located in the Capitol building, and members of the legislature can purchase supplies as well as personal items. If the members purchase personal items, a set of rules details how the members are to pay for them. The defendant will tell the court about the procedural rules that govern the stationery store. He will admit that he mistakenly charged personal items to his official expense account. He will also tell the court that he has already made restitution for these items and any others about which there may have been any speculation at all. However, there will simply be no evidence of any intent to improperly purchase these items,

as required by the criminal law. As a result, the government's evidence will be insufficient regarding the stationery store, just as it will be insufficient for each situation the government must prove.

Consider this portion of a closing argument by the prosecutor in the same case.

> Your Honor, we are here today because a man in a powerful political position ripped off the citizens of the United States. This is about a man who was elected into political office on at least ten different occasions, to serve the people and to serve his country. A man who, once in office, found that he had a lot of power. Now, our Constitution gives power to the representatives of the American people so they can serve the public. Those representatives, whom we elect, have our trust. They hold the key to our security and our hopes. Your Honor, we are here today because the defendant abused that power. He violated our trust. But worse still, he lied to and cheated the American people.

This argument, both in language and focus, is again much better calculated to appeal to a jury than to a judge who is required to articulate a legal basis for his or her conclusions. The language is somewhat condescending, and the argument seems designed to create a sense of personal betrayal. Is this good strategy for a prosecutor, who must prove every element of every crime charged beyond a reasonable doubt? Here is a better example of a prosecution closing argument.

> The government has demonstrated that the defendant, not his godson who mowed his lawn, not his cleaning or laundry servants, not his son-in-law, nor the engraver, but the defendant alone maintained detailed control over his payroll operations at all times. Only the defendant was responsible for submitting monthly payroll certification forms, detailing all the named employees, the dates they worked, and their duties. And only the defendant submitted these papers with his signature and no official duty entered on them. Therefore, Your Honor, the government has shown that the defendant knew that he was not supposed to pay these persons, but instead he charged their "salaries" to the government for their benefit or his own benefit in the form of cash kickbacks. These actions caused the government to pay more than $500,000 to so-called clerks of the defendant, by his concealment of material facts, embezzlement and conversion of public funds, and obstruction of justice. These are the facts, these are the actions of the defendant, and these are the crimes of the defendant.

This argument focuses on specific facts, and it connects those facts to the elements of the crimes with which the defendant has been charged. Such an approach meets the needs of the judge, because it gives him or her a basis for a ruling that is both within the law and consistent with the function of a trier of fact.

Here is one final example. If you were trying to convince a trial court not to allow a particular category of expert testimony at trial, how would you expect the judge to react to this argument in your trial brief?

> In *Smith,* the Supreme Court of Columbia noted the inherent weakness of expert testimony regarding the Battered Woman Syndrome when used in support of a claim of self-defense and declared such testimony "minimally relevant." Furthermore, as discussed above, even though such testimony may be "minimally relevant," it will almost always run afoul of Federal Rule of Evidence 403, and thus be deemed inadmissible. Federal Rule of Evidence 403, as are all the Rules of Evidence, is applied ad hoc, and in some cases a trial judge may not fully appreciate the amount of jury confusion that may result from the admission of such testimony. This situation gives rise to unpredictable determinations on the admissibility of such testimony. Accordingly, for the sake of judicial predictability, the Supreme Court of Columbia should adopt the position of several other jurisdictions and hold that expert testimony on the Battered Woman Syndrome is inadmissible.

Is the suggestion that the trial judge "may not fully appreciate the amount of jury confusion" likely to persuade the judge to rule in your favor? What is the trial court supposed to do with the suggestion that the state's highest court should change its previous ruling? You would demonstrate greater respect for the judge's ability to conduct a trial and be more likely to persuade the judge to rule in your favor if you made the argument this way:

> In *Smith,* the Supreme Court of Columbia noted the inherent weakness of expert testimony regarding the Battered Woman Syndrome when used in support of a claim of self-defense and declared such testimony "minimally relevant." Furthermore, as discussed above, even though such testimony may be "minimally relevant," it will almost always run afoul of Federal Rule of Evidence 403, and thus be deemed inadmissible. Because evidentiary rules are applied ad hoc in the particular circumstances of each trial, there is the possibility of unpredictable and inconsistent determinations on the admissibility of such testimony. Accordingly, to encourage judicial predictability, this court should hold that expert testimony on the Battered Woman Syndrome is inadmissible.

2. Use Appropriate Language

When you write for a trial court, write in a clear, concrete, straightforward manner. Make your arguments simple and easy to understand, and make sure you present them in an appropriately formal and respectful tone. If you were a trial judge reading this statement of facts in a trial brief, how would you react? This excerpt is from a brief written on behalf of a battered spouse accused of trying to murder her husband.

> Barbara Townsley asked her husband Nick to restrain his verbal outbursts, and then cautioned him of the high probability that the police would take him into custody if he failed to do so. Ignoring her advice, Nick loudly declared that he did not need instructions on how to live his life from someone whom he perceived to be a female dog. Nick then struck Barbara. This action prompted one of the members of the apartment community who had assembled to view the altercation to state his intention to notify the authorities.
>
> Barbara defended herself with the frying pan, which she had inadvertently brought outside with her, because she was washing it at the moment Nick rushed out the door. In the course of defending herself, Barbara hit Nick once in the head with the frying pan. Not even fazed by the blow, Nick jerked the frying pan from Barbara and struck her with it. Only by scrambling away did Barbara avoid another painful encounter with the cooking utensil.

The tone of the writing is highly inappropriate — it is sarcastic and suggests that the lawyer is not taking the case seriously. If the lawyer cannot convey outrage and sympathy for his or her own client, how is the judge supposed to react? In addition to suggesting a lack of respect for the client, the somewhat flippant use of language suggests a similar lack of respect for the court. Although the writer may have been trying to be creative and make the story interesting, the judge is not likely to see it that way. Here is a more direct and persuasive way to present the same facts.

> Barbara Townsley asked her husband Nick to stop yelling at her and then threatened to call the police if he did not stop. In response, Nick loudly declared that he did not need instructions on how to live his life from a "bitch." Nick then struck Barbara. This action prompted one of the neighbors to offer to call the police.
>
> Barbara defended herself with the frying pan, which she had inadvertently brought outside with her because she was washing it at the moment Nick rushed out the door. In the course of defending herself, Barbara hit Nick once in the head with the frying pan. Not even fazed by the blow, Nick jerked the frying pan from Barbara and struck her with it. Only by scrambling away did Barbara avoid more serious injury.

Does the next portion of the same trial brief sound like advocacy or a law review article? Think about how you might rewrite the passage to make it more persuasive to the judge who must decide whether to admit the evidence.

> The defendant in this case is pleading "not guilty" to all charges by asserting self-defense. In relying on self-defense, the defendant cites the

traditional theories associated with the doctrine, as well as the more recent theory of Battered Woman Syndrome. It is the position of the defendant that traditional self-defense can be proven sufficiently to result in the defendant's acquittal. The defendant contends that self-defense, when supported by Battered Woman Syndrome, meets the acquittal standard of preponderance of the evidence.

The highest court of this state has held that evidence of Battered Woman Syndrome is admissible as minimally relevant. *Smith v. State.* The holding is in accord with decisions of a majority of the states, a majority that is increasing with time. As the cases discussed below will show, there are compelling reasons for affirming and even strengthening the Supreme Court's decision in *Smith.* According to American Jurisprudence, numerous courts hold that expert evidence of the Battered Woman Syndrome is admissible, but some don't.

You need to focus much more directly on the role of the trial judge in this evidentiary dispute. You would rewrite the passage using more concrete language and explaining exactly what you intend to prove. Your rewrite might look something like this:

> Barbara Townsley is pleading "not guilty" to all charges because she was defending herself from an attack by her husband. In relying on self-defense, Ms. Townsley urges the court to hear expert testimony regarding Battered Woman Syndrome. This testimony will allow the jury to understand how the traditional elements of self-defense apply here.
>
> The highest court of this state has held that evidence of Battered Woman Syndrome is admissible. *Smith v. State.* This holding is in accord with decisions of a majority of the states, a majority that is increasing with time.

B. Writing for Appellate Judges

Most of us began writing for appellate judges in our first year of law school. Many introductory legal writing courses end with a moot court brief and appellate argument. How many of us really understood what it meant to be appearing in an appellate court? The phrase "standard of review" seemed like some arcane mantra that we were required to utter, but should not be required to comprehend.

There is no magic language that will persuade an appellate judge; writing clearly, concretely, and with appropriate formality will work in this context as well as it will in the trial context. Our focus in this section is on writing arguments that demonstrate an understanding of the role of the appellate judge. As with any other audience, if you write in a way that satisfies the appellate judge's expectations and gives the judge a reason to rule in your favor that is appropriate in the appellate context, you are much more likely to be persuasive.

The way to begin is to think about the function of an appellate judge. The judge typically must decide whether the judge or jury below made an error in applying the law. The appellate judge sees no evidence, hears no testimony, and can find no facts. On these matters, he or she must rely on the trial judge's evaluation. The appellate judge cannot begin to perform a legal assessment without knowing how much deference he or she is required to give the decision of the lower court. The issue of deference is why the concept of standard of review takes on such importance. The appellate judge is further constrained by other judicial rulings that might have precedential value. On the other hand, compared to the trial judge, the appellate judge has more freedom to consider social policies and trends in the law, at least where there is no clearly applicable binding precedent.

If you were an appellate judge, operating under these constraints, how would you react to this argument? The writer is arguing that the court should reverse the trial court's grant of summary judgment in favor of the appellees, a group of abortion protesters.

> Summary judgment was granted in favor of the appellees, Operation Cease and Desist, Terry Rand, Mary Rand, and Maria Leary. The court based its decision upon the premise that to bring an action under RICO, an economic motive is necessary. Appellant, The Pro-Choice Clinic, Inc., now urges this court to overturn summary judgment because an economic motive is not a requirement for invoking the provisions of RICO.
>
> One of the main reasons the District Court granted summary judgment for Cease and Desist was because the court chose to follow the holdings of a few Second Circuit cases. Although it may seem that these cases require an economic motive, in reality, they contradict themselves or were later limited by the Supreme Court.
>
> As shown earlier, the economic motive as found in *United States v. Ivic* rests on questionable legal grounds. In the same year, the Second Circuit, in *United States v. Bagaric*, conceded that "[i]t is clear that § 1962 does not, by its terms, require proof of ultimate improper economic motive."
>
> The *Bagaric* court stated that "motive itself is not generally an element of a particular offense. When Congress has required proof of motive it has generally done so for behavior not deemed blameworthy absent the immoral motive, and not otherwise punishable." This exception would not apply to the case at hand because here Cease and Desist admitted it illegally entered the Pro-Choice Clinic, which would be otherwise punishable and was eventually. The Court went on to say that "RICO demands no such inquiry . . . no additional scienter requirement is imposed by the statute. To carry out a deeper inquiry into long-term or ultimate motive would be to require adjudication of a factor traditionally deemed not exculpatory." The court in this case could not seem to make up its mind and therefore created an unsound decision. To follow a holding so inconsistent would be inappropriate.

How persuasive is an appellate court likely to find what can only be described as "whining" about the decisions of other courts? There is little real analysis in this argument — merely characterizations and expressions of frustration. Here is a way to approach the same argument with your audience's needs firmly in mind:

> The District Court granted summary judgment in favor of the appellees, Operation Cease and Desist, Terry Rand, Mary Rand, and Maria Leary. The court based its decision upon the premise that bringing an action under RICO requires an economic motive. Appellant, The Pro-Choice Clinic, Inc., now urges this court to overturn summary judgment because an economic motive is not a requirement for invoking the provisions of RICO.
>
> The District Court granted summary judgment for Cease and Desist in reliance on Second Circuit decisions. Although these cases may require an economic motive under some circumstances, they do not require such a finding in this case.
>
> In *United States v. Bagaric*, the Second Circuit conceded that § 1962 does not expressly require proof of ultimate improper economic motive. The court stated that "motive itself is not generally an element of a particular offense. When Congress has required proof of motive it has generally done so for behavior not deemed blameworthy absent the immoral motive, and not otherwise punishable." This exception would not apply to the case at hand because here Cease and Desist admitted that its members illegally entered the Pro-Choice Clinic, which is an otherwise punishable act. The Court went on to say that "RICO demands no such inquiry . . . no additional scienter requirement is imposed by the statute. To carry out a deeper inquiry into long-term or ultimate motive would be to require adjudication of a factor traditionally deemed not exculpatory." Similarly, the District Court should not have required proof of an economic motive in this case and should not have granted summary judgment.

Recall the example in Section I.A that argued the likelihood of jury confusion if expert testimony regarding Battered Woman Syndrome were allowed at trial. Although that passage is not likely to persuade a trial judge and, in fact, risked irritating the judge, it is well designed for an appellate court. It focuses on the likelihood of inconsistent results at the trial level and urges the court to rule in a way that would encourage consistency and efficiency throughout the system. Such an appeal acknowledges the ability of the appellate court to consider policy arguments and to rule in a way that has widespread precedential value. It is less effective at the trial level because a trial judge's rulings can affect only the case immediately before the court. Remembering such functional differences between the courts is one key way to enhance your persuasive powers.

II. WRITING FOR OTHER LAWYERS

We write to persuade other lawyers in many situations: We try to persuade our colleagues and superiors to adopt particular courses of action; we want our superiors to think we are capable and give us good evaluations, not to mention raises; and we want opposing counsel to see a matter from our client's perspective and offer a good settlement or agree to a specific provision in a transactional document. To accomplish these goals, we must write in a manner that is best calculated to have the desired result; that is, we must consider the needs and expectations of the individual we want to persuade.

What are the needs and expectations of attorneys to whom we are likely to write? We should assume that they are busy, that they are familiar with basic legal concepts and terminology but not necessarily with the specific area of the law we are writing about, and that they appreciate writing that conveys respect and formality appropriate for a law office. These expectations should lead us to write in a manner that includes these three characteristics:

- Efficiency
- Clear explanations of the law and the facts
- Professional tone

Consider this memo to a supervising attorney. The memo is supposed to evaluate the strength of the client's case and offer advice on whether to take the case. The client was "stalked" by a would-be suitor who harassed her by using e-mail. Now the client would like to sue for intentional infliction of emotional distress.

> The amalgamation of Mr. Partlow's conduct with the consequential impact on how Ms. Stalkey conducts her everyday affairs has, according to her, resulted in her being unable to sleep and sustaining significant emotional distress to the degree that she considered professional counseling. Does she have a sufficient cause of action? Let us first consider the elements of the tort of intentional infliction of emotional distress, most clearly enunciated in two cases, *Pavilon v. Kaferly*, and *Plocar v. Dunkin Donuts*.
>
> Both *Pavilon* and *Plocar* characterize the three essential elements of, and subsequent threshold for, finding intentional infliction of emotional distress. While the facts in *Pavilon* proved sufficient for the court to find grounds for a tort of intentional infliction, the court was not so easily persuaded by the complaint put forth in *Plocar*. And because you have asked me to ascertain the probability of success of Ms. Stalkey's claim, I feel it best to do so using a case that has withstood the scrutiny of a rigid standard, not one that has been found wanting. Furthermore, while the crucial test set forth in *Pavilon* is similar to that set forth in *Plocar* with regard to the core of the standard itself, there are slight differences in that *Pavilon* calls for truly extreme and outrageous conduct, thereby

making it a slightly more rigid test than *Plocar*. Because of these two factors and the fact that *Pavilon* is the more recent case, I will rely more heavily on its standard, as its precedential nature would prove much more persuasive overall.

The language of this memo is convoluted and overblown. The writer seems to be lecturing the audience and takes a very long time to get to the point. Indeed, the two paragraphs say very little. The reader is likely to find this memo frustrating and annoying. Here is a way you might rewrite this portion of the memo to better meet the needs and expectations identified above. The language does little more than provide context for the analysis to follow, but at least this version does so succinctly.

> Ms. Stalkey has been unable to sleep and is considering professional counseling. To determine whether she has a cause of action for intentional infliction of emotional distress, we must examine the governing cases, *Pavilon v. Kaferly* and *Plocar v. Dunkin Donuts*. The court in *Pavilon* found grounds for intentional infliction, but the court in *Plocar* did not. Because *Pavilon* is more recent and seems to apply a slightly higher standard to the defendant's conduct, this memo will focus on that case.

The next example offers too much in the way of personal editorializing and commentary. While the writer may believe everything in this paragraph, the lawyer trying to decide whether to take the case is looking for an analysis of facts and law, not suggestions on how the client can get her life in order!

> Clearly, Ms. Stalkey is distressed by the conduct of Mr. Partlow. I would definitely recommend that she visit a therapist and file a court-ordered injunction against Mr. Partlow to stop his activities. When one looks at the facts presented so far, however, I do not believe that we have a strong case against Mr. Partlow for the intentional infliction of emotional distress. Ms. Stalkey's case for proving severe emotional distress rests on the actions she took to protect herself, namely the rebuilding of her computer, replacement of the hard drive, and the refusal to use any on-line computer services. While I admit these actions are clearly expensive, I believe the defense would argue that they were neurotic overreactions to Mr. Partlow's actions. All Ms. Stalkey really had to do was change her computer code! This is a simple and very inexpensive procedure that would have stopped Mr. Partlow's access, if in fact he had the access claimed.

If you were to attempt to rewrite this paragraph to meet the needs of the audience, you would probably cut almost all of it. You might preserve the underlying facts as context for a serious discussion of whether she has suffered severe emotional distress. Everything else can be eliminated.

As a final example, consider this excerpt from a letter to opposing counsel in the same case. The writer was trying to establish a basis for making a settlement demand.

> We will argue to the court that it has a moral obligation to society to compensate for distress caused by stalkers. We are dealing with a person who has blatantly defied the warnings by the police and our client to commit actions that are causing distress and disruptions in Ms. Stalkey's life. He acknowledges that his own conduct could be construed as stalking, yet he continues with increased severity in his actions. We cannot allow individuals to suffer at the hands of others who knowingly cause distress in an extreme and outrageous manner under the pretense of professing love. Placing victims in fear to the point where it disrupts their personal lives is extortion.

The language of this letter is unprofessional and intemperate. It is not likely to encourage the recipient to pursue negotiations; rather, counsel will probably begin preparing for trial on the belief that settlement discussions will be antagonistic and ultimately useless. Here is one way you might rewrite to open the door to discussions while still articulating the basis for your client's claim.

> If forced to trial, we will argue that the court has an obligation to society to compensate for distress caused by stalkers. Your client defied warnings by the police and our client and committed actions that are causing distress and disrupting Ms. Stalkey's life. Ms. Stalkey should not have been made to suffer because of your client's professions of love. Placing victims in fear to the point where it disrupts their personal lives is conduct that requires compensation.

In all communications with other lawyers, efficiency and professionalism will enhance your ability to persuade. Your superiors will be more likely to appreciate and adopt your recommendations, and your opponents will be more likely to work with you in a constructive and productive manner.

You may have noticed a common thread throughout these two chapters on writing for particular audiences. Clear, concrete language and well-supported, well-organized arguments will work well with virtually any audience. Beyond that, remember to think about the needs and expectations of your specific audience. Are you using language the audience will understand? Are you making arguments that fit the audience's function? Is the tone of your writing appropriate for the audience and occasion? If you can answer yes to all of these questions, you will find that your writing is much more likely to have the persuasive impact you desire.

EXERCISES

1. Please rewrite this section of a trial brief to increase the likelihood that it would persuade the trial judge to permit expert testimony on Battered Woman Syndrome. Assume that you represent the defendant battered spouse. Then rewrite it for an appellate court. Assume that you represent the same client, who was convicted after the trial court barred expert testimony on Battered Woman Syndrome.

> In order to successfully assert a defense of self-defense, Barbara Townsley must prove by a preponderance of the evidence that she believed she was in imminent danger of unlawful bodily harm and that the use of such force was necessary to avoid the danger. All jurisdictions require satisfaction of the requirements. Jurisdictions differ on whether retreat is required and whether the reasonableness of the defendant must be evaluated according to a subjective or objective standard.
>
> When a battered woman asserts self-defense in a situation where attempted homicide occurs in the midst of a violent battering incident, a claim of self-defense is not extraordinary. A good chance of success exists because elements of self-defense, specifically the imminence of danger and the reasonableness of the deadly force, can be met in a traditional fashion.
>
> Although this case appears to meet the requirements of traditional self-defense, it is possible that the defense has concerns that Barbara Townsley's state of mind will be misunderstood by a jury. The jury may believe that Barbara Townsley had the opportunity to retreat or that she provoked the final series of events leading to the shooting, or both. The elements of self-defense would therefore not be met.
>
> To accommodate the perspective of a battered woman who attempts to kill in self-defense, and to counter the element of retreat in self-defense, the Columbia courts should strengthen the holding in *Smith* and allow testimony on Battered Woman Syndrome. A battered woman does not believe that she can leave her abusive husband. It is critical to a proper and complete defense to show the jury that she feared immediate danger when an ordinary person might not.

2. Please rewrite this portion of a memo to meet the needs of an attorney who is trying to decide whether to take the case. Your client was stalked by e-mail and wants to sue for intentional infliction of emotional distress.

> The first element requires that Partlow's behavior must be truly extreme and outrageous. John's behavior is analogous to the defendant's in *Pavilon* in that it was indecent and was an offensive and persistent sexual pursuit. However, it seems that absent any physical threats, abuse of a position of authority, and a knowledge that Susan

is particularly susceptible to emotional distress, it will be difficult to characterize the harassment as so outrageous "as to go beyond all possible bounds of decency, and to be regarded as atrocious, and utterly intolerable in a civilized community," as the courts have in these cases. However, the absence of these specific circumstances would not automatically preclude the recognition that John's conduct is truly extreme and outrageous. The allegations remain that he has frightened her, warned her that he has devised many methods to harass her, and that he has disregarded Susan's orders and the police's orders that he cease contact with her. The court does not rule that the cited behavior is the minimum standard, but it would not be difficult to distinguish a series of annoyances, and threats to annoy, which Susan's case consists of, from the serious behavior cited above. I would also like to point out that nothing in Susan's allegations provides proof that it was indeed John who sent the e-mail messages after the police told him to leave Susan alone. I have to admit that I am unfamiliar with ways to identify a sender of an anonymous e-mail, but I would suggest that this question be addressed if a complaint is in fact filed.

Based upon my findings, I feel that we would have a good chance at convincing the court that Mr. Partlow's actions against Ms. Stalkey constitute the tort of intentional infliction of emotional distress. I believe that the three elements for this tort have been met, and while there is an argument to the contrary, the argument in support of Ms. Stalkey's claim is the stronger one. The key focus is on whether or not Mr. Partlow's conduct was outrageous and excessive. The issues of intent and causation are pretty straightforward. What one person considers to be outrageous conduct, another may not. However, I feel the court in this instance will agree for the reasons argued above that the conduct of Mr. Partlow was outrageous and excessive, thus supporting Ms. Stalkey's claim of intentional infliction of emotional distress. The court should not wait to compensate stalking victims until they are actually physically harmed, for example, battery, rape, or even murder. To do so would encourage individuals to take the law into their own hands and make sure that any impending physical harm would not result.

Ms. Stalkey definitely does not have a clear cut-and-dried claim for intentional infliction of emotional distress, but I feel that a successful claim can be made. All elements for the cause of action can be met sufficiently. We will have to focus on the disregard of police warnings to prove that the extreme and outrageous conduct is present but in a different context than previous holdings. In addition, it is vital that we argue a moral policy argument aimed at compensation for stalking victims such as Ms. Stalkey. Following this strategy, we can produce a cause of action that has a reasonable chance of being ruled in our favor by the court.

CHAPTER 13

Five Pitfalls in Persuasive Writing

It is possible to take sound advice and apply it so rigidly that you fail to accomplish what you set out to do and even do the opposite of what you attempted. For example, you may wish to highlight your arguments and deemphasize those of your opponent. However, if you take your mission to the extreme, you may decide to omit discussing your opponent's arguments altogether. Then, when your opponent raises these arguments, they will gain more attention, particularly when your opponent points out that you ignored them.

Why do writers apply rules in a way that undercuts their persuasiveness? It is because they think that following a rule inevitably furthers their goals. What they fail to understand is that the goal is persuasiveness, and persuasiveness does not necessarily come from following a rule to an extreme. It comes from communicating effectively with your audience. In applying a rule, you have to use your judgment. You must ask: In the context of what I am writing, will this rule further my goal of communicating persuasively and if I apply this rule in an extreme way, will I further my goal or frustrate my efforts to reach it?

In this chapter, we discuss five common pitfalls in persuasive writing. A writer stumbles into a pitfall by taking a rule to an extreme and failing to use good judgment. Here are five guidelines designed to keep you from such errors:

1. Deal with Opposing Arguments
2. Avoid Excessive Detail
3. Avoid Rigidly Adhering to Formulaic Structures for Organizing Arguments
4. Avoid Long and Frequent Quotations
5. Avoid Excessive Citations

I. DEAL WITH OPPOSING ARGUMENTS

In this book, we encourage you to start off with arguments that favor you and then deal with opposing arguments. Some writers accept the first part of this advice, but decide that dealing with the opposing arguments will interfere with a seamless presentation of their argument. They therefore decide not to discuss the opposing arguments. Alternatively, they decide to mention the arguments only in passing, but not confront them directly. By not dealing with these arguments, the writers permit their opponents to raise them first and to create the framework in which the court will encounter the arguments. These well-meaning writers thus give an advantage to their opponents.

For example, suppose your client signed a contract to purchase a swimming pool for his backyard. After it was installed, your client discovered that he was being charged for the cost of hauling away the dirt that the contractor dug up to place the pool in the ground. You argue that the contract did not include a cost for this task. The small print, however, states that the customer will be responsible for "reasonable incidental expenses."

You might be tempted not to discuss this wording, because it weakens your argument or because you hope that your opponent might not raise the issue. Having performed adequate legal research, you know that the case law does not clearly predict whether or not the wording will control.

If you decide to ignore the wording, you take a big risk. It is prudent to assume that the opposing attorney has researched the same cases as you have and that a judge may bring up the issue on his or her own. Thus, your common sense tells you that hiding from an issue is unwise.

II. AVOID EXCESSIVE DETAIL

Stating facts in detail may give them more emphasis and can offer the reader a richer, more compelling story. However, too much detail can divert the reader's attention from your main theme. It might even lead the reader to focus on less relevant information to the point where the reader evaluates your argument on the basis of noncritical information.

Here is a complex example. Anthony Trol is a single twenty-seven-year-old who lives with his parents and has a steady job working for the city. He files for bankruptcy under Chapter 7 of the Bankruptcy Act, which would free him from having to repay any of his debts. His creditors argue that he should have to file under Chapter 13, which would require him to repay his debts gradually according to a three-year or five-year plan. The bankruptcy court agrees with the creditors. Trol, of course, would prefer not to have to pay his debts and appeals the court's ruling.

If you are opposing Trol's appeal, you could present the financial facts to the appellate court in a variety of ways. Here is one way:

Trol has stated that he was employed by the Town and that his monthly take-home pay totaled $1,000, net of federal, state, and local taxes. He has also stated that his monthly expenses totaled $600, consisting of rent ($300), food ($100), transportation ($50), clothing ($100), and recreation ($50), leaving him disposable monthly income of $400. In his statement of financial affairs, Trol also stated that he currently earns an annual gross income of $18,000.

Based on these sworn statements, the bankruptcy court concluded that Trol could repay 100% of his pre-petition debts in equal monthly payments of $200 under a three-year Chapter 13 plan, or $120 under a five-year plan. The court's worksheet indicated that Trol could repay his pre-petition debts without difficulty, because, after making monthly Chapter 13 plan payments, he would still have excess, disposable income of $200 per month under a three-year plan and $280 per month under a five-year plan.

Although your statement would be comprehensible to the judges and their clerks, you are presenting them with a considerable amount of information. To make the information easier to grasp, you might decide to reorganize it by starting with an introductory paragraph and then setting out the financial information in tabular form:

Because of the debtor's ample disposable income, the bankruptcy court found that under a three-year Chapter 13 plan, he could repay his debts by making equal monthly payments of $200. Alternatively, under a five-year plan, he could make equal monthly payments of $120.

GROSS INCOME	$18,000
NET MONTHLY INCOME	$1,000
MONTHLY EXPENSES	
Rent	300
Food	100
Transportation	50
Clothing	100
Recreation	50
TOTAL EXPENSES	$600
DISPOSABLE MONTHLY INCOME	$400
THREE-YEAR PLAN	
Pre-petition disposable income per month	$400
Ch. 13 monthly payments	$200
Ch. 13 disposable income	$200
FIVE-YEAR PLAN	
Pre-petition disposable income per month	$400
Ch. 13 monthly payments	$120
Ch. 13 disposable income	$280

Although this format might be more helpful, it still requires the court to sift through detailed information, perhaps more information than the court needs to reach a decision. Perhaps some members of the court may find themselves so immersed in information that they fail to focus on your main argument, that Trol can easily pay his debts under a Chapter 13 wage earner's plan. All the judges may need is the part of the chart explaining the three-year plan and the five-year plan and information on Trol's annual salary.

If you decided to present the information in textual, non-tabular form, you might present it this way:

> Because of Trol's disposable income of $400 per month, the bankruptcy court found that under a three-year Chapter 13 plan, he could repay his debts by making equal monthly payments of $200. Alternatively, under a five-year plan, he could make equal monthly payments of $120.

III. AVOID RIGIDLY ADHERING TO FORMULAIC STRUCTURES FOR ORGANIZING ARGUMENTS

"No rule is so general which admits not some exception," wrote the British scholar Robert Burton. His maxim certainly applies to a variety of rules instructing us on how to structure an argument. Although the standard rules frequently offer sound guidance, in some situations, they offer the wrong guidance. As with all rules on writing, we must test their applicability against the standard of good judgment: Will following this rule help me make an argument that is clear and persuasive?

For example, one organizational rule is to state the general rule of law first and then apply it. Suppose your client is a commercial tenant who stops paying rent, because it believes that the leased property is unfit for commercial use. The standard way to set out your client's position is to argue, first, that there is an implied covenant of fitness for use in commercial leases as well as in residential leases and, second, that the property in question is unfit for its intended use.

It is certainly acceptable to structure your argument in this manner. However, if the conditions of the property are dramatically unfit, you might well decide to reverse the order. The second argument (now your first argument) permits you to graphically describe the property's deficiencies at the beginning of your argument. Thus, you now enjoy the freedom to begin by emphasizing the hazards of a leaking roof, a faulty heating system, and an infestation of vermin. Once the court understands how these facts injure your client, it may be more open to accepting the other, more legal, part of your argument.

Here is another example. One standard rule is to play your strongest argument first. However, there may be unavoidable exceptions. We illustrate with a common tort doctrine: battery. As you know, a battery occurs when one person harmfully touches another person without his or her consent. If the court finds that your client harmfully touched another, you must argue that the person whom your client touched must have consented to such contact.

The Restatement elements required for establishing a battery are that (1) a person acts intending to cause a harmful or offensive contact with the person of the other or a third person, (2) a harmful contact with the person of the other directly or indirectly results, and (3) the person did not consent to such contact. Because of the nature of these elements, a court would expect you to establish the first and second elements before you argue the third element is also present. Yet, in your case, the third element is the critical one.

In this case, it probably would be unwise to start with the third element, because this organization of your argument would seem too unusual. A better solution would be to begin with a few sentences stating that the first two elements are clearly satisfied and then move on to a full argument concerning the third element. If there are minor issues concerning the first two elements, you could return to them after you complete your argument on the third issue. By organizing your argument in this way, you adhere to the organizational structure that the court expects, yet move rapidly into your major argument.

IV. AVOID LONG AND FREQUENT QUOTATIONS

Ask anyone what they do when they are reading a legal document and confront a long block quotation. The answer is always the same: "I try to skip it." Why, then, do writers use block quotations? The answer is that they are using quotations as appeals to authority. If it is persuasive to note that the court below or some other court agrees with your argument, quoting that court must increase the persuasiveness.

This conclusion obviously requires some significant qualifications. If the reader is not going to read the block quotation, its authoritative appeal is going to be minimal or non-existent. Shorter quotations are not necessarily the solution. The reader may be tempted to skip or skim them as well. Moreover, because the quotations are the product of a different writer, they may not harmonize well with your writing style and disrupt the flow of your writing.

The three standard guidelines remain sound. First, when possible, paraphrase the quoted material. You usually can phrase the statement as well as the original writer. As long as you provide a citation to your source, you will not be accused of stealing the work of another. Second, include a quotation when you are quoting words that the reader needs to construe to reach a decision. Third, include a quotation when it is particularly eloquent and effective in making a point.

For example, you are litigating a case in which the landlord refused to permit a tenant to assign his lease to a new tenant. Your jurisdiction follows the rule that a landlord cannot withhold its consent unreasonably. Because the issue is the reasonableness of the landlord's decision, you might be tempted to quote a passage from a prior court case that states the jurisdiction's rule:

> A restraint on alienation without the consent of the landlord of the tenant's interest in the leased property is valid, but the landlord's consent to an alienation by the tenant cannot be withheld unreasonably, unless a freely negotiated provision in the lease gives the landlord an absolute right to withhold consent.

Here, however, employing this block quote would be an error. The reader will have considerable difficulty understanding what the first twenty words mean. (They mean it is permissible for a lease to include a provision forbidding the tenant to sublet or assign the lease unless the landlord consents.) Moreover, this initial clause is irrelevant to your case. As a result, the reader may become confused about the meaning of the second clause, which is the relevant one. There is no reason for the reader to have to struggle with the third clause, because it does not apply to your case.

As an alternative, you might simply state the relevant part of the rule in your own words and include a citation to the relevant case:

> A lease may forbid the tenant from assigning the lease without the land-lord's consent; however, in this jurisdiction, the landlord may not withhold its consent unreasonably.

On the other hand, you might decide that the case will turn on the meaning of the word "unreasonably," and may wish to quote the words that the court must construe. In this case, you might draft this sentence:

> A lease may forbid the tenant from assigning the lease without the land-lord's consent; however, in this jurisdiction, "the landlord's consent to an alienation by the tenant cannot be withheld unreasonably. . . ."

If you see the merits of using a paraphrase or a brief quotation, but still are uncomfortable about excluding the entire quotation, you can use the paraphrase or brief quotation in the text and set out the entire quotation in a footnote.

Here is another example that returns us to the bankruptcy example we used earlier in this chapter. As you recall, Anthony Trol, the debtor, is seeking a Chapter 7 bankruptcy, which would free him from repaying any of his outstanding debts. However, the bankruptcy court rejects Trol's petition, because it believes that he could repay his debts gradually under a Chapter 13 plan, which would require him to repay his debts gradually according to a three-year or five-year plan. Trol appeals this decision. As an attorney for the creditors, you are drafting a brief in support of the bankruptcy court's decision. At the end of your Statement of Facts, you wish to report the bankruptcy court's rationale, because it supports your position. You might include the information by using a block quote:

> In dismissing Trol's Chapter 7 case, the court stated:
>
>> Trol has sufficient disposable income to liquidate all of his debts with relative ease and, in fact, he would still have $200 left over after his monthly payment to the Chapter 13 trustee, even under a three-year 100% plan. These cases are fact specific and in this instance the payment of these debts would not deprive the Debtor of adequate food, shelter, clothing, or other necessities. Because the numbers here are on a smaller scale than most does not alter or relieve the Debtor of his § 707(b) responsibility, and having failed to show cause why the case should not be dismissed under § 707(b), it is so ORDERED.

Upon reviewing the block quote, you might decide that it has all the negative qualities of a long quotation: in particular, it includes more information than the reader needs, it tempts the reader to skip over it, and it requires the reader to deal with a writing style that differs from yours. Therefore, you may decide to report the court's reasoning in your own words, but include some quotations from the original:

> In dismissing Trol's Chapter 7 case, the court noted that "[t]hese cases are fact specific and in this instance the payment of these debts would not deprive the Debtor of adequate food, shelter, clothing, or other necessities." According to the court's calculations, even under a three-year Chapter 13 plan, Trol could liquidate all his debts and still enjoy a monthly disposable income of $200. The court held that the Debtor's low income and very modest expenses did "not alter or relieve the Debtor of his § 707(b) responsibility. . . ."

Upon reading your redraft, you may decide that the two brief quotations disrupt your prose and distract the reader. You might conclude that the first quotation adds nothing special to the message you are trying to convey. Therefore, you might decide to redraft the passage this way:

> In dismissing Trol's Chapter 7 case, the court noted that cases dealing with substantial abuse are fact-specific, and here the Debtor could pay his debts under a Chapter 13 plan and still afford adequate food, shelter, clothing, and other necessities. More specifically, under a three-year 100% plan, the Debtor could make his monthly payment and still enjoy a disposable

income of $200. According to the court, "[b]ecause the numbers here are on a smaller scale than most does not alter or relieve the Debtor of his § 707(b) responsibility. . . ."

Upon reflection, you may decide that the second quotation does not sufficiently contribute to your message to justify including it. Therefore, you may decide to omit all quotations and put the court's reasoning into your own words. This is the choice we prefer.

> In dismissing Trol's Chapter 7 case, the court noted that cases dealing with substantial abuse are fact-specific, and here the Debtor could pay his debts under a Chapter 13 plan and still afford adequate food, shelter, clothing, and other necessities. More specifically, under a three-year 100% plan, Trol could make his monthly payment and still enjoy a disposable income of $200. Although his income and expenses are on a very modest scale, the court held that this consideration did not alter or relieve his § 707(b) responsibility.

As these examples demonstrate, you should use quotations sparingly. When you include a quotation, the burden is on you to justify your decision.

V. AVOID EXCESSIVE CITATIONS

All legal writers want to strengthen arguments by showing that sound precedent supports them. However, the attraction of citing authority can lead writers to cite too much authority. For example, look at the excessive number and length of footnotes in most law review articles. Perhaps excessive reliance on authority suggests that the writer is insufficiently confident about the persuasiveness of his or her argument. Cite authority only when necessary. Excessive citations do not strengthen your argument.

Here is an example. You are a Pennsylvania lawyer representing a client who is suing a hospital for malpractice. The trial court has granted the hospital's motion for summary judgment, and you are bringing an appeal. In your brief, you emphasize that in the case of summary judgment, the appellate court has a broad scope of review. In support of your argument, you offer this string cite:

> *LJL Transp., Inc. v. Pilot Air Freight Corp.*, 962 A.2d 639, 647 (Pa. 2009); *Washington v. Baxter*, 719 A.2d 733, 737 (Pa. 1998); *Albright v. Abington Memorial Hospital*, 696 A.2d 1159, 1165 (Pa. 1997); *Nationwide Mut. Ins. Co. v. West*, 807 A.2d 916, 918-19 (Pa. Super. 2002); *Grabowski v. Quigley*, 684 A.2d 610, 614 (Pa. Super. 1996), *appeal dismissed*, 717 A.2d 1024 (Pa. 1998).

In actuality, all you needed to include was a citation to the *Washington* case. It is particularly inappropriate to include a string cite for a point that is incontrovertible. Here *Washington* is the most recent state supreme court pronouncement on the subject and therefore sufficiently authoritative. You do not need to cite the earlier state supreme court cases and you certainly do not need to cite cases from the state's intermediate appellate court.

When might you decide to include a string citation? If you are arguing for a rule that is not well established, you may want to cite several favorable cases to show that the trend of the law favors the rule. If the only case in your jurisdiction that supports a rule is old, you may want to cite several cases from other jurisdictions, and perhaps a treatise or article, to show that the rule in the older case is still generally accepted law. If you are arguing that applying a rule to the facts of your case generates a favorable result, you may wish to cite several cases in which courts applied the rule to similar fact patterns and reached conclusions that favor your argument. In this last instance, be sure to follow each cited case with a brief parenthetical description of the case. However, in any of these situations, cite no more cases than are necessary to make your point.

EXERCISES

1. You represent the tenant in a dispute with her landlord. You are arguing that a landlord has a duty to make reasonable efforts to mitigate damages when a tenant defaults on a lease. In your jurisdiction, the highest court has not yet ruled on this issue. In support of your position, you discuss a favorable ruling by the Colorado Supreme Court:

   > Requiring the landlord to mitigate discourages economic waste and encourages productive use of the property. As the Colorado Supreme court has written:
   >
   >> Under traditional property law principles a landlord could allow the property to remain unoccupied while still holding the abandoned tenant liable for rent. This encourages both economic and physical waste. In no other context of which we are aware is an injured party permitted to sit idly by and suffer avoidable economic loss and thereafter to visit the full adverse economic consequences upon the party whose breach initiated the chain of events causing the loss.
   >
   > *Schneiker v. Gordon*, 732 P.2d 603, 610 (Colo. 1987).

   Please write a second draft in which you avoid using a block quote by either paraphrasing or using only brief, selected quotations.

2. In this case, a law student is suing the dean for false imprisonment. You represent the law student. The following passage comes from a Statement of Facts. Please revise to delete unnecessary facts that do not further your case.

On April 1, 2001, Olive W. Holmes, a third-year law student at The Law School, was arrested and charged with possession of drug paraphernalia. Dean Jones, the dean of The Law School, searched Ms. Holmes' locker and found marijuana seeds, potting soil, and pots. While walking by the open locker, Dean Jones noticed the seeds, and, because of his knowledge of controlled substances, recognized the seeds as marijuana seeds. The seeds were in plain view and not hidden by a coat, book, or other items in the locker. Dean Jones called the police and insisted that Ms. Holmes wait in his office until the police arrived.

While waiting in his office, Ms. Holmes asked Dean Jones if she could leave to take a scheduled law school exam. She promised that she would return afterward to talk to the police. Dean Jones refused to allow Ms. Holmes to leave his office. Ms. Holmes challenged the legality of the locker search, but to no avail. As a result, Ms. Holmes missed the exam and will have to repeat the class. Thus, the dean's refusal caused her to graduate one semester behind her class. Ms. Holmes spent a total of about four hours in Dean Jones' office.

At Ms. Holmes' preliminary hearing on April 20, the charge against her was dismissed when the individual who gave Ms. Holmes the materials admitted that she had told Ms. Holmes they were materials for starting an herb garden.

CHAPTER 14

Advocacy and Ethics

You would like to delay a proceeding. May you do so by making an argument that you know lacks any merit? You do not want to tell the court that the material evidence you offered was false. May you justify nondisclosure by relying on lawyer–client confidentiality? You know of a case in your jurisdiction that is directly adverse to your client's argument, and your opponent has not cited it. May you choose not to bring it to the court's attention? The answer to these questions is no. Advocacy has its limits.

Ethical rules place constraints on zealous advocacy. As you know, all states impose ethical regulations on attorneys. In most states, the regulations track the American Bar Association's Model Rules of Professional Conduct. In other states, the regulations track the ABA's earlier effort, the Model Code of Professional Responsibility.

In this chapter, we set out the major ethical rules governing advocacy. Because most states follow the Model Rules, we focus the discussion on them. In the footnotes, we provide references to the Disciplinary Rules (DRs) of the Model Code. With respect to the material covered in this chapter, the Model Rules do not contradict the Model Code; instead, they often offer more detailed provisions.

In this short chapter, we explain what the rules require. Rather than offer a detailed analysis, we acquaint you with the most pertinent rules. In this way, we seek to prevent you from committing the most typical violations. If you encounter a situation that raises difficult ethical questions, we hope that this chapter will serve as a starting point for detailed research.[1]

We can summarize the most pertinent ethical precepts in four rules:

1. Make only meritorious claims, defenses, and arguments.
2. Do not make false statements to a tribunal or fail to disclose material facts.

---

1. For detailed research, helpful sources include Monroe H. Freedman, *Understanding Lawyers' Ethics* (1990); Geoffrey C. Hazard, Jr. & W. William Hodes, *The Law of Lawyering: A Handbook on the Model Rules of Professional Conduct* (2d ed. 1990); Charles W. Wolfram, *Modern Legal Ethics* (1986).

3. Disclose adverse legal authority in the controlling jurisdiction.
4. In an ex parte proceeding, disclose all material facts.

I. MAKE ONLY MERITORIOUS CLAIMS, DEFENSES, AND ARGUMENTS

Model Rule 3.1 states:

> A lawyer shall not bring or defend a proceeding, or assert or controvert an issue therein, unless there is a basis in law and fact for doing so that is not frivolous, which includes a good faith argument for an extension, modification or reversal of existing law. A lawyer for the defendant in a criminal proceeding, or the respondent in a proceeding that could result in incarceration, may nevertheless so defend the proceeding as to require that every element of the case be established.[2]

Although you must argue your client's case persuasively, you must not bring frivolous proceedings, raise frivolous defenses, or argue issues in a frivolous way. According to Comment 2 accompanying Model Rule 3.1:

> The action is frivolous, however, if the lawyer is unable either to make a good faith argument on the merits of the action taken or to support the action taken by a good faith argument for an extension, modification or reversal of existing law.

The rule does not limit you to arguing settled law; you can make a good faith creative argument. Your argument is not frivolous if, in good faith, you seek to extend, modify, or reverse existing law. Moreover, your argument is not frivolous just because you believe that it will fail.

Rule 3.1 permits you as a criminal defense lawyer to require the government to prove all elements of its case without the defense's assistance. However, you still may not make frivolous arguments.

Here are two examples of frivolous arguments:

1. A lawyer argues lack of jurisdiction by contending that the federal government can punish only those crimes committed in the District of Columbia and that the federal income tax is unconstitutional.[3]

---

2. See Model Code of Professional Responsibility, DR 7-102(a); DR 2-109(A). Also worthy of attention is Rule 11 of the Federal Rules of Civil Procedure. When an attorney presents the court with a pleading, written motion, or other paper, Rule 11 requires the attorney to implicitly certify that to the best of the attorney's knowledge, information and belief, formed after a reasonable inquiry under the circumstances: (1) the paper is not being presented for an improper purpose; (2) the legal arguments are not frivolous; (3) the factual allegations have evidentiary support or are likely to after a reasonable opportunity for further investigation and study; and (4) the denials of factual contentions are warranted on the evidence or, if specifically so identified, are reasonably based on a lack of information or belief.

3. See *United States v. Collins*, 920 F.2d 619, 623-24, 628 (10th Cir. 1990).

2. Two doctors consult on a patient brought into the emergency room with a broken shoulder. The patient's lawyer brings an action against them for breaking the shoulder. After the lawyer learns the facts, he fails to drop the action.[4]

II. DO NOT MAKE FALSE STATEMENTS TO A TRIBUNAL OR FAIL TO DISCLOSE MATERIAL FACTS

Model Rule provisions 3.3(a)(1), (2) and (3) state that a lawyer shall not knowingly:

1. make a false statement of fact or law to a tribunal or fail to correct a false statement of material fact or law previously made to the tribunal by the lawyer;[5]
2. fail to disclose to the tribunal legal authority in the controlling jurisdiction known to the lawyer to be directly adverse to the position of the client and not disclosed by opposing counsel;[6]
3. offer evidence that the lawyer knows to be false. If a lawyer, the lawyer's client, or a witness called by the lawyer, has offered material evidence and comes to know of its falsity, the lawyer shall take reasonable remedial measures, including, if necessary, disclosure to the tribunal. A lawyer may refuse to offer evidence, other than the testimony of a defendant in a criminal matter, that the lawyer reasonably believes is false.[7]

According to Rule 3.3(c), these duties continue until the proceeding concludes.[8] Complying may require disclosing information otherwise protected by Rule 1.6, which requires the attorney to keep confidential information relating to the representation of the client. Nonetheless, Rules 3.3(a) and (b) prevail.

Rule 3.3(a)(3) states:

A lawyer may refuse to offer evidence that the lawyer believes is false.[9]

As these provisions make clear, when you communicate with a court or other tribunal, you must act with candor. You must not make material statements of law or fact that are false. When necessary to avoid assisting the client in a criminal or fraudulent act, you must disclose material facts.

---

4. See *Raine v. Drasin*, 621 S.W.2d 895, 898, 900-01 (Ky. 1981).
5. See DR 7-102(A)(5).
6. See DR 7-102(a)(3).
7. See DR 7-102(A)(4); 7-102(B)(2); 7-102(B)(1).
8. The Model Code of Professional Responsibility has no comparable provision.
9. The Model Code of Professional Responsibility has no comparable provision.

In addition, you may refuse to offer information that you reasonably believe to be false.

When you make a statement that purports to be based on your own knowledge, for example, in an affidavit, you must make only statements that you know are true or are based on a reasonably diligent inquiry.

If you learn that you have offered material evidence that is false, you must take reasonable remedial measures. In most cases, you must disclose that the evidence was false.

If you do not know that evidence is false, but have reasonable doubts about its truthfulness, you have the discretion to introduce it or withhold it.[10]

Here are four examples of violations of the duty of candor:

1. An attorney receives notice of a deportation hearing from the United States Immigration and Naturalization Service. He fails to notify his client or to appear at the hearing. The INS orders the client deported. In an appeal, the attorney states that he never received notice of the hearing.[11]
2. In a social security proceeding, an attorney advises his client not to mention her second marriage and calls her by the name she used before her remarriage.[12]
3. In a divorce proceeding, the court awards custody of the child to the husband. In violation of a court order, the wife leaves the country with the child. Although the wife's attorney knows where the wife and child are, he refuses to disclose that information to the court.[13]
4. An attorney forges his client's signature on a document and then notarizes it, fraudulently representing that he witnessed the signing.[14]

If you encounter the problems of perjury and suspected perjury while representing a criminal defendant, you will not find consistent guidance on what you should do. According to most authorities, you first should urge your client to correct false evidence. If that effort fails, most authorities would provide two alternatives. First, if possible, withdraw your representation. Second, make a disclosure to the court. It is also permitted to put your client on the stand if he or she insists on testifying, but to ask no questions if you believe the testimony may be perjured. The failure to ask questions sends a signal about your belief in the truthfulness of the testimony. Likewise, most authorities would permit you to withhold evidence if you have reasonable doubts about its truthfulness. On this general topic, see 1 Hazard & Hodes, supra note 1, § 3.3:213-3.3:218.

---

10. The Model Code of Professional Responsibility has no comparable provision.
11. See *Statewide Grievance Comm. v. Friedland*, 609 A.2d 645, 648-49 (Conn. 1992).
12. See *In re Ver Dught*, 825 S.W.2d 847, 850 (Mo. 1992).
13. See *Bersani v. Bersani*, 565 A.2d 1368, 1370-72 (Conn. Super. Ct. 1989).
14. See *In re Crapo*, 542 N.E.2d 1334, 1334-35 (Ind. 1989).

III. DISCLOSE ADVERSE LEGAL AUTHORITY IN THE CONTROLLING JURISDICTION

Model Rule 3.3(a)(2) states:

> A lawyer shall not knowingly fail to disclose to the tribunal legal authority in the controlling jurisdiction known to the lawyer to be directly adverse to the position of the client and not disclosed by opposing counsel.[15]

A close reading of the rule raises five points. First, you must disclose legal authority. Legal authority includes not just case law, but also statutes, regulations, ordinances, and administrative rulings.[16] If you fail to cite a pertinent adverse statute, for example, you can run afoul of the rule.

Second, you must disclose only adverse authority in the controlling jurisdiction. If you are litigating in a state trial court, you need to disclose adverse legal authority from state sources and from pertinent federal sources, for example, a decision by the United States Supreme Court. You need not disclose adverse cases decided in an adjoining state.

Third, you must disclose only authority directly adverse to your client's position. Even if the authority is not dispositive, it may be directly adverse and subject to the rule. For guidance in defining "directly adverse," Formal Opinion 280 (1949) of the American Bar Association Committee on Professional Ethics and Grievances is helpful.[17] It defines "directly adverse authority" as "directly adverse to any proposition of law on which the lawyer expressly relies, which would reasonably be considered important by the judge sitting on the case." The Committee offers this test:

> Is the decision which opposing counsel has overlooked one which the court should clearly consider in deciding the case?

Would a reasonable judge properly feel that a lawyer who advanced, as law, a proposition adverse to the undisclosed decision, was lacking in candor and fairness to him? Might the judge consider himself misled by an implied representation that the lawyer knew of no adverse authority?

Fourth, you must disclose adverse authority only when opposing counsel fails to disclose it.

Fifth, you still may argue that the adverse authority does not control in your case — for example, your case is distinguishable from the adverse case on the facts. Alternatively, you may argue that it is bad law. Presumably, you would make these arguments.

---

15. See DR 7-106(B)(1).

16. See 1 Hazard & Hodes, supra note 1, § 3.3:206, at 587.

17. For a reconfirmation of Formal Opinion 280, see ABA Comm. on Ethics and Professional Responsibility, Informal Op. 84-1505 (1984).

Even if we put aside the binding nature of the rule and the ethical duty to the tribunal, it makes practical sense not to hide important cases and other authorities. If the judge, the judge's clerk, or, belatedly, opposing counsel discovers the neglected adverse authority, you lose your credibility. As a result, you injure both your client and your reputation. Because your conduct may affect your success in future cases before the tribunal or against the same opposing counsel, you also injure your future clients.

Here are three examples of violations of this rule:

1. In a brief to an intermediate appellate court, an attorney states that there are no cases on point and fails to note a case by the same court that the court finds to be dispositive of the issue before it.[18]
2. A city and a state tax commission are litigating a property tax issue. While the case is on appeal, the legislature enacts a statute that moots the issue. Neither attorney brings the statute to the court's attention.[19]
3. Litigation ensues when a manufacturer terminates a truck dealership. The manufacturer fails to cite a state statute requiring good cause to terminate a franchise agreement with a licensed new motor vehicle dealer. The manufacturer's attorney argues that he had no obligation to inform the court, because he believes that the statute is unconstitutional and that he has no obligation to suggest unpleaded claims or theories to the opposing side.[20]

IV. IN AN EX PARTE PROCEEDING, DISCLOSE ALL MATERIAL FACTS

Rule 3.3(d) states:

> In an ex parte proceeding, a lawyer shall inform the tribunal of all material facts known to the lawyer that will enable the tribunal to make an informed decision, whether or not the facts are adverse.[21]

As the rule makes clear, in an ex parte proceeding — for example, an application for a temporary restraining order or a proceeding in which the opposing party defaults — you have an extensive duty of candor. Because no opposing attorney is present to make contrary arguments, your duty to the tribunal requires you to disclose more than the law and facts favorable to your client and more than the adverse legal authority required by Rule 3.3(a)(2).

---

18. See *Thomas v. Workmen's Comp. Appeal Bd.*, 629 A.2d 251, 253 (Pa. Commw. Ct. 1993).

19. See *City of Okla. City v. Oklahoma Tax Comm'n*, 789 P.2d 1287, 1297-1300 (Okla. 1990) (Opala, V.C.J., dissenting).

20. See *Dorso Trailer Sales, Inc. v. American Body Trailer, Inc.*, 464 N.W.2d 551, 554, 556-57 (Minn. Ct. App. 1990).

21. The Model Code of Professional Responsibility has no comparable provision.

As Comment 14 accompanying the rule states: "The lawyer for the repre-sented party has the . . . duty to make disclosures of material facts known to the lawyer and that the lawyer reasonably believes are necessary to an informed decision."

Here are two examples of violations of the rule:

1. An attorney sues his client for $4,000 in unpaid attorney's fees. In obtaining a default judgment, he fails to disclose that the client had already paid him $2,000 of that amount.[22]

2. Two attorneys representing separate plaintiffs win a favorable decision for a garnishment. The judge asks them to draw up a joint order for him to sign. While the process of jointly drafting the order goes on, one of the attorneys drafts an order providing recovery for only his client and submits it to a judge sitting in for the deciding judge. He fails to inform her of the material facts of the proceeding, notably the existence of another prevailing party.[23]

When it comes to legal ethics, there is some standard advice. Keep your nose clean. When faced with a choice, always take the high road. It is not bad advice.

---

22. See *Louisiana State Bar Ass'n v. White*, 539 So. 2d 1216, 1220 (1989).
23. See *Fitzhugh v. Committee on Professional Conduct*, 823 S.W.2d 896, 898-99 (Ark. 1992).

Magic Words: Writing with Flair

Some writers can put words together in a way that allows us to see what they see, feel what they feel, and know what they know. Sometimes they have a talent for using metaphors and imagery — words that create just the right mental picture. Sometimes they choose words that make an argument sound so simple and so right that it becomes irrefutable.

Writing with flair does not mean overwriting. Overwriting includes exaggerating and making your argument with overblown rhetoric that merely distracts. The type of rhetorical flair we are discussing here does not have those characteristics. Instead, it uses images that are easy to understand and that make an argument clearer and stronger. It uses carefully chosen, simple words to make a compelling argument.

In this appendix, we offer some personal favorites as examples of the magic you can accomplish with the right combination of words. Although most of these examples were originally delivered in spoken formats, the rhetorical techniques apply equally to messages that are intended to be read silently rather than listened to.

The first collection of excerpts includes some exceptionally effective mental pictures. The second offers particularly persuasive advocacy that depends on using simple, concrete words to make a straightforward, compelling argument. When appropriate, we offer observations on the techniques used by the writers in the hope that identifying specific techniques may give you some tools to use in creating your own rhetorical magic.

I. METAPHORS AND IMAGERY

A. Metaphors

The following examples demonstrate each writer's ability to use metaphors, implicitly comparing essentially dissimilar things to create a concrete picture of an abstract idea. For example, if you say an idea "limps" or "stumbles," you are using a metaphor to create a mental image of a weak idea. When we can "see" or "feel" an idea, we are more likely to understand, retain, and perhaps adopt it as our own.

We offer a selection of metaphors that ranges from well-developed, drawn-out images to quick, sentence-long "vision bites."

Andrew Hamilton defends Peter Zenger against charges of libel, August 4, 1735

Power may justly be compared to a great river; while kept within its bounds, it is both beautiful and useful, but when it overflows its banks, it is then too impetuous to be stemmed; it bears down all before it, and brings destruction and desolation wherever it comes. If, then, this be the nature of power, let us at least do our duty, and, like wise men who value freedom, use our utmost care to support liberty, the only bulwark against lawless power, which, in all ages, has sacrificed to its wild lust and boundless ambition the blood of the best men that ever lived.

Wendell Phillips protests the murder of abolitionist editor Elijah Lovejoy, Faneuil Hall, Boston, December 8, 1837

He [Lovejoy] took refuge under the banner of liberty amid its folds; and when he fell, its glorious stars and stripes, the emblem of free institutions, around which cluster so many heart-stirring memories, were blotted out in the martyr's blood.

Public opinion, fast hastening on the downward course, must be arrested. . . . Haply, we may awake before we are borne over the precipice.

Daniel Webster speaks in the United States Senate, March 7, 1850

[H]e who sees these states, now revolving in harmony around a common center, and expects to see them quit their places and fly off without convulsion, may look the next hour to see the heavenly bodies rush from their spheres, and jostle against each other in the realms of space, without causing the wreck of the universe. There can be no such thing as a peaceable secession.

Wendell Phillips speaks before the Massachusetts Anti-Slavery Society at the Melodeon, Boston, Massachusetts, January 27, 1853

We are perfectly willing—I am for one—to be the dead lumber that shall make a path for these men into the light and love of the people. . . .

Henry Thoreau pleads for John Brown, 1859

The Republican party does not perceive how many his failure will make to vote more correctly than they would have them. They have counted the votes of Pennsylvania & Co., but they have not correctly counted Captain Brown's vote. He has taken the wind out of their sails,—the little wind they had,—and they may as well lie to and repair.

John Fitzgerald Kennedy delivers his Inaugural Address, January 20, 1961

And if a beachhead of cooperation may push back the jungle of suspicion, let both sides join in creating a new endeavor, not a new balance of power, but a new world of law, where the strong are just and the weak secure and the peace preserved.

Reverend Martin Luther King, Jr., Letter from Birmingham Jail, April 16, 1963

But again I am thankful to God that some noble souls from the ranks of organized religion have broken loose from the paralyzing chains of conformity and joined us as active partners in the struggle for freedom. They have left their secure congregations and walked the streets of Albany, Georgia with us. They have gone down the highways of the South on tortuous rides for freedom. Yes, they have gone to jail with us. Some have been dismissed from their churches, have lost the support of their bishops and fellow ministers. But they have acted in the faith that right defeated is stronger than evil triumphant. Their witness has been the spiritual salt that has preserved the true meaning of the gospel in these troubled times. They have carved a tunnel of hope through the dark mountain of disappointment.

Reverend Martin Luther King, Jr. speaks at the Lincoln Memorial, August 28, 1963

But one hundred years later, the Negro still is not free. One hundred years later, the life of the Negro is still sadly crippled by the manacle of segregation and the chain of discrimination. One hundred years later, the Negro lives on a lonely island of poverty in the midst of a vast ocean of material prosperity. One hundred years later, the Negro is still languishing in the corner of American society and finds himself an exile in his own land. So we have come here today to dramatize a shameful condition.

In a sense we have come to the capital to cash a check. When the architects of our republic wrote the magnificent words of the Constitution and the Declaration of Independence, they were signing a promissory note to which every American was to fall heir. This note was a promise that all men — black men as well as white men — would be guaranteed the unalienable rights of life, liberty, and the pursuit of happiness.

But it is obvious today that America has defaulted on this promissory note insofar as her citizens of color are concerned. Instead of honoring this sacred obligation, America has given the Negro people a bad check — a check that has come back marked "insufficient funds." But we refuse to believe that the bank of justice is bankrupt. We refuse to believe that there are insufficient funds in the great vaults of opportunity in this Nation.

So we have come to cash this check. A check that will give us the riches of freedom and the security of justice.

I am not unmindful that some of you have come here out of great trials and tribulations. Some of you have come from narrow jail cells. Some of you have come from areas where your quest for freedom left you battered by the storms of persecution and staggered by the winds of police brutality. You have been the veterans of creative suffering. Continue to work with the faith that unearned suffering is redemptive.

I have a dream that one day on the red hills of Georgia the sons of slaves and the sons of former slaveowners will be able to sit down together at the table of brotherhood. I have a dream that one day even the state of Mississippi, sweltering with the heat of injustice, sweltering with the heat of oppression, will be transformed into an oasis of freedom and justice.

I have a dream that one day every valley shall be exalted, every hill and mountain shall be made low, the rough places will be made plain, and the crooked places will be made straight, and the glory of the Lord shall be revealed, and all flesh shall see it together. This is our hope. This is the faith that I go back to the South with. With this faith we will be able to hew out of the mountain of despair a stone of hope. With this faith we will be able to transform the jangling discords of our nation into a beautiful symphony of brotherhood. With this faith we will be able to work together, to pray together, to struggle together, to go to jail together, to stand up for freedom together, knowing that we will be free one day.

Richard Milhous Nixon delivers his Inaugural Address, January 20, 1969

The greatest honor history can bestow is the title of peacemaker. This honor now beckons America — the chance to help lead the world at last out of the valley of turmoil and on to that high ground of peace that man has dreamed of since the dawn of civilization.

Jesse Jackson speaks at the Democratic National Convention, July 1984

America is not like a blanket — one piece of unbroken cloth, the same color, the same texture, the same size. America is more like a quilt: many patches, many pieces, many colors, many sizes, all woven and held together by a common thread. The white, the Hispanic, the black, the Arab, the Jew, the woman, the native American, the small farmer, the businessperson, the environmentalist, the peace activist, the young, the old, the lesbian, the gay and the disabled make up the American quilt.

Patrick J. Buchanan speaks to the Daughters of the American Revolution, Constitution Hall, April 22, 1992

Like Gulliver, America is being tied down by the myriad tiny strands of this New World Order.

Mario Cuomo nominates Bill Clinton at the Democratic Convention, July 15, 1992

Supply-side operated from the naive Republican assumption that if we fed the wealthiest Americans with huge income tax cuts, they would eventually produce loaves and fishes for everyone. Instead, it made a small group of our wealthiest Americans wealthier than ever, and left the rest of the country the crumbs from their table — unemployment, bankruptcies, economic stagnation.

And this time, this time we cannot afford to fail to deliver the message — not just to Democrats, but to the whole nation — because the ship of state is headed for the rocks. The crew knows it, the passengers know it; only the captain of the ship, President Bush, appears not to know it. He seems to think — no, no, no — you see, the President seems to think that the ship will be saved by imperceptible undercurrents directed by the invisible hand of some cyclical economic god that will gradually move the ship so that at the last moment it will miraculously glide past the rocks. Well, prayer is always a good idea, but our prayers must be accompanied by good works. We need a captain who understands that and who will seize the wheel before it's too late.

Ronald Reagan addresses the Republican Convention, August 17, 1992

My dream is that you will travel the road ahead with liberty's lamp guiding your steps, and opportunity's arm steadying your way.

George H.W. Bush addresses the Republican Convention, August 21, 1992

And you just won't hear that inflation, the thief of the middle class, has been locked in a maximum-security prison.

Tony Blair addressing the Labour Party after 9/11, October 2001

That is what community means, founded on the equal worth of all. The starving, the wretched, the dispossessed, the ignorant, those living in want and squalor from the deserts of northern Africa to the slums of Gaza, to the mountain ranges of Afghanistan: they too are our cause. This is a moment to seize. The kaleidoscope has been shaken. The pieces are in flux. Soon they will settle again. Before they do, let us reorder this world around us.

B. Other Images

These examples suggest the possibilities of using language in a way that creates concrete, sometimes humorous images, without technically employing the metaphor device. There is no implied comparison here, merely a use of words that allows us to visualize some aspect of the writer's message in a way that makes it clearer, more dramatic, and more interesting. Again, we offer a range of examples that demonstrate the use of imagery in everything from single sentences to several paragraphs. The type of image you create will depend on your audience, the context, and the point you are trying to make.

Daniel Webster addresses the Senate, January 26-27, 1830

That all may be so; but if the tribunal should not happen to be of that opinion, shall we swing for it? We are ready to die for our country, but it is rather an awkward business, this dying without touching the ground! After all, that is a sort of hemp tax worse than any part of the tariff.

Wendell Phillips protests the murder of abolitionist editor Elijah Lovejoy, Faneuil Hall, Boston, December 8, 1837

Sir, when I heard the gentleman lay down principles which place the murderers of Alton side by side with Otis and Hancock, with Quincy and Adams, I thought those pictured lips [pointing to the portraits in the hall] would have broken into voice to rebuke the recreant American — the slanderer of the dead. The gentleman said that he should sink into insignificance if he dared to gainsay the principles of these resolutions. Sir, for the sentiments he has uttered, on soil consecrated by the prayers of Puritans and the blood of patriots, the earth should have yawned and swallowed him up.

Daniel Webster addresses the United States Senate, March 7, 1850

And, now, Mr. President, instead of speaking of the possibility or utility of secession, instead of dwelling in those caverns of darkness, instead of groping with those ideas so full of all that is horrid and horrible, let us come out into the light of the day; let us enjoy the fresh air of Liberty and Union; let us cherish those hopes which belong to us; let us devote ourselves to those great objects that are fit for our consideration and our action; let us raise our conceptions to the magnitude and the importance of the duties that devolve upon us; let our comprehension be as broad as the country for which we act, our aspirations as high as its certain destiny; let us not be pygmies in a case that calls for men.

Frederick Douglass speaks in Rochester, New York, July 4, 1852

To drag a man in fetters into the grand illuminated temple of liberty, and call upon him to join you in joyous anthems, were inhuman mockery and sacrilegious irony. . . .

Fellow citizens, above your national, tumultuous joy, I hear the mournful wail of millions! Whose chains, heavy and grievous yesterday, are, today, rendered more intolerable by the jubilee shouts that reach them.

Wendell Phillips addresses the Massachusetts Anti-Slavery Society at the Melodeon, Boston, Massachusetts, January 27, 1853

You load our names with infamy, and shout us down. But our words bide their time. We warn the living that we have terrible memories, and that their sins are never to be forgotten. We will gibbet the name of every apostate so black and high that his children's children shall blush to bear it. Yet we bear no malice — cherish no resentment. . . .

Elizabeth Cady Stanton, 1872

These boys and girls are one today in school, at play, at home, never dreaming that one sex was foreordained to clutch the stars, the other but to kiss the dust. . . .

John Fitzgerald Kennedy delivers his Inaugural Address, January 20, 1961

The world is very different now. For man holds in his mortal hands the power to abolish all forms of human poverty and all forms of human life.

Mario Cuomo addresses the Democratic Convention, July 17, 1984

The difference between Democrats and Republicans has always been measured in courage and confidence. The Republicans believe that the wagon train will not make it to the frontier unless some of the old, some of the young, some of the weak are left behind by the side of the trail.

The strong, the strong, they tell us, will inherit the land!

We Democrats believe in something else. We Democrats believe that we can make it all the way with the whole family intact.

And we have more than once.

Ever since Franklin Roosevelt lifted himself from his wheelchair to lift this nation from its knees. Wagon train after wagon train. To new frontiers of education, housing, peace. The whole family aboard. Constantly reaching out to extend and enlarge that family. Lifting them up into the wagon on the way. Blacks and Hispanics and people of every ethnic group and Native Americans — all those struggling to build their families and claim some small share of America.

To succeed we will have to surrender some small parts of our individual interests, to build a platform we can all stand on, at once, and comfortably, proudly singing out. We need a platform we can all agree to, so that we can sing out the truth for the nation to hear, in chorus, its logic so clear and commanding that no slick Madison Avenue commercial, no amount of geniality, no martial music will be able to muffle the sound of the truth.

It is a mortgage on our children's future that can only be paid in pain and that could bring this nation to its knees.

But there's another part to the shining city; the part where people can't pay their mortgages . . . ; where students can't afford the education they need and middle-class parents watch the dreams they hold for their children evaporate.

In this part of the city there are more poor than ever. And there are people who sleep in the city streets, in the gutter, where the glitter doesn't show. There is despair, Mr. President, the faces that you don't see, in the places that you don't visit.

The struggle to live with dignity is the real story of the shining city. And it's a story that I didn't read in a book, or learn in a classroom. I saw it and lived it, like many of you. I watched a small man with thick calluses on both his hands work 15 and 16 hours a day. I saw him once literally bleed from the bottoms of his feet, a man who came here uneducated, alone, unable to speak the language, who taught me all I needed to know about faith and hard work by the simple eloquence of his example. I learned about our kind of democracy from my father. And I learned about our obligation to each other from him and from my mother. They asked for a chance to work and to make the world better for their children, and they asked to be protected in those moments when they would not be able to protect themselves. This nation and this nation's government did that for them.

Bill Clinton addresses the Democratic Convention, July 17, 1992

An America in which the rich are not soaked — but the middle class is not drowned, either.

Ronald Reagan addresses the Republican Convention, August 17, 1992

Until then, when we see all that rhetorical smoke billowing out from the Democrats, well, ladies and gentlemen, I'd follow the example of their nominee — don't inhale.

George H.W. Bush addresses the Republican Convention, August 21, 1992

Now, the Soviet bear may be gone, but there are still wolves in the woods. It is a body caught in a hopelessly tangled web of PACs, perks, privileges, partisanship and paralysis. Every day, every day, Congress puts politics ahead of principle and above progress. [This last example demonstrates the use of alliteration — the repetition of initial sounds for dramatic effect. — EDS.]

Barack Obama, The Audacity of Hope (2007)

Maybe the critics are right. Maybe there's no escaping our great political divide, an endless clash of armies, and any attempts to alter the rules of engagement are futile. Or maybe the trivialization of politics has reached a point of no return, so that most people see it as just one more diversion, a sport, with politicians our paunch-bellied gladiators and those who bother to pay attention just fans on the sidelines: We paint our faces red or blue and cheer our side, and if it takes a late hit or cheap shot to beat the other team, so be it, for winning is all that matters. But I don't think so.

II. SIMPLE APPEALS

Sometimes the purity and simplicity of an argument are such that we cannot help but be persuaded. If the writer can identify objective principles with which the reader must almost certainly agree and attach those principles to the idea the writer is trying to convey, the reader is likely to be swept along to the writer's intended conclusion almost without realizing it. If the writer can also employ simple, concrete, perhaps even eloquent language that makes the idea easy to understand and believe in, the likelihood of persuasion becomes even greater. Here are some examples:

Red Jacket responds to a missionary at a council of chiefs of the Six Nations, 1805

Brother, you say there is but one way to worship and serve the Great Spirit. If there is but one religion, why do you white people differ so much about it? Why not all agreed, as you can all read the book?

Brother, we are told that you have been preaching to the white people in this place. These people are our neighbors. We are acquainted with them. We will wait a little while and see what effect your preaching has upon them. If we find it does them good, makes them honest, and less disposed to cheat Indians, we will then consider again of what you have said.

Elizabeth Cady Stanton keynotes the first Woman's Rights Convention in Seneca Falls, New York, July 19, 1848

The right is ours. The question now is: how shall we get possession of what rightfully belongs to us? We should not feel so sorely grieved if no man who had not attained the full stature of a Webster, Clay, Van Buren, or Gerrit Smith could claim the right of the elective franchise. But to have drunkards, idiots, horse-racing, rum-selling rowdies, ignorant foreigners, and silly boys fully recognized, while we ourselves are thrust out from all the rights that belong to citizens, it is too grossly insulting to the dignity of woman to be longer quietly submitted to. The right is ours. Have it, we must. Use it, we will. The pens, the tongues, the fortunes, the indomitable wills of many women are already pledged to secure this right. The great truth that no just government can be formed without the consent of the governed we shall echo and re-echo in the ears of the unjust judge, until by continual coming we shall weary him.

The world has never yet seen a truly great and virtuous nation, because in the degradation of woman the very fountains of life are poisoned at their source. It is vain to look for silver and gold from mines of copper and lead. It is the wise mother that has the wise son. So long as your women are slaves you may throw your colleges and churches to the winds. You can't have scholars and saints so long as your mothers are ground to powder between the upper and nether millstone of tyranny and lust. How seldom, now, is a father's pride gratified, his fond hopes realized, in the budding genius of his son! The wife is degraded, made the mere creature of caprice, and the foolish son is heaviness to his heart. Truly are the sins of the fathers visited upon the children to the third and fourth generation. God, in His wisdom, has so linked the whole human family together that any violence done at one end of the chain is felt throughout its length, and here, too, is the law of restoration, as in woman all have fallen, so in her elevation shall the race be recreated.

Frederick Douglass speaks in Rochester, New York, July 4, 1852

It is admitted in the fact that Southern statute books are covered with enactments forbidding, under severe fines and penalties, the teaching of the slave to read or to write. When you can point to any such laws in reference to the beasts of the field, then I may consent to argue the manhood of the slave. When the dogs in your streets, when the fowls of the air, when the cattle on your hills, when the fish of the sea and the reptiles that crawl shall be unable to distinguish the slave from a brute, then will I argue with you that the slave is a man!

What, am I to argue that it is wrong to make men brutes, to rob them of their liberty, to work them without wages, to keep them ignorant of their relations to their fellow men, to beat them with sticks, to flay their flesh with the lash, to load their limbs with irons, to hunt them with dogs, to sell them at auction, to sunder their families, to knock out their teeth, to burn their flesh, to starve them into obedience and submission to their masters? Must I argue that a system thus marked with blood, and stained with pollution, is wrong?

George Graham Vest served as U.S. Senator from Missouri from 1879 to 1903 and became one of the leading orators and debaters of his time. This speech is from an earlier period in his life (1855) when he practiced law in a small Missouri town. It was given in court while representing a man who sued another for the killing of his dog. During the trial, Vest ignored the testimony, and when his turn came to present a summation to the jury, he made the following speech and won the case:

Gentlemen of the Jury: The best friend a man has in the world may turn against him and become his enemy. His son or daughter that he has reared with loving care may prove ungrateful. Those who are nearest and dearest to us, those whom we trust with our happiness and our good name may become traitors to their faith. The money that a man has, he may lose. It flies away from him, perhaps when he needs it most. A man's reputation may be sacrificed in a moment of ill-considered action. The people who are prone to fall on their knees to do us honor when success is with us, may be the first to throw the stone of malice when failure settles its cloud upon our heads.

The one absolutely unselfish friend that man can have in this selfish world, the one that never deserts him, the one that never proves ungrateful or treacherous is his dog. A man's dog stands by him in prosperity and in poverty, in health and in sickness. He will sleep on the cold ground, where the wintry winds blow and the snow drives fiercely, if only he may be near his master's side. He will kiss the hand that has no food to offer. He will lick the wounds and sores that come in encounters with the roughness of the world. He guards the sleep of his pauper master as if he were a prince. When all other friends desert, he remains. When riches take wings, and reputation falls to pieces, he is as constant in his love as the sun in its journey through the heavens.

If fortune drives the master forth, an outcast in the world, friendless and homeless, the faithful dog asks no higher privilege than that of accompanying him, to guard him against danger, to fight against his enemies. And when the last scene of all comes, and death takes his master in its embrace and his body is laid away in the cold ground, no matter if all other friends pursue their way, there by the graveside will the noble dog be found, his head between his paws, his eyes sad, but open in alert watchfulness, faithful and true even in death.[1]

Elizabeth Cady Stanton, 1872

When there is a demand for healthy, happy, vigorous, self-reliant women, they will make their appearance. But with our feeble type of man-hood the present supply of vanity and vacuity meets their wants. Woman, as she is today, is men's handiwork. With iron shoes, steel-ribbed corsets, hoops, trains, high heels, chignons, panders, limping gait, feeble muscles, with her cultivated fears of everything seen and unseen, of snakes, spiders, mice and millers, cows, caterpillars, dogs and drunken men, firecrackers and cannon, thunder and lightning, ghosts and gentlemen, women die ten thousand deaths, when if educated to be brave and self-dependent, they would die but one.

---

1. *http://www.historyplace.com/speeches/vest.htm.*

William Jennings Bryan addresses the Democratic National Convention, July 8, 1896

You come to us and tell us that the great cities are in favor of the gold standard; we reply that the great cities rest upon our broad and fertile prairies. Burn down your cities and leave our farms, and your cities will spring up again as if by magic; but destroy our farms and the grass will grow in the streets of every city in the country.

Clarence Darrow makes his closing argument in the Leopold and Loeb case, Chicago, 1924

Your Honor stands between the past and the future. You may hang these boys; you may hang them by the neck until they are dead. But in doing it you will turn your face toward the past. In doing it you are making it harder for every other boy who in ignorance and darkness must grope his way through the mazes which only childhood knows. In doing it you will make it harder for unborn children. You may save them and make it easier for every child that sometime may stand where these boys stand. You will make it easier for every human being with an aspiration and a vision and a hope and a fate. I am pleading for the future; I am pleading for a time when hatred and cruelty will not control the hearts of men. When we can learn by reason and judgment and understanding and faith that all life is worth saving, and that mercy is the highest attribute of man.

Clarence Darrow makes his closing argument in the Henry Sweet trial, May 19, 1926

Let us take a little glance at the history of the Negro race. It only needs a minute. It seems to me that the story would melt hearts of stone. I was born in America. I could have left it if I had wanted to go away. Some other men, reading about this land of freedom that we brag about on the Fourth of July, came voluntarily to America. These men, the defendants, are here because they could not help it. Their ancestors were captured in the jungles and on the plains of Africa, captured as you capture wild beasts, torn from their homes and their kindred, loaded into slave ships, packed like sardines in a box, half of them dying on the ocean passage; some jumping into the sea in their frenzy, when they had a chance to choose death in place of slavery. They were captured and brought here. They could not help it. They were bought and sold as slaves, to work without pay, because they were black. They were subject to all of this for generations, until finally they were given their liberty, so far as the law goes — and that is only a little way, because, after all, every human being's life in this world is inevitably mixed with every other life and, no matter what laws we pass, no matter what precautions we take, unless the people we meet are kindly and decent and human and liberty-loving, then there is no liberty. Freedom comes from human beings, rather than from laws and institutions.

I do not believe in the law of hate. I may not be true to my ideals always, but I believe in the law of love, and I believe you can do nothing with hatred. I would like to see a time when man loves his fellow man and forgets his color or his creed. We will never be civilized until that time comes. I know the Negro race has a long road to go. I believe that the life of the Negro race has been a life of tragedy, of injustice, of oppression. The law has made him equal, but man has not. And, after all, the last analysis is: what has man done, and not what has the law done? I know there is a long road ahead of him before he can take the place which I believe he should take. I know that before him there is sorrow, tribulation and death among the blacks, and perhaps the whites. I am sorry. I would do what I could to avert it. I would advise patience; I would advise tolerance; I would advise understanding; I would advise all those things which are necessary for men who live together.

Sir Winston Churchill, Their Finest Hour, House of Commons, June 18, 1940

Of this I am quite sure, that if we open a quarrel between the past and the present, we shall find that we have lost the future.

Ronald Reagan addresses the Republican Convention, August 17, 1992

In America our origins matter less than our destinations, and that's what democracy is all about.

Mary Fisher addresses the Republican National Convention, August 23, 1992

Tonight, I represent an AIDS community whose members have been reluctantly drafted from every segment of American society. Though I am white, and a mother, I am one with a black infant struggling with tubes in a Philadelphia hospital. Though I am female, and contracted this disease in marriage, and enjoy the warm support of my family, I am one with the lonely gay man sheltering a flickering candle from the cold wind of his family's rejection.

Tonight, HIV marches resolutely toward AIDS in more than a million American homes, littering its pathway with the bodies of the young. Young men, young women, young parents, young children. One of the families is mine. If it is true that HIV inevitably turns to AIDS, then my children will inevitably turn to orphans.

I want my children to know that their mother was not a victim. She was a messenger. I do not want them to think, as I once did, that courage is the absence of fear; I want them to know that courage is the strength to act wisely when most we are afraid. I want them to have the courage to step

forward when called by their nation, or their party, and give leadership —
no matter what the personal cost. I ask no more of you than I ask of myself,
or of my children.

To my children, I make this pledge: I will not give in, Zachary, because
I draw my courage from you. Your silly giggle gives me hope. Your gentle
prayers give me strength. And you, my child, give me reason to say to
America, "You are at risk." And I will not rest, Max, until I have done
all I can to make your world safe. I will seek a place where intimacy is
not the prelude to suffering.

I will not hurry to leave you, my children. But when I go, I pray that you
will not suffer shame on my account. To all within the sound of my voice,
I appeal: Learn with me the lessons of history and of grace, so my children
will not be afraid to say the word AIDS when I am gone. Then their children, and yours may not need to whisper it all. God bless the children, and
God bless us all. Good night.

George W. Bush, 9/11 Speech

Today, our fellow citizens, our way of life, our very freedom came under
attack in a series of deliberate and deadly terrorist acts. The victims were in
airplanes, or in their offices; secretaries, businessmen and women, military
and federal workers; moms and dads, friends and neighbors. Thousands of
lives were suddenly ended by evil, despicable acts of terror.

The pictures of airplanes flying into buildings, fires burning, huge structures collapsing, have filled us with disbelief, terrible sadness, and a quiet,
unyielding anger. These acts of mass murder were intended to frighten our
nation into chaos and retreat. But they have failed; our country is strong.

III. LEGAL WRITING

Here are some examples of actual legal writing using some of the writing
tools we have talked about — imagery, simple appeals, and other effective
use of language. In the last two examples, we see judges who have a sense
of humor about what they are doing and the subject of their writing.

Morrison v. Olsen, 487 U.S. 654, 699 (1988) (SCALIA, J., dissenting). Scalia recognizing that contemporary constitutional interpretation has drastic implications on the separation of powers.

That is what this suit is about. Power. The allocation of power among
Congress, the President, and the courts in such fashion as to preserve the
equilibrium the Constitution sought to establish. Frequently an issue of this
sort will come before the Court clad, so to speak, in sheep's clothing: the
potential of the asserted principle to effect important change in the equilibrium of power is not immediately evident, and must be discerned by a
careful and perceptive analysis. But this wolf comes as a wolf.

Brief for American Civil Liberties Union, et al. as Amici Curiae Supporting Respondent, Texas v. Johnson, 491 U.S. 397, 109 S. Ct. 2533 (1989), 1989 WL 1127779, 27.

Even if the State's interest in preserving the flag as a symbol of nationhood were a legitimate interest unrelated to the suppression of expression, there is no basis upon which this Court can conclude that burning the flag undermines that interest. Cf. *Tinker*, 393 U.S. at 508. It is because the flag is such a powerful symbol that people choose to burn it to express dissent. Far from diminishing the flag's symbolic value, such politically expressive flagburning is a reminder of the freedom this country affords its political dissidents.

Stambovsky v. Ackley, 169 A.D.2d 254, 257 (1991) (from the majority opinion).

From the perspective of a person in the position of plaintiff herein, a very practical problem arises with respect to the discovery of a paranormal phenomenon: "Who you gonna call?" as a title song to the movie "Ghostbusters" asks. Applying the strict rule of caveat emptor to a contract involving a house possessed by poltergeists conjures up visions of a psychic or medium routinely accompanying the structural engineer and Terminix man on an inspection of every home subject to a contract of sale. It portends that the prudent attorney will establish an escrow account lest the subject of the transaction come back to haunt him and his client — or pray that his malpractice insurance coverage extends to supernatural disasters. In the interest of avoiding such untenable consequences, the notion that a haunting is a condition which can and should be ascertained upon reasonable inspection of the premises is a hobgoblin which should be exorcised from the body of legal precedent and laid quietly to rest.

The first two paragraphs in Chief Justice Roberts's dissent from the denial of certiorari in Pennsylvania v. Dunlap, No. 07-1486.[2]

October 14, 2008

Officer Sean Devlin, Narcotics Strike Force, was working the morning shift. Undercover surveillance. The neighborhood? Tough as a three-dollar steak. Devlin knew. Five years on the beat, nine months with the Strike Force. He'd made fifteen, twenty drug busts in the neighborhood.

Devlin spotted him: a lone man on the corner. Another approached. Quick exchange of words. Cash handed over; small objects handed back. Each man then quickly on his own way. Devlin knew the guy wasn't buying bus tokens. He radioed a description and Officer Stein picked up the buyer. Sure enough: three bags of crack in the guy's pocket. Head downtown and book him. Just another day at the office.

---

2. *http://www.supremecourtus.gov/opinions/08pdf/07-1486.pdf.*

Review Exercise

PERFORMANCE EXAMINATION

Most states now require some form of performance examination as part of their bar exams. Performance exams frequently require the preparation of persuasive documents such as demand letters and briefs. Therefore, we have created a sample performance examination as your review exercise.

Performance exams typically include two major components — the File, which provides the factual information you need to complete the assignment, and the Library, which provides the requisite legal information. Depending on the state, performance exams may be ninety-minute exams or three-hour exams. You should follow your instructor's directions regarding how to complete this assignment.

FILE

TO: Associate
FROM: Partner
RE: Starkey Case

As you know, we represent Kris Malden, who has been sued for stalking Sandy Starkey. Pleadings and discovery are now complete, and we are ready to file a motion for summary judgment. We simply don't believe that Malden's conduct, however reprehensible, amounted to stalking under the law. Included in this memo you will find the facts the parties have managed to stipulate to, the facts upon which the parties disagree, and the applicable statutory and case law. I am including the criminal stalking statute, although this is a civil case, because there are no cases under the civil statute and so we will need to use the criminal cases to help define the terms in the civil statute. This should be persuasive to the court, since the language of the two statutes is nearly identical.

Stipulated Facts
    1. Prior to April 1, 2010 Kris Malden and Sandra Starkey had a pleasant working relationship at Playtime, a company that designs computer games. Malden is a senior Vice President at the company; Starkey is Executive Secretary to the Chief Executive Officer.

2. On or about April 1, 2010, Kris Malden asked Sandra Starkey to "go out" with him.
3. Sandra Starkey refused to "go out" with Kris Malden.
4. Between April 1, 2010 and September 30, 2010, Kris Malden asked Sandra Starkey to "go out" with him approximately nine times.
5. Between April 1, 2010 and September 30, 2010, Kris Malden called Sandra Starkey at her home approximately 15 times.
6. If Sandra Starkey's husband answered the phone, Kris Malden hung up.
7. Kris Malden told Sandra Starkey he would try to convince her husband there was "something going on" between Starkey and Malden so her husband would divorce her.
8. In September and October 2010, Kris Malden posted Sandra Starkey's first name, address and telephone number on his web site *www.iamtheman.com*.
9. Along with Sandra Starkey's address and phone number, Kris Malden posted, "For a good time call Sadistic Sandy, she welcomes all comers. Don't worry if she says 'no', she really means 'yes.' Don't worry about her husband; he likes to watch."
10. Men called and came to the Starkey residence uninvited and made sexual advances toward Sandra Starkey after seeing Kris Malden's web site.
11. Sandra Starkey's husband had to remove these trespassers from the residence, and on one occasion the police had to remove a trespasser.
12. Sandra Starkey confronted Kris Malden near the end of September 2010, and told him to stop calling her and to remove her name and phone number from his web page.
13. Kris Malden did not comply with this first request to remove information from the web page.
14. Sandra Starkey confronted Kris Malden on or about October 6, 2010 and specifically demanded he take all information regarding her off his web site.
15. Kris Malden removed all references to Sandra Starkey from his web site on or about October 16, 2010.
16. Kris Malden did not at any time follow Sandra Starkey.
17. Kris Malden did watch Sandra Starkey on security cameras at work.
18. Kris Malden did not at any time make any explicit physical threats and/or threatening gestures toward Sandra Starkey.
19. Kris Malden did not at any time make a written or verbal threat to hit, punch, rape, kill or otherwise physically harm Sandra Starkey.
20. Sandra Starkey has never sought a restraining order against Kris Malden.
21. Kris Malden has ceased all contact with Sandra Starkey except contact that is necessary for work purposes.
22. Sandra Starkey has lost sleep and suffered from nightmares as a result of the stipulated events.

The main disagreement between the parties relates to Malden's intent. He says he was just having a little fun, and wanted to get Starkey's attention. She argues that this went way beyond fun and that he knew or should have known that his actions would put her in fear if not actual danger. She does not argue that he personally intended to hurt her.

Please draft a brief in support of our summary judgment motion.

LIBRARY

§ 1708.7 Stalking; tort action; damages and equitable remedies

(a) A person is liable for the tort of stalking when the plaintiff proves all of the following elements of the tort:

(1) The defendant engaged in a pattern of conduct the intent of which was to follow, alarm, or harass the plaintiff. In order to establish this element, the plaintiff shall be required to support his or her allegations with independent corroborating evidence.

(2) As a result of that pattern of conduct, the plaintiff reasonably feared for his or her safety, or the safety of an immediate family member. For purposes of this paragraph, "immediate family" means a spouse, parent, child, any person related by consanguinity or affinity within the second degree, or any person who regularly resides, or, within the six months preceding any portion of the pattern of conduct, regularly resided, in the plaintiff's household.

(3) One of the following:

(A) The defendant, as a part of the pattern of conduct specified in paragraph (1), made a credible threat with the intent to place the plaintiff in reasonable fear for his or her safety, or the safety of an immediate family member and, on at least one occasion, the plaintiff clearly and definitively demanded that the defendant cease and abate his or her pattern of conduct and the defendant persisted in his or her pattern of conduct.

(B) The defendant violated a restraining order, including, but not limited to, any order issued pursuant to Section 527.6 of the Code of Civil Procedure, prohibiting any act described in subdivision (a).

(b) For the purposes of this section:

(1) "Pattern of conduct" means conduct composed of a series of acts over a period of time, however short, evidencing a continuity of purpose. Constitutionally protected activity is not included within the meaning of "pattern of conduct."

(2) "Credible threat" means a verbal or written threat, including that communicated by means of an electronic communication device, or a threat implied by a pattern of conduct or a combination of verbal, written, or electronically communicated statements and conduct, made with the intent and apparent ability to carry out the threat so as to cause the person who is the target of the threat to

reasonably fear for his or her safety or the safety of his or her immediate family.

(3) "Electronic communication device" includes, but is not limited to, telephones, cellular telephones, computers, video recorders, fax machines, or pagers. "Electronic communication" has the same meaning as the term defined in Subsection 12 of Section 2510 of Title 18 of the United States Code.

(4) "Harass" means a knowing and willful course of conduct directed at a specific person which seriously alarms, annoys, torments, or terrorizes the person, and which serves no legitimate purpose. The course of conduct must be such as would cause a reasonable person to suffer substantial emotional distress, and must actually cause substantial emotional distress to the person.

(c) A person who commits the tort of stalking upon another is liable to that person for damages, including, but not limited to, general damages, special damages, and punitive damages pursuant to Section 3294.

(d) In an action pursuant to this section, the court may grant equitable relief, including, but not limited to, an injunction.

(e) The rights and remedies provided in this section are cumulative and in addition to any other rights and remedies provided by law.

(f) This section shall not be construed to impair any constitutionally protected activity, including, but not limited to, speech, protest, and assembly.

§ 646.9 Stalking

(a) Any person who willfully, maliciously, and repeatedly follows or harasses another person and who makes a credible threat with the intent to place that person in reasonable fear for his or her safety, or the safety of his or her immediate family, is guilty of the crime of stalking, punishable by imprisonment in a county jail for not more than one year or by a fine of not more than one thousand dollars ($1,000), or by both that fine and imprisonment, or by imprisonment in the state prison. . . .

(e) For the purposes of this section, "harasses" means engages in a knowing and willful course of conduct directed at a specific person that seriously alarms, annoys, torments or terrorizes the person, and that serves no legitimate purpose.

(f) For purposes of this section, "course of conduct" means two or more acts occurring over a period of time, however short, evidencing a continuity of purpose. Constitutionally protected activity is not included within the meaning of "course of conduct."

(g) For the purposes of this section, "credible threat" means a verbal or written threat, including that performed through the use of an electronic communication device, or a threat implied by a pattern of conduct or a combination of verbal, written, or electronically communicated statements and conduct made with the intent to place the person that is the target of the threat in reasonable fear for his or her safety or the safety of his or her family and made with the apparent ability to carry out the threat so as to cause the person who is the target of the threat to reasonably fear for his or her safety or the safety of his or her family. It is not necessary to prove that the defendant had the intent to actually carry out the threat. The present incarceration of a person making the threat shall not be a bar to prosecution under this section. Constitutionally protected activity is not included within the meaning of "credible threat."

(h) For purposes of this section, the term "electronic communication device" includes, but is not limited to, telephones, cellular phones, computers, video recorders, fax machines, or pagers. "Electronic communication" has the same meaning as the term defined in Subsection 12 of Section 2510 of Title 18 of the United States Code.

(1) For purposes of this section, "immediate family" means any spouse, parent, child, any person related by consanguinity or affinity within the second degree, or any other person who regularly resides in the household, or who, within the prior six months, regularly resided in the household.

PEOPLE v. UECKER
Mar. 24, 2009

FACTS

Count 1 — Stalking of M.:

M. is a service representative at the Social Security Administration in Shasta County. Her first encounter with defendant was at her work parking lot around the end of May or beginning of June 2006 when she noticed him sitting by her white Mustang between noon and 1:00 p.m. Defendant was on his bicycle, parked three to four feet from her car. M. commented that bicycling was good exercise. Thereafter, defendant would be beside M.'s car every day when she would go to lunch, even when her lunch hour varied. They would exchange greetings, and defendant sometimes would try to engage M. in further conversation. On occasion M. would oblige, but she always would say she had to get back to work because she was running late. She was polite to defendant because her job taught her to treat human beings with kindness and respond to their conversation. This pattern continued week after week, month after month.

About the same time defendant starting hanging around M.'s car, he started leaving notes for her on her car. The first note included his telephone number and read as follows: "If you want to go riding bicycles, give me a call." M. ripped up the note and threw it away because she "wasn't interested."

In September, M. started parking on the street because she no longer needed the shade the original parking spot provided and somebody else had started parking in her spot. Defendant approached her at her new spot and asked whether she was trying to "get away from [him]." She said "[n]o." He continued showing up at her new parking spot, leaving her notes and trying to engage her in conversation. One of these notes read as follows: "I'm not a homeless guy. I have a job. I have a roof over my head. I want to go out with you." She threw it away and did not talk to him about the note. His behavior was beginning to concern M., and she decided she needed to "prepare for stuff" "if he got crazy or something." She bought Mace and started taking "evasive" actions by moving her car.

But defendant persisted. His next note was a Christmas card that read as follows:

> "[M.],
>
> I hope you have a nice holiday season! I know how we met is a little rare, and I look like a transient on the side of the road but I can assure you I do have a full time job and a roof over my head. [Smiley face.] Listen, no strings attached, if ever you want to call sometime just to talk, I'm open for it, if you haven't lost my number? Its [sic] really nice talking to you as an attractive, mature lady! I'm not looking for anything super serious but I wouldn't mind the companionship on a cold, rainy day, sipping hot chocolate. [Smiley face.]
> Danny
> P.S. Nice car. [Smiley face.] I like it better than the Mustang." (Capitalization omitted.)

M., who had bought a Toyota Camry a week before, was concerned and terrified defendant knew her every move. She went inside her workplace and talked with the administrative secretary for management, Nancy Patterson, and told her the following: "Something's not right. This man just doesn't go away. And I don't know what to do anymore. I thought I could handle it on my own." M. had now become so fearful of defendant she stopped going out in the evenings and shopping and had her girlfriend stay with her a few times.

The next day, M. was so scared she parked in another location that was 10 feet from her work's exit. As she was walking out of work, defendant approached her on his bicycle and asked if she got his Christmas card. She thanked him but "[f]irm[ly]" said she was "not interested" because she was "seeing someone" and asked whether his statement about her being a mature woman implied she was old. Defendant said "no," "got mad," and asked why she had been flirting with him. She said she had not been and was simply responding to his conversation. She then announced she had to go pick up her son, and defendant left.

The following day, M. took a much later than normal lunch because her son was very ill. She did not see defendant but received the following note:

> "[M.],
>
> I'm not on my bike anymore. The weather is too cold, wet or unpredictable.
>
> I'm in a small brown truck w/ a camper shell. I still spend my lunch hour here because its [sic] quiet. I don't like to keep leaving notes on your car. Would much rather talk to you. [Smiley face.]

Ok so you're not mature! You're an immature trouble making brat!
Now what? [Smiley face.]

What's a guy gotta do to get a call from a beautiful woman? I'll be
here tomorrow if you want to see me. You sure have some funny lunch
hours. [Smiley face.]

Dan."

When M. read this note, she "really freaked out." She "started to realize
that this is more than just someone interested in dating, that this guy is just
watching [her] every move." She "started parking way down the road" so
defendant would not be able to see her car, had people walk her to her car,
and alerted the guard at her workplace. As with the last note, M. gave it to
Patterson. M. did not call the police herself because office protocol required
her to go through management.

Patterson spoke to her manager, Linde Ballentine, about the situation,
and Ballentine called M. into her office. M. told Ballentine defendant had
been leaving notes on her car, "he was now scaring her with some of the
things in the notes, [and] that she didn't know how to interpret them." M.
was crying on and off, was shaky, and had to sit down several times.

The following day, December 19, Ballentine saw defendant in his truck
eating lunch. He was positioned "with a good view of the entry to the
parking lot where the cars come in" and of the "employee entrance." Management then contacted law enforcement.

Count 2 — stalking of J.:

J. is a part-time real estate agent in Shasta County who began her career
in November 2006. To generate business, she posted real estate advertisements with her photograph and phone number in local newspapers and
magazines.

At the end of November or early December 2006, J. received a phone
message from "Danny" saying he was looking for a "livable shack in the
boonies for less than 60,000 dollars." J. returned his call, and when she had
found a couple of houses that might work, she asked for his last name so
she could mail the information to him. Defendant said it was "Eucker."

Defendant then began calling J. a couple of times a day both on her
cellular phone and her office line. She thought his messages were "a little
too comfortable and playful." He joked about his friends coming over and
"rid[ing her] horses" after she mentioned she liked the country and had
horses. He told her she had a "really cool voice" and he could "[p]robably
talk to [her] all day." That message left her with a "haunting and violating
feeling." In reference to a listing of property she had found him in "[n]ot the
greatest area," he asked if she ever went to check the places out and hinted
she should take him there. She had no intention of doing so because she
"wanted to make sure [she] was coming back." She pressed him for information to help him qualify for a loan, but he never provided any and
simply wanted more listings.

During the second week of phone calls, defendant left a message stating he had something to tell J. He then laughed and said, "Oh, no, never mind. If you're curious enough, you'll call back." When J. did not call back, defendant called her a couple of days later and asked if she had received his message. When she said she had, defendant asked her, "Do you like surprises?" J. responded that she was "[n]ot particularly fond of them."

By now, J. was questioning defendant's credibility. He had said a friend had referred him to her, which she knew was a lie because defendant was her first client. J. decided to check Megan's Law database to see if defendant was listed. When she tried Danny "Eucker" nothing came up. When she tried Danny "Uecker" she saw defendant's picture with his residence address listed as a hotel. J. drove by the hotel several times to look at the trucks parked there, since defendant had told her he drove a truck. She "wanted to get a visual of every truck in there, so in case he pulled up behind [her, she] would know" and "wouldn't get caught off guard."

At some point after she learned defendant was a "sex offender," defendant left a message for her saying he wanted to come by the office. J. responded by parking her car "far out in the parking lot backwards, so it wouldn't look like a real estate car," putting her hair in a knot, wearing sweats, and "frump[ing] on in." She asked coworkers to let her know if anybody came to the door looking for her.

A couple of days after their last phone contact, defendant left the following "irate" message: "I guess that's what you realtors do, you just drop us." J. responded with the following message: "I'm a little offended that, you know, you would speak to me that way because I had been trying to help. Every step of the way. And didn't really appreciate that." She falsely told him she was quitting the residential real estate business to focus on commercial real estate and she would send him to someone who could help him. Thereafter, J. decided not to host open houses and asked her manager whether she could put someone else's photograph in the advertisements.

Defendant called J. back about three times after her last message. The first two messages were lengthy and extremely apologetic. In one, defendant said the following: "I started this with you, [J.], because you didn't treat me like everybody else—some other realtors. So, with all due respect, I'd like to finish this with you. But I want to handle this with you—I want you to handle this or at least handle my issues, anyway." The message scared her. In another, defendant said the following: "I'm sorry. I shouldn't have yelled at you like that. I had some words with a buddy at work. It wasn't your fault, but I want you to finish what you've started here with me. I know you're doing the commercial thing, but I want you to finish what you started with me." J.'s reaction to the second message was, "this guy is like talking to a girlfriend or something . . . [i]t just . . . didn't s[i]t well, either." The third said, "Hey, I just want, you know, out of Dodge and by now, you probably know why."

J. reported defendant's conduct to law enforcement on December 13, 2006. She was afraid of defendant and felt trapped by him.

In all, defendant called her about 30 times over a three-week period, and of those calls, six to 10 were direct conversations.

Defendant was arrested on December 21, 2006.

DISCUSSION

I. Sufficient Evidence Supported Both Stalking Convictions

Defendant contends there was insufficient evidence he stalked either M. or J. As we will explain, he is incorrect.

A. Statutory Definitions

The Legislature has defined the crime of stalking as follows:

"Any person who willfully, maliciously, and repeatedly follows or willfully and maliciously harasses another person and who makes a credible threat with the intent to place that person in reasonable fear for his or her safety, or the safety of his or her immediate family. . . ." (§ 646.9, subd. (a).)

"'[H]arasses' means engages in a knowing and willful course of conduct directed at a specific person that seriously alarms, annoys, torments, or terrorizes the person, and that serves no legitimate purpose." (§ 646.9, subd. (e).)

"'[C]ourse of conduct' means two or more acts occurring over a period of time, however short, evidencing a continuity of purpose. Constitutionally protected activity is not included within the meaning of 'course of conduct.'" (§ 646.9, subd. (f).)

"'[C]redible threat' means a verbal or written threat, including that performed through the use of an electronic communication device, or a threat implied by a pattern of conduct or a combination of verbal, written, or electronically communicated statements and conduct, made with the intent to place the person that is the target of the threat in reasonable fear for his or her safety or the safety of his or her family, and made with the apparent ability to carry out the threat so as to cause the person who is the target of the threat to reasonably fear for his or her safety or the safety of his or her family. It is not necessary to prove that the defendant had the intent to actually carry out the threat. The present incarceration of a person making the threat shall not be a bar to prosecution under this section. Constitutionally protected activity is not included within the meaning of 'credible threat.'" (§ 646.9, subd. (g).)

B. Standard of Review

"The standard of review is well settled: On appeal, we review the whole record in the light most favorable to the judgment below to determine whether it discloses substantial evidence — that is, evidence that is reasonable, credible and of solid value — from which a reasonable trier of fact could find the defendant guilty beyond a reasonable doubt. [Citations.] '[I]f the verdict is supported by substantial evidence, we must accord due deference to the trier of fact and not substitute our evaluation of a witness's credibility for that of the fact finder.' [Citation.] 'The standard of review is the same in cases in which the People rely mainly on circumstantial evidence. [Citation.]' Although it is the duty of the [finder of fact] to acquit a defendant if it finds that circumstantial evidence is susceptible of two interpretations, one of which suggests guilt and the other innocence [citations], it is the [finder of fact], not the appellate court which must be convinced of the defendant's guilt beyond a reasonable doubt.' " (*People v. Snow* (2003) 30 Cal. 4th 43, 66 [132 Cal. Rptr. 2d 271, 65 P.3d 749].)

C. There Was Sufficient Evidence Defendant Stalked M.

Defendant argues there was insufficient evidence of all three elements of stalking, namely: (1) following or harassing another person; (2) making a credible threat; and (3) intending to place the victim in reasonable fear for her safety. We take each element in turn, finding sufficient evidence supported all three.

The first element of stalking is "willfully, maliciously, and repeatedly follow[ing] or willfully and maliciously harass[ing] another person." (§ 646.9, subd. (a).) Here, there was sufficient evidence to support this element. After M. told defendant firmly she was not interested in him, he got mad. The next day after she had taken a much later lunch hour than normal, defendant left a note calling her derogatory names. The day after this note, defendant positioned himself in his car with a good view of the employee entrance. From this evidence, a reasonable jury could have found defendant purposefully (i.e., willfully) followed M. on more than one occasion (i.e., repeatedly) with the intent to disturb or annoy her (maliciously) after she told him she was not interested in him and refused to acquiesce in his requests to go out with him.

The second element is "mak[ing] a credible threat," which includes a threat implied by a pattern of conduct or a combination of verbal and written communicated statements and conduct. (§ 646.9, subds. (a), (g).) Here, defendant's pattern of conduct, his written notes, and verbal statements implied he was going to do whatever it took to get M. to go out with him, reasonably causing M. to fear for her safety. Almost every workday for approximately seven months, defendant followed M. and/or placed notes on her car. He would always find her or her car no matter what time she had taken her lunch hour or in what location she had parked her car. When she told him firmly she was not interested in him, he got mad. The next day, defendant tracked her car down yet again, left her a note stating he did not like to keep leaving notes on her car, she was an "immature trouble making brat" and asking, "Now what" and what he had to do to get a call from a beautiful woman. When M. read this note, she "really freaked out," "started parking way down the road" so defendant would not see her car and had people walk her to her car. The next day, he returned again and positioned himself with a good view of the employee entrance. From this evidence, a reasonable jury could have found that defendant made an implied threat to her safety in that he was going to do whatever he needed to get M. to go out with him and that she reasonably feared for her safety. His persistence lasted seven months with no signs of abating, his last conversation with M. and his last note to her evidenced hostility toward her, and his final action of positioning himself where he could see her comings and goings at work signaled he was not going to take no for an answer.

The third element of stalking is intending to place the victim in reasonable fear for his or her safety. Here, defendant's intent was evidenced by comments in two notes he left for M. explicitly alerting her he had been tracking her. The first was when he mentioned her new car within the first week she purchased it. The second was when he mentioned she had "funny lunch hours." From these comments, a reasonable jury could conclude defendant wanted M. to know he had been watching her while she was parked at work and keeping track of her schedule to place her in fear of her safety.

Taken as a whole, therefore, there was sufficient evidence to support the jury's verdict that defendant stalked M. within the meaning of section 646.9.

D. There Was Sufficient Evidence Defendant Stalked J.

Defendant makes a similar sufficiency-of-the-evidence argument with respect to J., challenging all three elements of the crime. Again, we find sufficient evidence to support the stalking conviction.

As to the first element, there was no evidence defendant followed J., so we focus on the evidence he harassed her within the meaning of the statute. Defendant called J. under the guise of searching for a "livable shack in the boonies for less than 60,000 dollars." It was apparent defendant's contact with J. was not directed toward the legitimate purpose of buying real estate, as he refused her request to provide her information to help him qualify for a loan, would not give her the correct spelling of his name, and would not tell her the truth about how he got her contact information. When she tried to cut off contact with him, defendant kept calling her, leaving her one irate message about realtors dropping customers and another message that he wanted to "finish this with [her]" and wanted her to "handle [his] issues." Defendant left her feeling afraid and trapped. This evidence was sufficient to support the element of harassment.

The second element is making a credible threat. Here, defendant's pattern of conduct in calling J. over 30 times in three weeks despite her desire to cut off contact with him, and his verbal statements in those calls, implied a threat that caused her to reasonably fear for her safety. He left messages for J. that were "a little too comfortable and playful," ones that left her with a "haunting and violating feeling," and ones that scared her. He told her he wanted a house in the boonies and then hinted she should take him out in her car to look at the properties. He told J. that she had a "really cool voice" and he could "[p]robably talk to [her] all day." He left a message saying he had something to tell her, laughed, and then told her if she was curious enough, she would call back. When she did not, he asked her if she liked surprises. He left a message saying he wanted to come by the office. She changed her parking habits and dress to hide from defendant and would not hold open houses. When she did not return this call, he left her an irate message about realtors dropping their clients. When she told him that she was quitting the residential real estate market, he still persisted in calling her. In his last messages, he cryptically told her he wanted to "finish this with [her]," wanted her to "handle [his] issues," and he wanted "out of Dodge and by now, [she] probably kn[e]w why." It was after this series of calls that J. contacted law enforcement.

Taken as a whole, this conduct implied a threat to J.'s safety. She knew defendant is a sex offender and defendant's last comment to J. indicated he knew that she knew. He intimated he wanted to be alone with her, made suggestive comments about her voice, asked if she liked surprises, told her he wanted to come by the office, was irate when she tried to get rid of him, and left cryptic messages on her answering machine. Simply put, this pattern of unrelenting conduct over the course of three weeks that toward the end became hostile and demanding, perpetrated by someone who is a sex offender and had no legitimate interest in real estate, was sufficient to satisfy this element.

The third element is intending to place the victim in reasonable fear for his or her safety. Here, it can be inferred defendant intended to place J. in reasonable fear for her safety from his persistent phone contacts with her despite her attempts to end them, his apparent knowledge that she knew he is a registered sex offender, and his hostile and demanding tone in one of his last messages. This evidence supported not only the conclusion J. reasonably feared defendant and had reason to fear him but also that he acted with the intent to induce that fear. (*People v. Falck* (1997) 52 Cal. App. 4th 287, 299 [60 Cal. Rptr. 2d 624].)

DISPOSITION

The judgment is affirmed.

PEOPLE v. FALCK
Jan. 27, 1997

Appellant George F. Falck stands convicted of stalking, a violation of Penal Code section 646.9, subdivision (a). Appellant raises issues of the sufficiency of the evidence to support his conviction. We find that the evidence is sufficient to support appellant's conviction, and accordingly affirm the judgment.

At the time appellant committed the acts at issue here, former section 646.9, as applicable here, provided:

"(a) Any person who willfully, maliciously, and repeatedly follows or harasses another person and who makes a credible threat with the intent to place that person in reasonable fear for his or her safety, or the safety of his or her immediate family, is guilty of the crime of stalking, punishable by imprisonment in a county jail for not more than one year or by a fine of not more than one thousand dollars ($1,000), or by both that fine and imprisonment, or by imprisonment in the state prison. . . .

"(d) For purposes of this section, 'harasses' means a knowing and willful course of conduct directed at a specific person that seriously alarms, annoys, torments, or terrorizes the person, and that serves no legitimate purpose. The course of conduct must be such as would cause a reasonable person to suffer substantial emotional distress, and must actually cause substantial emotional distress to the person. 'Course of conduct' means a pattern of conduct composed of a series of acts over a period of time, however short, evidencing a continuity of purpose. Constitutionally protected activity is not included within the meaning of 'course of conduct.'

"(e) For purposes of this section, 'credible threat' means a verbal or written threat implied by a pattern of conduct or a combination of verbal or written statements and conduct made with the intent and the apparent ability to carry out the threat so as to cause the person who is the target of the threat to reasonably fear for his or her safety or the safety of his or her immediate family. The present incarceration of a person making the threat shall not be a bar to prosecution under this section. . . .

"(i) For purposes of this section, 'immediate family' means any spouse, parent, child, . . ."

FACTS

Appellant has been diagnosed as suffering from schizophrenia. His ability to control his impulses is reduced unless he receives and takes antipsychotic medication. Although appellant graduated from college, received an M.B.A. and served in the army, receiving an honorable discharge, he has been unable to obtain employment since 1978 or 1979, apparently declining into homelessness until 1982 or 1983 when he was given a place to sleep by the Resurrection Lutheran Church.

In 1982, when appellant was 35 or 36, he began to frequent a Nations' Hamburgers restaurant. There he noticed, and became fixated with, a 19-year-old woman working at the restaurant. He sent her 12 black roses. One or two days later he began to send her letters at the restaurant, identifying himself as George Frederick and writing about astrology and how they were meant to be together for eternity. Appellant sent the victim two or three letters a day. The manager of the restaurant told appellant he would be arrested if he came into the restaurant again. Appellant did go into the restaurant again, the police were called, and appellant was arrested. Appellant was put on six months court probation and ordered to stay away from the victim.

For 12 years appellant almost managed to comply with this admonition, although he did not cease thinking about the victim. He obtained a copy of her birth certificate. He obtained some pictures of her from her high school yearbook. He learned from county records that she had married. He tried to call her at two different telephone numbers over this period of time, but was unsure if she was the person who answered the telephone. In November 1994, appellant stopped taking the medication prescribed for his mental condition, and shortly thereafter embarked on the course of conduct leading to the charges filed against him in this case. Appellant explained at trial that he believed that if he had been able to continue seeing the victim in 1982 they would have married. He believes that astrology is God's system for creating different types of people. In late 1994 to early 1995, his study of astrology and the movement of the planets convinced him that the time was right to try again to get together with the victim. He felt that it was nearly imperative that he contact her.

Appellant telephoned the victim at her home in January 1995, identifying himself as "George Frederick," and stating: "I found you. I can tell by your voice." The victim hung up immediately and called the police. Appellant called again. The victim's husband answered, but disguised his voice as the victim's. Appellant, believing himself to be talking to the victim, said that they were deemed by God to be together forever, and spoke about astrology. The victim's husband identified himself, telling appellant not to call again. Appellant called the next morning, again reaching the victim's husband. The husband told appellant that a police report had been filed. The victim and her husband changed their telephone number. The victim received no further calls from appellant. She began, however, to receive letters from him. Appellant sent the victim pictures of her and pictures of himself. He sent her pornographic pictures cut from a magazine, putting captions on them explaining that they were intended to represent the victim. Appellant's letters were sprinkled with astrological references, with discussions of the sexual acts appellant wished to experience with the victim and his anticipation of their impending marriage. In addition, appellant placed a personal advertisement in the newspaper, which the victim read, that recited that appellant had to contact her, that he loved her and had to find her and that he wanted to marry her.

Appellant was arrested on February 3, 1995. The police searched his apartment. They found pictures of the victim in various places. They found written notes referring to astrological matters linking appellant's name to the victim's. One of the notes referred to the date March 21, 1982. Appellant told the police that March 21, 1982, was the date he and the victim were married. Some of the notes referred to the victim by her first name and appellant's last name. The police also found Hustler Magazines, some with cutout spaces corresponding to the pictures sent to the victim, and a copy of the advertisement placed by appellant in the newspaper. At a police interview following his arrest, appellant openly discussed his obsession with the victim. Appellant's statements were coherent but rambling. He discussed the victim, astrology, his need to be dominated sexually, his past, his illness, and his intention to marry the victim. He explained that he had obtained the victim's pictures from high school yearbooks obtained at the library. He stated that he could not keep away from the victim, and asked the interviewing officer to take him to the victim or at least to give her his telephone number.

By the time of the trial, appellant was again taking medication. He told the jury that he never had intended to cause any harm to the victim or to frighten her. He had wanted to marry her, but had no intention of forcing her to marry him. He stated that his interest in the victim had faded, and that he no longer was in love with her or wanted to marry her.

DISCUSSION

Sufficiency of the Evidence

Appellant contends that the evidence fails to support the verdict. The question, of course, is not whether there is evidence from which the jury could have reached some other conclusion, but whether, viewing the evidence in the light most favorable to respondent, and presuming in support of the judgment the existence of every fact the trier reasonably could deduce from the evidence, there is substantial evidence of appellant's guilt — i.e., evidence that is credible and of solid value — from which a rational trier of fact could have found the defendant guilty beyond a reasonable doubt.

Appellant here contends that the record is devoid of evidence that he made a "credible threat," or that he made that threat with the intent to place the victim in reasonable fear for her safety or the safety of her immediate family.

A. Evidence of Credible Threat

At the time of appellant's communications with the victim, a "credible threat" was defined as "a verbal or written threat or a threat implied by a pattern of conduct or a combination of verbal or written statements and conduct made with the intent and the apparent ability to carry out the threat so as to cause the person who is the target of the threat to reasonably fear for his or her safety or the safety of his or her immediate family." (§ 646.9, former subd. (e).) Section 646.9 does not require that the defendant actually intend to carry out the threat. It is enough that the threat causes the victim reasonably to fear for her safety or the safety of her family, and that the accused makes the threat with the intent to cause the victim to feel that

fear. In addition, in determining whether a threat occurred, the entire factual context, including the surrounding events and the reaction of the listeners, must be considered.

Appellant's communications with the victim were peppered with references to astrology and to appellant's intention of spending eternity with
her. Appellant wrote about sexual acts in which he wished to engage with
the victim. He sent her pornographic pictures. He wrote such things as,
"I need you and want to charge ahead on my RD 350 Yamaha road and
street racer into your body beginning our eternity of marital bliss as God
intended it." In a letter informing her of his lifetime accomplishments he
told her that he was very good with an M-16 automatic rifle weapon.
In another letter he wrote that he knew she was a "hard woman to handle."
He wrote: "You're better off with me, I can heal your wounds. Give me the
chance. Please don't be married to anyone but me. God created us for each
other." He wrote that the victim was his "only chance to keep from hurting
and leaving beautiful women." We have little difficulty in perceiving a
credible threat in these letters. They disclose an obsessive desire to engage
in sexual acts with the victim. They disclose an obsessive desire to marry
her and be with her. The references to eternity and to appellant's proficiency with a rifle reasonably could be construed as an intention to kill the
victim and commit suicide so that they might spend eternity together. They
can be construed as a threat to kill the victim or her husband if she did not
agree to appellant's wishes. It also is relevant that appellant once sent the
victim a dozen black roses, a gift with sinister overtones. Appellant made it
abundantly clear that his desires took precedence over the victim's wishes.
His obsession continued over 12 years notwithstanding that the victim
did not know him, had evidenced no desire whatsoever to know him
and indeed had taken steps to ensure that he would not contact her. Finally,
it is a sad truth, and one commonly reported, that persons such as
appellant, in the grips of an obsession, have killed or harmed the object
of that obsession, even while maintaining that they have no desire to
cause harm. In short, the evidence not just slightly, but overwhelmingly,
supports the finding that the victim not only actually feared appellant, but
had cause to fear him. Appellant's conduct, accordingly, conveyed a credible threat.

B. Evidence That Appellant Intended to Place the Victim in Fear for Her Safety

Appellant, the only person who had actual knowledge of his intent in
communicating with the victim, testified that he had no intention to cause
fear in the victim. He claimed that he loved the victim, would never harm
her and had no desire to make her afraid. Intent, however, can be inferred
from circumstantial evidence. Indeed, it is recognized that "[t]he element of
intent is rarely susceptible of direct proof and must usually be inferred
from all the facts and circumstances disclosed by the evidence."
(*People v. Kuykendall* (1955) 134 Cal. App. 2d 642, 645, 285 P.2d 996.)

Here, it can be inferred that appellant intended to cause fear in the victim from the fact that he insisted on maintaining contact with her although she clearly was attempting to avoid him, and although he had been warned away by the police, the court, and the victim's husband. In addition, appellant's letters were peppered with his desire to engage in sexual acts with the victim, acts which often included elements of bondage or violence. Appellant sent the victim black roses, symbolic of death. He referred to being together with her for eternity. He referred to his prowess with a rifle. All this evidence not only supports the conclusion that the victim feared appellant and had reason to fear him, but that he acted with the intention of inducing that fear. Substantial evidence supports the jury's verdict.

CONCLUSION

The judgment is affirmed.

PEOPLE v. HALGREN
Sept. 3, 1996

FACTUAL AND PROCEDURAL BACKGROUND

Melissa Gonzales met Halgren at a grocery store on September 9, 1994. He asked her if he could practice his Spanish with her. During their conversation he learned where she worked and that she was divorced. She showed him a picture of her child. She refused his invitation to have lunch.

The next day, Halgren telephoned Gonzales at the office where she worked as a receptionist and asked her to lunch. She refused, telling him she had a boyfriend. During their conversation she said she came from Killeen, Texas. The following day he telephoned again and asked her to lunch. She said she was going grocery shopping during her lunch hour because that evening she planned to cook dinner for her boyfriend. She told him he could come along on the shopping trip, but did not expect he would. At noon he arrived at her office. She refused his invitation to ride in his car, but said he could follow her.

At the market Halgren attempted to take Gonzales's shopping list; she said she could do it herself. She thought he seemed jittery. She found him annoying and told him he talked too fast and looked bowlegged. These comments did not discourage Halgren, and he ran down the aisle slapping his calves with his boots. Gonzales told him he was acting strange. He followed her through the check stand and outside, where he offered to help with her bags. When she refused, he pulled a badge from his pocket. She asked if he were a police officer, and he replied, "All you need to know is that I'm really important." Upon her return to her office, she told the other receptionist, Lorena Torres, about her experience.

Gonzales did not hear from Halgren again until October 26, when he called her office and asked if he were speaking to Miss Killeen, Texas.

Gonzales hung up. He called her several times that day and she and Torres began keeping a log of his calls. When Torres answered she thought Halgren sounded angry that she was trying to protect Gonzales. During one call Halgren demanded to speak to the manager, who told him to stop calling because he had no business with the company. During his last call that day, Halgren told Gonzales he only wanted talk to her. She told him to leave her alone, she had called police and a telephone trap would be set.

When Gonzales arrived home that evening, there was a message from Halgren on her answering machine. It stated: "Hi, Melissa, this is [Halgren]. I don't know why you are being so rude to me and such a bitch. You are fat and ugly and repulsive. You make me want to vomit. So you are going to have to talk to me sometime."

A short time later, Gonzales was talking on her telephone with a friend when she heard a clicking sound indicating she had an incoming call. She switched to the other line and heard Halgren say, "So, are you ready to talk to me now?" She switched back to the first call and tried to ignore further clicks, but there were so many she and her friend could not continue their conversation. She answered the other line and heard Halgren say, "You are going to have to talk to me." She yelled, "I want you to leave me alone. I don't know you. I don't want to know you. Stop calling me." Halgren yelled back, "Bitch, you don't know who you are messing with. I am going to call you whenever I want to, and I am going to do to you whatever I want to." Gonzales testified she was terrified for herself and her son. She unplugged her telephone and the next morning changed her telephone number to an unlisted one and notified her son's preschool about the harassment.

On October 28, Gonzales stayed home from work. That day several of her co-workers saw Halgren pacing around their office. Police were notified.

Each day from October 29 until November 8 there were a total of 25 to 30 hang-up calls and calls from Halgren to Gonzales' office. On November 2, he called and said, "God, I've missed you. You look great today in black." She was wearing black that day. During another call he told her she would be sorry she had been so rude to him.

On November 8, Gonzales' co-workers saw Halgren outside their office building. The police were called. Halgren telephoned Gonzales and she attempted to keep him on the line. He said, "All I want to do is be close to you. I don't understand your rudeness. Why won't you talk to me? You are going to have to talk to me sometime." He said he was not going to let her be rude to him and either "I'm going to fix you" or "I'm going to fix this."

Police located the telephone booth from where Halgren had called Gonzales. When he saw them walking toward him, he said, "I'm not a stalker or anything," and hung up. After Halgren's arrest, police found two knives, a small holster, and a rotating light beacon inside his car and a Swiss army knife and a badge in his pocket.

Defense Case

Frank Gregory Jennings testified he and Halgren met Gonzales and her son at a Mission Valley mall, where they had gone to pass out business cards advertising Halgren's services as a stripper for parties. Jennings said Halgren sometimes wore a police uniform costume when he performed.

Police officer Craig Myrom testified he took reports of some of Halgren's calls. He stated based on conversations with Gonzales he considered the case an annoying phone call case, not a stalking case.

Halgren's girlfriend, Jean Malana, testified Halgren sometimes wore a police uniform and badge and used the other police-related items in his car when he performed as a stripper.

DISCUSSION

Substantial Evidence of a Credible Threat Supports the Conviction

Halgren contends his conviction is not supported by substantial evidence because his statements to Gonzales, viewed objectively, were not credible threats. He argues he never threatened her or her child with physical harm.

The court must look at the whole record and determine whether evidence of each essential element is substantial. "The reviewing court presumes in support of the judgment the existence of every fact the jury could reasonably deduce from the evidence." (*People v. Bloom* (1989) 48 Cal. 3d 1194, 1208, 259 Cal. Rptr. 669, 774 P.2d 698.)

Sufficient evidence supports the judgment. Halgren repeatedly telephoned Gonzales, insisting she speak with him after she had clearly explained she was not interested. He left a message on her home telephone and demanded she talk with him there. He told her she would be sorry she had been so rude. He appeared at her office when she was not there, positioning himself where he could watch people leave the building. On the day he was arrested he told her she would pay for her rudeness and he would "fix her" or "fix this." These statements were a credible threat with a clear intent to place her in fear for her safety. Coupled with the repeated harassing telephone calls, they constitute substantial evidence that supports his conviction of felony stalking.

DISPOSITION

The judgment is affirmed.